Halliday: System and Function in Language

Halliday:
System and Function in Language

Selected Papers edited by
G. R. Kress

Oxford University Press

Oxford University Press, Walton Street, Oxford OX2 6DP

LONDON GLASGOW NEW YORK TORONTO DELHI
BOMBAY CALCUTTA MADRAS KARACHI
KUALA LUMPUR SINGAPORE HONG KONG TOKYO
NAIROBI DAR ES SALAAM CAPE TOWN SALISBURY
MELBOURNE AUCKLAND
and associated companies in
BEIRUT BERLIN IBADAN MEXICO CITY

Library Edition ISBN 0 19 437127 1
Paperback Edition ISBN 0 19 437062 3

© *Selection and editorial matter*
Oxford University Press 1976

First published 1976
Second impression 1981

Printed in Hong Kong

Contents

Preface

The volume is a selection from about 90 books, articles, reviews, lectures and working papers, many unpublished. It contains none of Halliday's papers on language teaching, stylistics, sociolinguistics, applied linguistics. Four of the papers printed here were previously unpublished (2, 9, 10, 11) and they appear in full; of the three which I judged to be relatively difficult of access (1, 4, 12), only 4 is significantly reduced: it is a section from a much larger paper. With the other papers I felt able to make more substantial cuts: thus only about a third of 'Categories of the theory of grammar' appears here. In particular I left out those parts of the argument which were concerned with setting the theory in the context of the linguistic debate of the time. This has given to some parts a slightly ahistorical feel. It has been my concern to give a substantial introduction to Halliday's linguistic theory, and enough material to provide readers with a working knowledge of systemic grammar. The full bibliography of Halliday's writings will give help to readers who wish to go further. One omission which I continue to mourn is *Grammar, Society and the Noun*, a beautifully articulate statement about the place of linguistics in the human sciences; however, there was no room to print it in full, and it seemed impossible to cut.

It is a pleasant duty to acknowledge help and advice: Professor Strevens gave me most helpful ideas about the possible shape for the volume very early on. My friend and colleague Dr Robert Hodge has been an ever-patient and discerning sounding board. Matthew Huntley of Oxford University Press guided the volume through the most difficult stages of proofs, and his help was invaluable. But above all my thanks are due to Professor Halliday, who made available to me a copy of everything he had written and still had in his possession, and who provided the up-to-date bibliography. With unfailing generosity and courtesy he has been available for advice and help, while showing heroic restraint at all other times. What errors of fact or judgement may inhere in this volume are thus due to regrettable obstinacy on my part.

G.R.K., Norwich, April 1976

Introduction

The purpose of this volume is to bring together those of M. A. K. Halliday's papers which demonstrate clearly his theoretical standpoint, and which show the origins and the development of Halliday's thinking about language. In the two possible approaches to a study of language—the socially oriented and the psychologically oriented—Halliday is clearly within the first. So the papers also attempt to show what questions a sociologically oriented theory asks about language. These are crucial questions for those whose work involves them in precisely that border area where sociological problems and language are closely connected. There is the further question whether it matters what kind of a theory we are using for this specific purpose. This question is rarely asked: most often, when it is asked, the answer has been that it does not matter. Sociolinguists are now working with models which are at best neutral with respect to this question, and most frequently are positively opposite in their main thrust.

Halliday's most recent writings are characterized by a strong functional bias. In many of his papers (e.g. Chapter 2 of this volume) his purpose is to specify the functions which language has in society, and then to establish what reflection these functions find in the structure of the language itself. Some of the non-technical papers (e.g. 'Relevant models of language') have attracted much attention, so that it has seemed to some people that Halliday has performed a switch of theories, and that his earlier writings on language are divorced from the later, sociolinguistic, functionally oriented work. If this were the case, then we would have simply another example of an interesting set of questions about society and language, but a set of questions unrelated to a formal linguistic theory, and in particular, unrelated to the formal theory known as systemic grammar.

But the interest of Halliday's work lies precisely in the necessary connection between the form of the theoretical framework, and the set of questions which flow from it. To illustrate this point it is necessary to examine in some detail the origins of Halliday's theory.

First then the antecedents. Three names figure prominently in Halliday's thought: Malinowski, Firth, and Whorf. Malinowski's anthropological fieldwork in Polynesia demonstrated to him the impossibility of 'translating' terms and texts from the language of one culture to the language of another. Yet if language is a self-contained system, which can be described in terms of itself, and whose meanings can be made explicit entirely in terms of itself (as structuralists generally assume) this is puzzling. Malinowski's answer was that language is far from self-contained; it is entirely dependent on the society in which it is used. And in two senses: first, it has evolved in response to the specific demands of any given society, so that its nature and use reflect specific characteristics of that society; secondly, its use or any instance of its use in that society is entirely context dependent. '. . . utterance and situation are bound up inextricably with each other and the context of situation is indispensable for the understanding of the words' (from 'The problem of meaning in primitive languages'). Malinowski distinguished between the immediate *context of utterance*, and a general (and generalizable) *context of situation*. Closely related to this is Malinowski's definition of meaning as derived, 'not from a passive contemplation of the word, but from an analysis of its functions, with reference to the given culture'. The major functions of language which Malinowski identified in one Polynesian society are: the pragmatic function (language as a form of action), the magical function (language as a means of control over the environment) and the narrative function (language as a storehouse of useful and necessary information through its preserved accounts of history).

Halliday uses Malinowski in several ways. Firstly, he takes over the definition of meaning as function in context (initially through the mediation of Firth). Secondly, he accepts Malinowski's characterization of language as multi-functional, and while he does not take over any one of the major speech functions defined by Malinowski, he makes use of them in several ways: Halliday's interpersonal, ideational, and textual functions incorporate some of the facets pointed to in Malinowski's functions. In particular, there is quite a strong affinity between Malinowski's pragmatic and Halliday's interpersonal function.

Several of Malinowski's early and contentious notions (e.g. those of a primitive language) are ignored by Halliday. Malinowski drew a parallel between the phylogenetic aspect of language development generally, and the ontogenetic aspect of language development in the child. Malinowski felt that the categories which he discovered in language had developed in response to needs of the societies which used language. Halliday sees the language development of the child in a similar manner: the child has certain needs, and expresses these in sound. This is very much a functional view: in a specific context the child has a specific need and he uses sound to express that need. The 'meaning' of that sound is its function in the context. Initially the child has a large range of needs, so that the uses he makes of sound, the functions, are also large in number. The process of language development for the child is one in which he learns to express his needs in the conventionalized functions of the language which is spoken around him, and in the conventional structures which are available for their expression. This is due to the fact that the child is growing into a society which already has an established and conventional way for expressing certain needs. For 'primitive man' (who for Halliday would be some pre-historic ancestor of modern man, but who for Malinowski might be Polynesian man) there is no such restrictive context, there is no language around him which dictates the development of the expression of his needs. Thus 'primitive man' fashions for himself the form of expression of his needs: he shapes language to reflect the uses he wants to make of it. Thus in this 'Urlanguage' the use of any linguistic item is an action which expresses directly the need underlying it. Using language is an action like other actions, its function is the expression of meanings. Malinowski expressed this in a somewhat unfortunate way, so that he spoke of 'speech as a mode of action, rather than a countersign of thought'. Obviously he did not mean that the people he was studying did not and could not think; though the phrase 'Language, in its developed ... scientific functions, is an instrument of thought ...' could give rise to such an interpretation. Halliday expresses this in a related but uncontroversial manner: to use language is to mean (just as to use a knife is to cut). From this derive his initially odd statements such as 'Learning how to mean' for the title of an article on child language.

Halliday relates Malinowski and Whorf, and the link can be made most easily through the Malinowskian notion that language in its structure mirrors the real categories derived from the practical uses both of the child and of 'primitive man'. Not that Whorf operated with a category even remotely related to 'primitive man' or 'primitive culture'. One of his finest characteristics must be the sensitivity which he showed to the richness and subtlety of the aboriginal American Indian cultures and languages which he studied. But like Malinowski Whorf insisted on the link between the cultural organization and the reflection of this in the structure of the language.

Whorf, unlike Malinowski, was a grammarian; one consequence of this was that he used language as a starting point for his work, that is, he viewed the relation between language and culture from the point of view of language. That Whorf stressed the importance of language in ordering society, rather than deriving the nature of language from social structures, is therefore not surprising. Another consequence was that Whorf actually looked for and attempted to describe the grammatical categories which he felt shaped the philosophy, worldview, or conceptual organization of the culture he was studying. These categories, he realized, were unlikely to be expressed directly, in the surface organization of the language. His interest therefore focused on a distinction between what he called overt and covert categories. An overt category is one which has an explicit formal representation on the surface (e.g. the category *plural* in English), a covert category is one which does not (e.g. the category *animate* in English). Whorf was thus concerned with what is now regarded as deep grammar. Working in the linguistic background of the twenties and thirties, Whorf naturally concentrated on morphological categories in the main, though his concerns were precisely those of modern grammatical theories, that is, to provide descriptions of the deeper grammar of language. Whorf's analyses led to what might be called typologies of language. The particular types which he established were SAE (Standard Average European) on the one hand, and American Indian, and particularly Hopi, on the other.

This typological use of his theory has sometimes been seen as the major thrust of Whorf's work, and the notion of linguistic relativity which arises from it has become characterized as the Whorf (−Sapir) hypothesis. Halliday's use of Whorf concentrates however on the other and more important aspects of Whorf's theory: the clear acceptance of the relation of language and culture, a view of language as the embodiment of a conceptual system and an explicit attempt to describe the relevant linguistic categories needed in any account of the deep grammar of a language.

What then of Firth? Malinowski was not a linguist. Whorf was an exceedingly penetrating thinker about language, who substantiated his hypotheses with careful linguistic fieldwork. But Whorf did not attempt to establish a linguistic theory, and his descriptive work is quite neutral with respect to any particular descriptive framework. Firth however was first and foremost a linguist. He accepted Malinowski's view of the relation between language and society; in particular he accepted Malinowski's definition of meaning as function in context. To understand Firth it is necessary at the very least to understand Malinowski, and to see Firth, the linguist, in the linguistic context of the twenties and thirties. Certainly, Malinowski's general view of the setting of language was widely accepted (e.g. Wittgenstein's *Philosophical Investigations*); the predominant, strictly linguistic, theory however was that of de Saussure. His term *état de langue* was widely taken up by linguists and the task of linguistics seen to lie in the twofold purpose of describing this *état*, and in developing the methods necessary for doing this in the manner of the natural sciences. For de Saussure this *état* was a self-contained and rigid entity, certainly so far as the individual speaker is concerned. The individual receives his *langue* from the community in which he grows up. The *langue* is the property of the community, beyond the influence of the individual. The individual is therefore quite unable to influence and change the *langue*. Two important considerations follow from this: first, the entity to be described is static; second, the entity to be described is not *langue* as manifested in the use of the individual (for which de Saussure used, significantly, another term, *parole*), but the abstract entity *langue* which exists quite apart from the individual's uses of it. Thus linguists following de Saussure strictly are bound to concentrate on the description of a self-contained abstract entity, rather than on the contextually determined linguistic uses of language by the individual. The conception of the nature of the object and the methodology developed for describing it, namely structuralism, were therefore intimately linked. De Saussure's structuralism makes use of two crucial and related categories: *syntagm* and *paradigm*. Relations between an item and other items present in a structure are *syntagmatic;* relations between an item and other items not present in the structure are *paradigmatic*. The two categories thus represent two basically different principles of organization for any linguistic theory. Those theories which have become known in a general and not strictly accurate way as *structural* have tended to focus on the syntagmatic aspect of language.

The problem for Firth therefore was this: despite overt rejection of de Saussure (particularly of de Saussure's dichotomies, or de Saussure's view of language as a homogeneous whole) he was working within the general Saussurean framework. Yet he wished to develop a theory which incorporated Malinowski's term context of situation (though generalized to the more usable category of situation types) and his view of meaning as function in context. The first step had to be an attempt to develop a methodology that allows the linguist to provide a coherent description of language in these terms. The problems are these:

1. If the meaning of linguistic items depends on cultural context, one needs to establish sets of categories which link linguistic material with the cultural context.

2. The notion *meaning is function in context* will have to find formal definition, so that it can be used as a principle working throughout the theory; that is, the smallest linguistic item must be describable in these terms just as much as the largest.

3. The theory has to provide for a continuity of description; it has to allow the linguist to relate the statement of function in context of the smallest to that of the largest linguistic unit.

Firth attempted to solve these problems by a formalization of the notion of paradigm, while retaining the notions of structure and of syntagm from de Saussure. The theory has as a result come to be known as System Structure Theory. But to take the points raised above in turn. First, most linguists and most linguistic theories do agree in broad outline about the units to be used in the description of language (at the very least this can be said of those units used to describe, in commonly used terms, surface structures). But absolutely no such agreement exists when it comes to the description of socio-cultural units: although Firth had addressed himself to this problem as early as 1935 in his important paper *The Technique of Semantics*, with very few exceptions (the most outstanding of these being Mitchell's *The Language of Buying and Selling in Cyrenaica*) the questions were not even being asked until very recently. That is, neither linguists nor sociologists were attempting to connect the two disciplines in a sufficiently serious fashion to lead to the establishment of the necessary categories. One of the problems is size: the micro-level of linguistics does not readily match the macro-level of sociology. It had also been felt by many linguists (and changes in this view really are extremely recent—where there are changes) that while linguistic behaviour rests on the shared knowledge by speakers of a finite set of abstract rules, which could be enumerated and described, the same was not true of social behaviour, which was seen as infinitely variable and not rule governed. This is not and was not the view of sociologists; the concept of role, for instance, depends on the assumption of a community's sharing of a set of rules of social behaviour. Neither sociologists nor linguists had asked the question: what are the appropriate categories for the statement of the context of the largest linguistic units. In fact, even now most linguists would refuse to recognize these as relevant questions for a linguist to be asking.

Firth had made an attempt to develop a theory which would accomplish this first requirement. He had set out the following categories which were, he felt, necessary in any description of linguistic events.

A. The participants: persons, personalities and relevant features of these
   (i) The verbal action of the participants
   (ii) The non-verbal action of the participants
B. The relevant objects and non-verbal and non-personal events
C. The effect of the verbal action. (Firth, 1957b)

These raise the question of the discontinuity of units from different levels. To explain: if we talk about the phoneme / d / we refer to the context of phonological structure. There is no discontinuity there. Phonological structures are abstract linguistic entities. They in turn operate as basic units in a syntactic context. There is a very minor discontinuity there, that between syntax and phonology, but the important point is that the description refers to linguistic units. When we come to the border area between language and the social context in which it operates, we are dealing with two different sets of entities. One set is from the social level, and the other from the linguistic. And it is theoretically impossible to link units of the one kind to units of the other. There simply is no basis for stating relations or connections. That is, unless the theory regards linguistic behaviour as one form of social behaviour; and here we return to the opposition between the view of language as a self-contained system, psychological in its orientation, and the view of language as a context-dependent entity, sociological in its orientation. The former theory (which one might characterize as an internal theory) will have precisely the difficulty pointed to; the latter (which one might characterize as an external theory) will not.

It would of course be totally wrong to pretend that this is an either/or matter. An internal theory can attempt to make the link with the larger context just as an external theory of language will have to provide a full description of the internal structure of the utterance. The main question is always about the main thrust of the approach: certain questions are more likely to arise from one approach rather than from another. An external theory is more suited to providing a description with no discontinuity from the socio-cultural to the purely linguistic units.

To take up the second point raised above, the development of a linguistic theory based on the notion of function in context. Firth did this by means of the concept of *system*. This is a theoretical term, not to be understood as the ordinary use of the word 'system' (say in a sentence such as *I can't get her out of my system* or *It's a rotten system where you have to work five days a week*) nor to be confused with de Saussure's technical use of the term. For Firth a system is an enumerated set of choices in a specific context. This gives rise to two sets of contexts for any item. First, the context of the other possible choices in a system, and second, the context in which the system itself occurs. To give an example from phonology: in a phonological structure CVC, such as s—rVC, a system operates at the place marked with a —, namely, a system composed of the items which are possible alternatives in that position. In English the possibilities are $/ k /$, $/ t /$, and $/ p /$ (exemplified by words such as s*t*rike, s*p*ring, s*c*rap). The paradigmatic context for any term in this system is therefore provided by the set of alternatives in that system; the paradigmatic context for $/t/$ is $/k/$ and $/p/$. But to establish the system in the first place we need a description of the context in which precisely these choices are possible. For a start we need to know that in the structure CVC the initial C is a consonant cluster (as against a single consonant) and that it is the maximal initial consonant cluster for English, (as against clusters such as s*l*ide). C_1, the initial consonant, is then described as $C_aC_bC_c$. Now we can state that the system operating at C_b in the structure $C_aC_bC_cV$ C is as described above. It is easy enough to demonstrate that a statement of the context of the system is necessary. Consider the structure C_aC_b V C: if we wished to describe the system at C_b we would find that it comprised the terms $/t/$ $/k/$ and $/p/$ as well as $/l/$ $/m/$ $/n/$ (i.e. s*t*ick, s*k*ip, s*p*eck, s*l*ick, s*m*ack, s*n*ick). Thus a changed context gives rise to a system comprising six terms, as against three previously. The description of a system depends on the statement of the context in which it occurs.

To restate: contextual statement is both

1. a statement of the other terms in the system which provide the (paradigmatic) context for the *term* under consideration and

2. a statement of the context in which the *system* operates.

The latter can be made

(a) in terms of the sequential/structural context and

(b) in terms of a system's context of other systems in which it operates (this point will be discussed below).

Firth's theory of language encompasses 1 and 2 (a), but it does not develop 2 (b). It might be useful at this point to see to what extent Firth's theory allows for a description of language in terms of *function in context*. First then, a linguistic unit operates in two contexts: (a) in the context of the other terms in a system and (b) as a member of a system it operates in the context of syntagmatic structures. Thus contextual statement of the linguistic unit is achieved. Functional labelling of the units of syntagmatic linguistic structure is necessary through the theoretically prior employment of the notion of system. For Malinowski meaning was the function in (the social) context of the (largest) linguistic item; Firth extended that notion successfully to the description of all linguistic units, and showed the potential of this notion as a basis for a linguistic theory. The 'meaning' of /t/ say, in the system operating a C medial in a syllable initial consonant structure would be defined (a) by its potentiality of occurrence in a three-term system and (b) as the function of the system of which it is a member in that context. However, in the process the term 'meaning' has become somewhat metaphorical in its use. Firth never regarded *semantics* as a separate area of linguistics; and the answer to that apparently curious omission lies in precisely this: the principle underlying all linguistic description was the statement of the function of linguistic items in their context, and that for Firth was meaning. Thus all the linguist's activity was about the statement of meaning, about semantics. There could, for him, be absolutely no reason for talking about a separate level of semantics.

The importance of Firth for Halliday lies in the attempt which Firth made to provide the linguistic component to go with the sociolinguistic insights of Malinowski. The two important categories are:

1. *context of situation*, that is, a view of language as closely dependent on stateable general types of situation which influence language. From here Firth developed his theory of the multiplicity of 'languages' within the total language. This is an important insight which Halliday took over and developed in his work on *register*.

2. *system*, which in re-defined form has become the major formal category in Halliday's theory.

These are not the only influences: for instance, Halliday uses Firth's category of *collocation* in his work on lexis (see pp. 73–83 in this volume);

but they are the significant ones. Halliday made no use of Firth's work in prosodic analysis, which many followers of Firth regard as Firth's major achievement. To the extent that this is so, and to the extent that the content of Halliday's theory depends more strongly on Malinowski and Whorf, the label Neo-Firthian which has been applied to him obscures the main thrust of Halliday's thinking about language.

Two shortcomings of Firth's theory must now be mentioned. One which might of itself be trivial, and one which is not. The trivial first: Firth never attempted to provide a fully worked out and systematic exposition of his theory. His theoretical statements are nowhere presented as a fully-fledged model. Had Firth made the attempt to state his theory in a coherent fashion, he might well have noticed and overcome the more significant shortcoming. That consists in a serious gap, namely in the interrelation of parts of the model. Firth did not provide a set of terms or categories which could systematically relate all the descriptive statements on all levels to each other. To express this in terms of statement of function in context, he did not show what the contexts of all linguistic units were and how these were to be related. Using the phonological example: once the context of all systems on the phonological level have been stated, a formal device is needed for stating what the contexts for these new largest phonological units are, and how they are to be related. Thus once we have enumerated all the systems in all possible C V C structures, we need to know in what structures the syllables themselves occur, and what systems they form at each choice-point (structural/functional place) in those larger structures. Only in this way can the theory relate the smallest to the largest linguistic unit, and the statement of the function in context of a phoneme be related to the statement of the function in context of the utterance.

If the theory was not to continue to exist on the level of highly illuminating but isolated statements about language, and about possible approaches to the study and description of language, there was a clear need for the tightening up and regularization of these theoretical sketches. From his earliest statements on, Halliday attempted to provide a coherent theoretical framework for his descriptive linguistic work. Chapter 4 in this volume shows this clearly. The theory outlined in this extract makes use of the following abstract theoretical categories; *unit*, *element*, and *class*. The *unit* is 'that category to which corresponds a segment of the linguistic material about which statements are to be made'. Segments are of differing size, and these will have to be given names which will themselves become terms in the theory. The *element* is the category which corresponds to a structural place in the structure of the *unit*. The *class* is the category which corresponds to the 'exhaustive inventories of forms classified as operating at a given place in the structure of the unit next above'.

It might be useful to discuss these categories in terms of the phonological example used above, and then to state the difference between this theory and Firth's. In that discussion the *unit* is a syllable. The structure of the unit is CVC. It has three structural places, thus three *elements* C V C, more precisely, C (syllable initial) V C (syllable final). At each of these elements operates a *class*, that is, an exhaustive system of terms. This system is composed of units from the level next below. Units of one level are terms in systems of classes which are elements operating in places in the structure of units at the next level above. The phonemes /t/ /p/ /k/ are terms in the system C cluster medial which is a class representing an element (namely cluster medial consonant in a syllable initial consonant structure) in the unit syllable, which is the unit of the next level above.

Halliday assumes that the direction of analysis is from the top downwards, so that the largest unit is defined first, the elements in the structural places described, the classes operating at each element then enumerated. The latter step produces a description of the units next below; the procedure is repeated downwards, until the smallest linguistic unit is reached. Halliday says that 'it is assumed that a downward direction of procedure, from the larger to the smaller unit, is methodologically acceptable without explicit justification'. However, in a theory which attempts to provide a description of language in terms of function (of linguistic units) in context, this is the necessary direction: the structure of the larger unit specifies the context of the classes, which are systems composed of terms from the level next below. In this approach classes of systems are defined by the place at which they operate, so of necessity the place has to be specified first, and thus the structure of the larger unit, before the system can be defined. Structural labels such as first consonant, second consonant (in a consonant cluster) are not sufficiently specific to enable the linguist to define the system operating at that point. Functional labels such as cluster-initial, cluster-final, are needed. Thus the basic orientation of the linguistic theory outlined is functional rather than structural (but see chapter 5, 5·3, p. 65).

The difference between Firth's theory and Halliday's in the extract from 'Grammatical categories in modern Chinese' lies in the following:

1. Halliday's theory is explicit.

2. It provides a framework within which it is possible to state the relationship of units on all levels to each other (i.e. the relation of *unit* to *element* and *element* to *class*).

3. It provides a statement of the context of all linguistic units (i.e. by the downward direction of analysis).

4. It illustrates the theoretical basis for the basically functional character of the theory.

On the further question of the relation between 'purely linguistic' levels and the socio-cultural settings of language events, Halliday, in this early work, confines himself to asserting the desirability of relating these levels. The following [p. 37] is representative: 'This (i.e. that the sentence is the largest unit described) does not exclude the possibility, and even necessity, of making contextual statements about some larger unit. Such statements would give meaning at another level to features accounted for in the grammatical statement, and may be required to complete an otherwise only partial systematization of the material. *One could set up a unit of contextual statement features of which would determine grammatical features.*' (my italics). As he points out, such statements and descriptions of contextual features are given in 'Grammatical categories in modern Chinese' but on an *ad hoc* basis. The point to notice is that the theoretical framework exists at this stage for making such statements, and for extending the description in this direction.

The term 'system' is not one of the primary categories in this theory; it is used to describe classes, and it is secondary to that term. While the theory put forward in 'Grammatical categories in modern Chinese' is explicit in the sense that it shows the relationship among a set of terms, several additional terms need to be introduced. These terms can be derived from those defined above but it is undesirable that theoretically necessary terms remain implicit.

The paper 'Categories of the theory of grammar', which was published in 1961, tidies up these shortcomings. The primary grammatical categories used are *structure*, *unit*, *class*, and *system*. *Element* is omitted (the term *element* continues to be used in the theory, but it is now a secondary category; similarly with *place*); the new terms are *system* and *structure*. *Structure* is necessary to define the likeness of units. Unless the internal structure of a unit is known, one cannot describe what other units are like it, or are the same. A structure is 'an arrangement of elements ordered in places'. *Element* is derived from *structure*, as an item occupying a structural place in a specified relation to other items, or to the structure as a whole. In effect, *element* is the term for the functionally labelled structural place. To use the earlier example again: CVC is a *structure* with three places 1, 2, 3; each place can be filled by a *unit* from the level next below. The *elements* on the other hand are *syllable initial consonant, syllable final consonant,* and *syllabic vowel.* The introduction of the new term *system* allows a necessary re-definition of the term *class* in the 1956 theory. Now *class* can be used to designate a collection of *units* defined as identical through their potentiality of occurrence at the same element in the structure of the unit next above. The systematic statement of choices at the element operating in the structure of the unit on the next higher level is now accounted for by the term *system*. Each element is represented by a class of units from the level next below. As noted earlier, the element s.i.cons. has itself a structure, or rather, a set of structures, such as CCC,CC,C, with the elements as defined earlier. Thus a system of classes emerges, each class with a specific and enumerable set of choices.

The categories of system, structure, class and unit are related to each other by three *scales: rank, delicacy* and *exponence. Rank* is reasonably transparent as a theoretical term; it relates the units to each other in a hierarchy. This is implied, in the earlier theory, in the relation of element and class, where the structural elements of one unit are classes of the unit next below. In the 1961 theory, the relation of rank is implied in the relation between structure, element and class in the same way. *Delicacy*, similarly, is transparent: it reflects the fact that linguistic descriptions can be made in varying degrees of fineness, subtlety, or *delicacy*. In the example above the syllable can be described as CVC. A more delicate description states the possibilities of structure that exist at each element; at the syllable initial consonant: C, CC, CCC; at the syllabic vowel the possible choices: V, VV, VVV; at the syllable final consonant: C, CC, CCC, CCCC. At each element in these secondary structures further steps in delicacy can be taken, depending on the purpose for which the linguist is using the description. *Exponence*, finally, is the scale which relates the abstract categories of the theory to their (abstract or concrete) *exponents*. That is, abstract grammatical categories have to find representation at some point; this 'representation' can be by other abstract categories (as when elements are expounded by classes, which are expounded by units from the rank below, and so on), or it may be through concrete exponents, as happens when increases in the delicacy of analysis yield not further classes of units, but actual lexical categories. (See especially chapter 5, pp. 70–72, and chapter 7.)

The categories in the 1961 theory have equal theoretical status. Certain theoretical tendencies are still left implicit, and the most important among these is that concerning the status of system. The notion of meaning as function in context becomes a possible organizing principle for a theory of language through the use of the term system. It is true, as Halliday says, that all the categories can be derived from any one of the categories. But in as far as the categories of *structure, class,* and *unit* are used in most linguistic theories (though obviously with theory specific definitions), it seems clear that *system* is the crucial category. The question is not so much one of logical possibility, but of the basic theoretical orientation. A formal theory based on the notion of meaning as function in context must give central place to the category of system. The other extracts in the second section of this volume illustrate the emergence in Halliday's thinking of system as the crucial theoretical concept. In the paper 'Chain and choice in language' Halliday states clearly that *chain* (syntagm) and *choice* (paradigm) represent two distinct alternative possibilities of organization for a linguistic theory.

The paper 'Deep grammar: system as semantic choice' acknowledges the previously latent status of system. It is now seen as the category which has definitive importance for the theory: the principle of choice is primary. Deep grammar consists of the totality of the systems of language; meaning arises from choices made within systems; structure is the device for giving these choices physical sequential representation. Thus for Halliday the link is between 'deep' systemic choice, non-sequential, abstract, non-physical, and 'surface' manifestation, realization, in sequential, physical structure. All structure is surface, and all systemic choice is deep. One implication of this approach is a careful attitude toward structure: the structure itself and every element of structure represent a systemic choice. It is therefore impossible to dismiss certain features of structure as 'merely surface'. The correspondence between all items of structure and their features in systems must be established and is demanded by the theory.

The pronounced functional character of Halliday's more recent writing is therefore implicit in the theory outlined as early as 1956. If one wished to provide a characterization of the theory as it exists from about 1966 onwards, it might be as follows. The structure in which language operates is socio-cultural. From the structural place in which it operates (quite analogous to the derivation of function as above) it derives its largest functions which are:

1 the function to establish, maintain, and specify relations between members of societies

2 the function to transmit information between members of societies and

3 the function to provide texture, the organization of discourse as relevant to the situation.

The first function Halliday calls the *interpersonal* function, the second the *ideational*, and the third the *textual*. Each of these functions makes a contribution to the structure, so that a grammatical structure is a composite pattern in which one melodic line derives from each—Halliday uses the analogy of polyphonic music.

From these functions derive the semantic systems of the language. Thus, in English, the major systems of the clause are *mood* (deriving from the interpersonal function), *transitivity* (deriving from the ideational function) and *theme* (deriving from the textual function). Similarly the nominal group, verbal group and other constituent types have systems deriving from all three functions. Choice within a system is meaning, as defined earlier: so these systems represent the meaning potential of language. Halliday does recognize a semantic level (his earlier term 'contextual level' was an unfortunate choice in this respect). It is close to Lamb's 'semology', but though Halliday is quite convinced of the tri-stratal organization of language he is, as he himself admits, very uncertain as to the location of the boundary between semantics and grammar.

This then is the theory. Language is a social activity. It has developed as it has, both in the functions it serves, and in the structures which express these functions, in response to the demands made by society and as a reflection of these demands. This is far from an anti-universalistic position. Malinowski said that 'It would be both preposterous and intellectually pusillanimous to give up at the outset any search for deeper forces which must have produced these common, universally human features of language' (Malinowski 1923). As I attempted to show earlier, Whorf's significance to Halliday lies not in his relativistic stance, but in his attempt to uncover grammatical, cognitive categories which could be seen to underlie and give rise to conceptual orientations of society. Halliday's position would be that the statement of the totality of all systems in one language would differ from that of another language: the search for universals is then best conducted through a comparison of the full systemic potential of different languages. Similarly with Halliday's formal linguistic theory: the theory attempts at all times to provide categories which are universal.

In his most recent work Halliday has concentrated on integrating the various aspects of his thinking into a coherent framework under the general rubric of what he calls 'social semiotics' (the social system, or the culture, as a semiotic construct). This is the theme of a number of his recent publications—in particular his essay 'Language as social semiotic' in *The First LACUS Forum*, and his discussion with Herman Parret in the latter's *Discussing Language*. The theme is that language is explainable only as the realization of meanings that are inherent in the social system, the meanings that constitute the culture. It is of course not the only form of their realization; but it is its place in the broader environment of other semiotic systems that has shaped its evolution and determines its nature and functions.

This Halliday sees as coming under four headings.

1 The linguistic system itself, which he interprets in terms of the functional categories of ideational, interpersonal and textual discussed above —the 'functional components of the semantic system', in his own terms. The interpretation of contemporary English in these terms will be seen in his forthcoming *Meaning of Modern English*, to be published by Oxford University Press. As far as the formal properties of the system are concerned, Halliday claims that Lamb's stratificational model is largely compatible with his own conceptualization of how language is organized.

2 The development of the system in the child, on the subject of which he has just completed a book *Learning How to Mean*, based on detailed observations of his own and setting forth a general hypothesis about

how (and why) a child constructs the functional semantic system of the mother tongue.

3 The text, that is the instantiation of the 'meaning potential' in actual contexts of situation. Apart from studying natural conversation, which Halliday has always regarded as a sine qua non of the understanding of the linguistic *system* (and has himself been doing for many years), he has just completed a joint study, together with his wife Ruqaiya Hasan, on the subject of cohesion (the non-structural element of texture) in modern English (*Cohesion in English*).

4 The fourth heading is the social structure; and here the most important influence on Halliday's work has been Bernstein. Halliday makes extensive use of Bernstein's ideas to provide the social theory that he is convinced must be incorporated into any explanation of language; an example is his use of Bernstein's theory of codes, as the principle whereby the culture regulates the range of meanings, or register, that is typically associated by its members with particular social contexts.

The integrated picture can be apprehended both in relation to the system itself and in relation to the development of the system by a child. The child learns the mother tongue interactionally, in the context of learning the culture through the mother tongue. In the same way language has evolved in the context of its use in the social construction of reality—a phrase that Halliday borrows from the title of Berger and Luckmann's well-known book on the sociology of knowledge. This is what determines the form that human language has taken (our brains could have constructed symbolic systems of many other kinds).

Most recently of all Halliday has returned to an investigation that he began pursuing ten and more years ago, into the way in which the context of situation is, in Dell Hymes' phrase 'constitutive of' the text. Halliday is convinced that it is possible to show a systematic relationship between the text, the linguistic system, and the situation, provided that the situation is interpreted not as the material environment (in however abstract terms) but as a semiotic structure whose elements are social meanings, and into which 'things' enter as the bearers of social values. He reinterprets the concept of *field*, *tenor* (originally 'style') and *mode*, first set out in *The Linguistic Sciences and Language Teaching*, in these terms, and attempts to show how these are linked to the ideational, interpersonal and textual components of the system. Using children's texts as examples, he tries to show how the systemic options represented in the text reflect the semiotic properties of the situation as expressed in this way. It remains to be seen how far such an attempt can be successful; but Halliday is surely right in claiming it as an important goal of linguistic and sociolinguistic studies.

Section One

System and Function

1 A brief sketch of systemic grammar

I should like to describe to you in outline something of the work that my colleagues and I have been doing in the realm of grammatical description and theory. I hope to make six points about the grammar. The name 'systemic' is not the same thing as 'systematic'; the term is used because the fundamental concept in the grammar is that of the 'system'. A system is a set of options with an entry condition: that is to say, a set of things of which one must be chosen, together with a statement of the conditions under which the choice is available.

First, then, the grammar is based on the notion of choice. The speaker of a language, like a person engaging in any kind of culturally determined behaviour, can be regarded as carrying out, simultaneously and successively, a number of distinct choices. At any given moment, in the environment of the selections made up to that time, a certain range of further choices is available. It is the system that formalizes the notion of choice in language.

In chapter 9 you can see system networks, taken from the grammar of the English clause. The system network is the grammar. The grammar of any language can be represented as a very large network of systems, an arrangement of options in simultaneous and hierarchical relationship. The network is open-ended. To the left of each arrow is the entry condition; to the right, joined by a brace, is the set of two or more options which make up the choice. So for example given the entry condition 'clause' there are three simultaneous choices to be made: from transitivity, mood and theme. (For speech a fourth choice is added: information.) There are various ways in which selection in one option may serve as a condition of entry to another; these are illustrated on page 14. In addition to the simple entry condition (if restricted then either intransitive or transitive) there are the two types of junction: conjunction (if both non-middle and identification then either active or

Extract from 'Systemic Grammar' *La Grammatica; La Lessicologia* Rome: Bulzoni (Atti del I e del II Convegno di Studi, Società di Linguistica Italiana), 1969.

passive) and disjunction (if either modulated or modalized is selected, then there is a choice from both uncommitted/committed and neutral/oblique).

Second, the description of a sentence, clause or other item may be just a list of the choices that the speaker has made. The system network specifies what are the possible combinations of choices that could be made; each permitted path through the network is thus the description of a class of linguistic items. Thus the description of a linguistic item is the set of features selected in that item from the total available. Such a description is at the same time a statement of its relationship to other items: reference to the grammar shows that *John threw the ball* relates to *did John throw the ball?*, *the ball John threw*, *the ball was thrown by John* &c., which differ from it, and from each other, in respect only of certain specified options.

Third, the term 'structure' has not yet been mentioned, and in fact considerations of structure are delayed till the latest possible. By 'structure' we may understand the representation of an item in terms of its constituents, with the linearity that such a representation implies: if *John threw the ball* is said to 'consist of' a subject *John* and a predicate *threw the ball* it is implied that one comes before the other, or at least that their relation is expressible in terms of linear sequence. Obviously the description of a language must at some stage take cognizance of succession in real time; the problem is at what point to introduce linearity into the description. The linear arrangement of the parts of a sentence does not figure, here, in the most abstract representation of that sentence; structure is treated as a mechanism whereby the speaker realizes or makes manifest the choices he has made. The concept of realization has been familiar in linguistics for a long time, though it has been called by different names; in English, exponence, implementation, manifestation as well as realization. The options selected by the speaker are 'realized' as structures; and there are two aspects to a structure, the bracketing and the labelling, each of which needs to be considered.

Fourth, then, two principal types of bracketing have been used in linguistics, which we might refer to as 'maximum bracketing' and 'minimum bracketing'. The former is what is known as 'immediate constituent' analysis; the latter has been called 'string constituent' analysis and is often associated with the 'slot and filler' account of structure. With minimum bracketing the fewest possible layers of structure are introduced into the description: the tree has a much smaller number of levels in it. In a systemic description the bracketing is minimal, for three reasons. First, any bracketing more than the necessary minimum is redundant, because the information it contains is recoverable from the systemic part of the description: its function is to show how sentences are related to one another and this is shown in terms of options.

Second, the significance of the bracketing is that it indicates where a new set of options is open to the speaker: each node is the point of origin for a set of systems, so that again the determining factor is that of choice. Finally, non-minimal bracketing tends to be self-contradictory. The clause *John threw the ball*, minimally bracketed, is a three-element structure, and this represents its structure as the realization of options in transitivity, Actor Process Goal. If we then consider its structure as a message, assuming one possible reading in which *the ball* is marked out by intonation as 'new' information and *John threw* as 'given', the clause will be structured into two constituents: Given (John threw) New (the ball); and if we introduce another dimension of structure, that of theme—rheme, we shall need a third analysis: Theme (John) Rheme (threw the ball), still in two parts but with the break at a different place. Thus any item may have not just one structure but many. Since there may be a number of simultaneous structures superimposed on one another in this way, minimal bracketing is the most neutral; in the present example, only a tree corresponding to the first bracketing is an adequate representation of all three.

Fifth, and closely related to the last point, is the question of labelling. There are two ways of labelling: according to structural function, and according to class. Functional labelling will indicate for example that the structure is one of actor—process—goal, or theme—rheme, or modifier—head and so forth. Class labelling will indicate such things as noun phrase, verb phrase, noun, verb, adjective or adverb. It is not always obvious what the difference between the two is. In terms of the present grammar, they are interpretable by reference to the underlying notion of choice. A class is a statement of 'choices now open'; for example the label 'noun phrase' means that there are options of singular/plural, count/mass, specific/non-specific and so on. A function is a statement of 'choices already made': thus 'subject' means that indicative has been selected, 'goal' means that transitive has been selected, &c. The two types of labelling thus as it were face different ways in relation to the concept of choice. Since structure is fully predictable, being derived from the systemic representation, the primary labels used here are functional ones. But the analysis of structural function is componential; in *John threw the ball*, *John* has a composite function of actor and given and theme and subject and possibly others as well. Thus the element of a structure, the constituent, is a complex of structural functions each of which represents some choice that the speaker has made in the planning of that sentence.

Sixth, since the structure is regarded as the realization of systemic choices, the grammar has to indicate how the particular choices made by the speaker are realized in structural terms. To each of the options on p. 14, such as indicative, imperative &c., we may append a realization statement showing the contribution made by the selection of that option to the structure of the sentence: for example, the realization statement accompanying the option 'indicative' would be 'subject is present in the string'. These are thought of as statements of relationship rather than as rules.

A realization statement may take various forms. Certain options are realized by the presence of a particular function in the structure, like indicative above, or 'restricted' realized by the presence of the function 'actor'. But other options have the effect of mapping two structural functions one on to the other: of conflating them into a single element. For example in *John threw the ball*, *John* is both subject and actor (the definition of 'subject' lies outside the present discussion, but it is treated here as a modal function, whose position in sequence varies with the choice of mood: declarative *John threw*, interrogative *did John throw*); but there is no need for the subject and the actor to be the same element —we could have the passive form *the ball was thrown by John* in which *the ball* is now subject though it is not actor but goal. There must therefore be a particular option whereby the speaker decides to conflate the roles of actor and subject: this would be the option 'operative'. The realization statement of the feature 'operative' specifies that subject and actor form a single element. There are altogether five types of realization statement which are needed to relate the structure of sentences to the options selected. A complete structure is thus a sequence of elements, composed of functions any of which may extend across more than one element; it is bracketed at each rank and where there is recursion, where an option provides for going round a loop and returning to an earlier choice.

The six points I have made could be summarized as follows. One, the underlying notion in the grammar is that of choice, and this is represented through the concept of a system, which is a set of options together with a condition of entry. Two, the description of any sentence or other item in the language takes the form of a statement of the options that have been selected in that sentence. Three, the structural representation of a sentence is derived by realization from the systemic one, so that the latter is the more abstract ('deeper'). Four, the structural representation is minimally bracketed. Five, the structural labelling is functional and componential, the element of structure being a complex of functions realizing different options. Six, the systemic and the structural descriptions are related by realization statements which show the structural contribution of the options in the grammar.

2 The form of a functional grammar

The study of the social functions of language—of 'language and social man'—has for a long time occupied an important place in linguistics as a field of theoretical investigation. It is natural that we should want to gain some understanding of how language is used, so that the search for valid principles of language use is perhaps the most obvious and immediate goal of such enquiries. But an equally significant question, for the linguist, is that of the relation between the functions of language and language itself. If language has evolved in the service of certain functions, that may in the broadest sense be called 'social' functions, has this left its mark in determining the nature of language? It is the purpose of this paper to suggest that it has, and that this fact is one that may be systematically reflected in the construction of a grammar. A 'complex grammar' will be understood here as a grammar that is functionally complex: one whose components are functional in origin (see note below).

We must distinguish two sub-questions, and rule out one of them. It is obvious that the social functioning of language determines the pattern of language *varieties*, in the sense of diatypic varieties, or registers; the register range, or verbal repertoire, of a community or an individual derives from the range of social uses of language in the context of the particular culture. But this diatypic variety is itself a form of patterned selection within the language system, which must therefore be such as to accommodate it. The more fundamental question, and the one with which we shall be concerned here, is then: is the social functioning of language reflected in linguistic structure—that is, in the internal organization of language *as a system*? It seems reasonable to expect that it will be; and it was in fact said to be by Malinowski, who wrote in 1923 that 'language in its structure mirrors the real categories derived from the practical attitudes of the child . . .'. In Malinowski's

This paper, entitled 'On Functional Grammars', was read to the Seminar on the Construction of Complex Grammars, Cambridge, Mass., June 1970. It was published in a revised version in Basil Bernstein (ed.) *Class Codes and Control Vol. II*, London: Routledge & Kegan Paul, 1973. This is the original version, previously unpublished.

view all uses of language, throughout the many stages of cultural evolution, had left their imprint on linguistic structure, although 'if our theory is right, the fundamental outlines of grammar are due mainly to the most primitive uses of language' (Malinowski, 1923).

It was in the language of young children that Malinowski saw most clearly the functional origins of the language system. His formulation was in fact 'the practical attitudes of the child, and of primitive or natural man'; but he later modified this view, realizing that linguistic research had demonstrated that there was no such thing as a 'primitive language'—that all adult speech represented the same highly sophisticated level of linguistic evolution. Similarly all uses of language, however abstract, and however complex the social structure with which they were associated, were to be explained in terms of very elementary functions. It may still be that the developing language system of the child in some sense traverses, or at least provides an analogy for, the stages through which language itself has evolved; but there are no living specimens of its ancestral types, so that any evidence can only come from within, from the study of the language system and its acquisition by the child.

Malinowski's ideas were somewhat ahead of his time, and were not backed up by any language acquisition studies. Nor, perhaps, would it have helped very much if they had been, since anyone at the time thinking about how a child learnt his native language was likely to think in terms of the acquisition of sounds: control of the means of articulation, and perhaps, at most, mastery of the sound system, or phonology, of the language in question. It was only as the focus of attention gradually shifted, towards the acquisition of meanings rather than simply the acquisition of sounds, that such studies became relevant to the point at issue. We can trace the stages in the development of this interest, more or less level by level. The next step is to think of language acquisition in terms of words; the child has to acquire a vocabulary, and language competence is then equated with the size of the lexicon. Next it comes to be thought of as the mastery of structures—of the grammar, in the traditional sense of this term. Only recently has language acquisition come to be seen as the mastery of linguistic functions, and it is this perspective that is needed here, in which learning language is learning the uses of language and the meaning potential associated with them; the structures, the words and the sounds are the realization of this meaning potential. Learning language is learning to mean.

With language acquisition seen as the acquisition of a meaning potential, it becomes possible to consider the Malinowskian thesis seriously, since we can begin by looking at the relation between the child's linguistic structures and the uses he is putting language to. But first we ought to ask what the notion of language serving certain functions really implies. What do we mean by the 'social functions of language', in terms of the daily life of homo grammaticus, the talking ape?

A way into this is to consider certain very specialized uses of language, such as the bidding system of contract bridge, or other game languages. The bidding language may be thought of as a system of meaning potential: a range of options open to the player as performer and receiver. This potential, which is what I understand by Hymes' 'communicative competence', is neutral as to speaker and hearer since it is shared; it presupposes speaker, hearer and situation—in terms of the language system, a set of options and the ability to select appropriately within them, to say 'four hearts' at the right place. I prefer to talk of 'meaning potential' because I am interested in what the speaker (or hearer) can do, not in what he knows; and while the two are, to a certain extent, different ways of looking at the same thing, the ethnographic perspective does have somewhat different implications from the psychological one.

There are many 'restricted languages' of this kind, in games, systems of greetings, musical scores, weather reports, recipes and numerous other generalized situation types. The simplest case is one in which the text consists of only one message unit, or a string of message units linked by 'and'; a well-known example is the set of a hundred or so cabled messages that one was permitted to send home while on active service in wartime, a typical expression being $61 + 92$, decoded perhaps as 'happy birthday and please send DDT'. Here the meaning potential is simply the list of possible messages, as a set of options, together with the option of choosing more than once, perhaps with some specified maximum number.

The daily life of the individual talking ape does not revolve around options like this, although much of his speech does take place in fairly restricted contexts in which the options are limited and the meaning potential is in part rather closely specifiable. Buying and selling in a shop, going to the doctor, having one's hair cut are all situation types in which the language is not as a whole restricted but where there are certain definitely restricted patterns; similarly one can say more or less what one likes on the telephone, but there are prescribed ways of beginning and ending the conversation. These all relate to delimitable social functions of language—in the widest sense, to what we use language for, and what we expect to achieve by using language that we could not achieve without it. (To gain some insight into this it is helpful to consider everyday tasks and ask oneself how much more difficult they would be to carry out if one had to do so without language.)

We could set out to write a list of 'uses of language' by the adult; such a list could be indefinitely prolonged, and would be of no real interest. The social functions of language are significant to the extent that they shed light on language, so that we will be interested in identifying a given function if we find we can specify some or all of the meaning potential associated with that function. And we shall be interested even more if we find that, by doing so, we can account for certain features in the structural organization of language.

With this in mind we may look at the relation between the child's linguistic structures and the uses to which he is putting language. The language system of the very young child is, effectively, a set of restricted varieties; and it is a characteristic of young children's language that its internal form reflects rather directly the function that it is being used to serve. What the child does with language tends to determine its structure. This relatively close match between structure and function can be seen from a consideration of some parts of the system as it might be of a very young child; we can see how the structures that he has mastered are direct reflections of the functions that language is being required to serve in his life.

Figures 1–3 on pages 11–13 represent such a system; or rather, they represent three possible components of a total system where the total number of such components is low—say between three and six. Each such component is the grammar corresponding to just one function that the child has begun to control. By the 'instrumental' function I mean the use of language for the purpose of satisfying material needs: the 'I want' function, including 'I don't want'. In this example the child has developed a meaning potential here consisting of two simultaneous options: positive and negative desire, and three categories of object of desire, food, clothing and toys. Under one combination of circumstances, namely the conjunction of 'food' and 'positive', there is a further option in his meaning potential, since here he has learnt that he can demand not only a first instalment but also a supplementary one, 'more'. (Note that this particular child cannot do this in the negative; he has not yet learnt to mean 'no more'.) With clothing and toys the option does not arise. In the system 'basic' versus 'supplementary', therefore, the term 'basic' is the unmarked one, where 'unmarked' is defined as that which must be selected if the conditions of entry into the system are not satisfied.

Each option in the meaning potential is expressed, or realized, by some structure-forming element. In the instrumental component there are just three: the object of desire, the negative element, and the quantifier. The child's selection of a particular combination of options within his meaning potential is thus realized in the form of a structure; but it is a structure in which the elements are very clearly related to the underlying function which the language is being made to serve. For example, there is obviously a connection between the 'instrumental' function of language and the presence, in the derived structure, of an element having the structural function 'object of desire'. (What is significant is

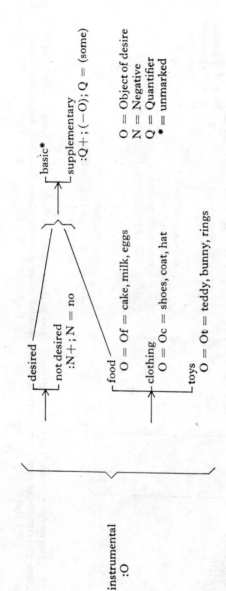

FIGURE I

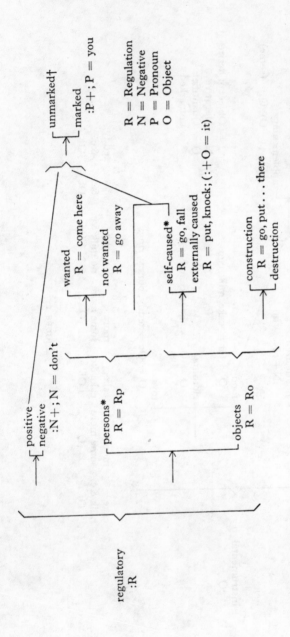

FIGURE 2

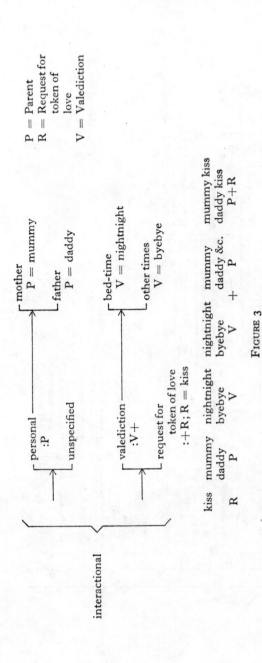

FIGURE 3

Figures 1–3: key to structural formulae

:X	'X is added'
X+	'X precedes (other element)'
+X	'X follows (other element)'
…X	'X is final'
−X	'X is deleted'
( )	'optionally'

[Note: All systems on pp. 11–13 are fictitious. For real systems in the language of a child see items 37 and 45 in Appendix II at the end of this book.]

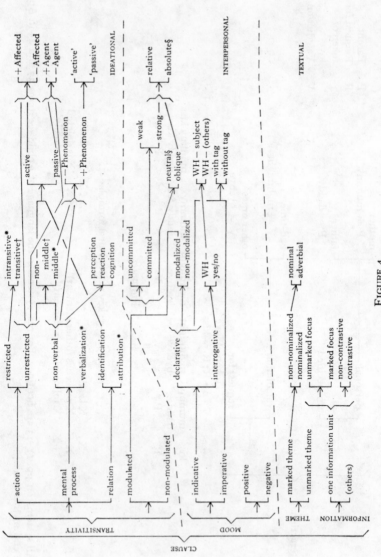

FIGURE 4

Figures 1–4: summary of notational conventions

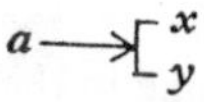

$a \longrightarrow \begin{bmatrix} x \\ y \end{bmatrix}$ there is a system x/y with entry condition a (if a, then either x or y)

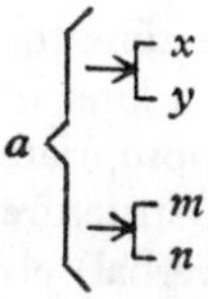

$a \begin{cases} \to \begin{bmatrix} x \\ y \end{bmatrix} \\ \\ \to \begin{bmatrix} m \\ n \end{bmatrix} \end{cases}$ there are two simultaneous systems x/y and m/n, both having entry condition a (if a, then both either x or y and, independently, either m or n)

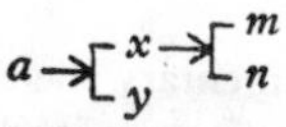

$a \to \begin{bmatrix} x \\ y \end{bmatrix} \to \begin{bmatrix} m \\ n \end{bmatrix}$ there are two systems x/y and m/n, ordered in dependence so that m/n has entry condition x and x/y has entry condition a (if a then either x or y, and if x, then either m or n)

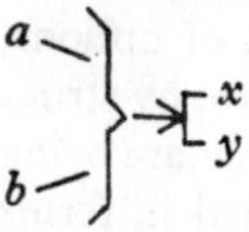

$\left. \begin{array}{c} a \\ \\ b \end{array} \right\} \begin{bmatrix} x \\ y \end{bmatrix}$ there is a system x/y with compound entry condition, conjunction of a and b (if both a and b then either x or y)

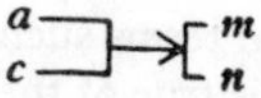

$\left. \begin{array}{c} a \\ c \end{array} \right] \to \begin{bmatrix} m \\ n \end{bmatrix}$ there is a system m/n with two possible entry conditions, union of a and c (if either a or c, or both, then either m or n)

$a^* \ldots x^*$ (or any paired symbol) x is unmarked with respect to a (if a, then always x)

x^* x is unmarked with respect to all environments (if any tangential feature, then always x). Note: a tangential feature is the non-dominant term in a dominant system, e.g. a in

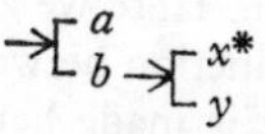

$$\to \begin{bmatrix} a \\ b \end{bmatrix} \to \begin{bmatrix} x^* \\ y \end{bmatrix}$$

not, of course, the label itself but the fact that we are forced to identify a particular category, to which a label such as this then turns out to be appropriate.)

The proto-grammar represented here is thus a functional one in the two distinct but related senses in which the term is used in linguistics: it is an account of the functions of language, and at the same time the elements of its structures are also functional elements. It is a kind of 'case grammar', although the notion of case is perhaps less appropriate than the related notion of element of structure in system-structure theory, since case is usually restricted to dependent (non-verbal) elements whereas here the entire structure is shown as a configuration of functions.

We have assumed for purposes of illustration a very elementary stage of language learning: for example the child whose grammar is described here has only two-element structures. We could just as well have chosen another stage; the emphasis is on the form of the language system. It consists of a meaning potential, represented as a network of options, deriving from a particular social function and realized, in turn, by structures whose elements derive from the functional meanings that are being expressed. These elements are more appropriately described in terms such as 'object of desire'—which, as we have said, clearly relates to the 'I want' function of language—than in 'purely' grammatical terms such as 'pivot'. I shall be suggesting later that exactly the same is true of the structural functions of the adult language, which likewise have their origin in the social functions of language, though merely in a slightly more subtle way. Even such an apparently 'grammatical' function as 'subject' is clearly relatable to language use (in fact the notion of a 'purely grammatical' function is absurd).

The same principle is present in the other two components here illustrated. One is of the 'regulatory' function of language: the use of language to control the behaviour of others—to manipulate the persons and, with or without their help, the objects in the environment. This is the 'do as I tell you' function. Here we also find the option of positive and negative, and also a distinction between persons and objects in the grammar—a distinction that is made here on two grounds: first, that persons are merely required to be either present or absent, whereas objects may also be required to be built up or broken down, and second, that the actions of persons are self-caused only, whereas those of objects may be either self-caused or externally caused ('go there' or 'put it there'). It should be stated that it is a particular interpretation of the child's emergent notion of transitivity which chooses to analyse 'put it there' as an instruction to an object to get itself put somewhere, rather than to a person to do something with an object. This could no doubt be tested in various ways, but it is immaterial to the present discussion since it would be just as easy to represent the system in the grammar the other way round.

The other example is of the 'interactional' function: the child's use of language as a means of personal interaction with those around him, the function of 'me and my mummy'. I have assumed, but again for the sake of illustration only, an English middle-class family type with mummy and daddy as the significant personal roles; and I have postulated two types of linguistic interaction—valedictions, and requests for a sign or token of love. Again, we have the elements of structure and their derivation from the options in the meaning potential. The network shows what the child can do, in the sense of what he can mean, and the structural statement shows how he does it—how the meanings are expressed through functional configurations.

In another paper[1] I have suggested what may be the basic set of functions that language has for the child, listing the instrumental, the regulatory, the interactional, the personal, the heuristic, the imaginative and the representational (the last was badly named, and would have been better called 'informative', since it referred specifically to the use of language for exchange of information). These are what I mean by the generalized social functions of language in the context of the young child's life. When the child has acquired the ability to use language to some extent in one of these functions, however limited the grammatical and lexical resources he can bring to bear, then he has built up a network of options, a meaning potential, for that function, and can manipulate some structural configurations, however elementary, of elements relating to the function in question.

The social functions which language is serving in the life of the child thus determine both the available options and the structural realizations of those options. This can be seen clearly in the language of young children once we concede that language acquisition is, basically, the acquisition of the social functions of language and of a meaning potential associated with them. However, although this connection between language function and the language system is clearest in the case of young children's language, it is actually, I think, a feature of language as a whole. The system of natural language can best be explained in the light of the social functions which language has evolved to serve. Language is as it is because of what it has to do. Only, the relation between language function and language structure will appear much less directly, and in more complex ways, in the fully developed adult system than in children's language.

To say this is in effect to claim, with Malinowski, that ontogeny does in some way provide a model for phylogeny. We cannot examine the

1. 'Relevant Models of Language' *The State of Language* (*Educational Review* 22.1), 1969. 26–37.

origins of language; but if we can show that natural language in its adult form is explainable in terms of social function, and that the language of the child, in its various stages, is derivable from the functions that the child makes language serve for him at that particular stage of his maturation, then we have at least something to discuss in relation to the nature and origins of the language system.

It is characteristic, it seems, of the utterances of the very young child that each one is functionally simple: that is, each utterance serves just one function. If an utterance is instrumental in function, seeking the satisfaction of some material need or desire, then it is just instrumental and nothing else. This represents a very early stage of language development, and it is shown in our grammar by the fact that each utterance is totally specified by just one network. To derive the utterance *more milk!* we need only the instrumental system network, which fully describes its structure.

The adult language bears very clearly the marks of its humble origins in a system such as this one. But it differs in various fundamental ways, of which perhaps the most fundamental is that adult utterances are functionally complex. That is to say, each adult utterance, with a few broadly specifiable exceptions, is serving more than one function at the same time. For example, when after the recent Football Association Cup Final match between Leeds and Chelsea a friend of mine who is a Londoner greeted me with *I see that Chelsea trounced Leeds again*, he was conveying a certain piece of information (which he guessed I probably knew already), referring it to our shared experience, expressing his pleasure and triumph (I am a Leeds supporter, and he knows it), and relating back to some previous exchange between us. The problem for a sociolinguistic theory is: what is there in the adult language which corresponds to the functional systems, or sets of meaning potential, in the language of the young child? What, in fact, is the relation of the fully developed language system to the social functions of the adult language, and can we explain something of the form that languages take by examining this relation?

In one sense, the variety of social functions of language is, obviously, much greater in the adult. He does more different things, and in a great many of his activities he uses language; he has a very broad diatypic spectrum. Yet there is another sense in which his functional variety is much poorer, and we can perhaps appreciate this if we approach it from the child as point of departure. Among the child's uses of language there emerges, I think rather late, the use of language to communicate a content; that which I referred to in a general way as the 'representational' function. It would probably be clearer—as I suggested above— if one were to use a more specific term in the first instance, since what happens later can be seen as the broadening and deepening of this use to a more general function that could properly be called 'representational'. Be that as it may, during the course of childhood and adolescence this function gradually comes to predominate. Eventually it comes completely to dominate—if not the adult's use of language, at least his thinking about language, so that if one suggests to the adult that language has other functions than that of communicating ideas, or content, he is frankly amazed. Yet this is a very minor and rather late function as far as the child is concerned, and many problems of adult-child communication, especially in the primary school, arise from the adults' failure to grasp this fact. This is well illustrated by adult renderings of nursery rhymes, which tend to be very dramatic, with an intonation and rhythm appropriate to the content; this is meaningless to the child, for whom the language is not content—it is language in its imaginative function, and should be expressed as patterns of sounds and words and structures and meanings. (A similar failure has been known to occur when actors have recorded foreign language courses, where their renderings can only focus the students' attention on the content function of the language.)

What happens, then, in the course of maturation is a process we might call 'functional reduction' whereby the original functional diversity of the child's language—a set of fairly discrete functions, each with its own meaning potential and therefore its own grammar—is replaced by a much more highly organized and more abstract, but also much simpler, functional system. The immense functional diversity of adult language usage—immense, that is, if one simply asks 'in what activities of daily life does language play a part?'—is reduced in the internal organization of the language system to a very small set of functional components, or 'macro-functions'. These are the highly abstract linguistic reflexes of the multiplicity of social uses of language. There are innumerable social purposes for which adults use language; but these are not represented directly, one by one, as functional components in the internal organization of language, as are those of the child. This, besides immeasurably complicating the system, would make it virtually impossible for different functions to be combined in the utterance in the way the adult requires. Instead, they are represented indirectly in the language system through 'macro-functions' of a very general kind—which are still recognizable, nevertheless, as being the underlying demands which we make on language and which it must serve in order to fulfil the more specific social purposes which we require of it.

One of these macro-functions is the representational, or, as I shall prefer to call it, the 'ideational'. For the child, the use of language to express a content is a special case of language use, just one function among many; but with the adult, this function of language comes to be involved in one way or another in practically all uses of language in which he engages. Whatever the adult is doing with language, he needs to exploit its generalized ideational potential, its potentiality for expressing a content in terms of his experience of the real world. There is almost always an ideational element in adult speech, with the exception of certain types of utterance like *how do you do?*; this is an abstract function underlying nearly every specific use of language. It is already beginning to emerge in certain of the specific functions of child language, although not the earliest ones; and no doubt it develops out of these in the course of the gradual separation of 'function' from 'use' that marks the development of the adult system. But in the child language it is (in principle) one utterance: one function, whereas in the adult language it is (again in principle) every utterance: all functions—in the new, abstract sense of macro-function. All utterances have an ideational component in them; but they all have something else besides.

The macro-function is still a meaning potential, although the potential is now very vast and complex. And—the main point—the structures of the adult language are still recognizably functional, given the generalized 'macro-function' concept. That is to say, corresponding to (i.e. realizing the options in) the ideational function of language are structures whose elements are recognizable as elements in our interpretation of our experience, our experience of the world around us and inside us. So, for example, the clause *Sir Christopher Wren built this gazebo* is, structurally, a configuration of the functions 'agent' (*Sir Christopher Wren*), 'process: action: creation' (*built*) and 'goal: resultant' (*this gazebo*), in which the categories 'agent', 'process' and 'goal', and their sub-categories, are categories of our experience, and reflect our understanding of the external world. The function which language is serving here, that of encoding our experience in the form of 'content', still determines not merely the available options but also the structural realizations thereof.

Once again, the categories are not arbitrarily set up from outside language, either casually or as an extralinguistic theory of knowledge. It is the internal structure of language, the grammatical organization as we find it, empirically, which leads us to analyse the clause in this way—though, of course, once we identify the underlying functions this may lead us to select one rather than another of a number of possible structural interpretations. Structural functions such as 'agent' and 'process' are significant in relation to the meaning potential of the ideational element in language. The clause is the structural unit wherewith we express a particular part of that meaning potential—our experience of the processes of the external world, including also the processes of our own consciousness, thinking, seeing, liking, talking and so on. These are encoded, in English, and probably most other languages, into three types of structural element: the process itself, the participants in the process (animate and inanimate), and the attendant circumstances. This is the basis of the very widespread three-way distinction of constituents of the clause into verbals, nominals and the rest (adverbials, in the broader sense). Thus the clause, in the adult language, is the entry point into a network of options which constitute the meaning potential for the expression of processes: options in the types of process that we recognize, the various participant functions that may be associated with them, and so on, down to the actual names—the words of the language— which, by and large, represent the most delicate distinctions that the system embodies.

'Transitivity' is the name for this particular range of meaning potential—the encoding of our experience of processes. To put it another way, transitivity is the ideational component in the meaning of the clause. Figure 4 on page 14 sets out the most generalized options within the transitivity system of English (see also chapter 9). The right hand column in Table 1 (pp. 22–3) shows how these are realized in the form of structures; and it can be seen that the structure-forming elements— process, affected, agent, phenomenon, and the like—are still, like those of the protolanguages we looked at earlier, functional in origin. These terms are of course only names, and have no status in the description; but, as before, they are motivated names. If we find, for example, that the grammar of English embodies as a distinct syntactic category a structural element expressing the external causer of a process, it is reasonable to label it 'agent'; whether we did so or not, it would remain valid as a structural function, one which derives from the social function that language serves in expressing our experience of processes and the participants in them.

The clause, however, is not confined to the expression of transitivity. The ideational function may dominate adult intuitions about language, but in the adult language system other functions coexist with it. Again however there is a contrast with that of the child. In the adult system all the non-ideational elements in language are as it were rolled into one; there is just one 'macro-function' which embodies all use of language to express social and personal relations—all forms of the speaker's intrusion into the speech situation and the speech act. With the child, these are differentiated; his use of language to interact with others is, at first, rather distinct from his use of it to express his own personality or his attitudes and feelings. Later, all these components are fused, in the system of language, to form a single generalized 'interpersonal' component at this more abstract functional level. In the clause, the interpersonal element is represented by mood and modality: the selection by the speaker of a particular role in the speech situation, for himself and for the hearer, and of judgments, assessments of probability and the like.

TABLE I

clause	:Proc.Af; Mo.Prop; Th.Rh; Th+Rh
action	Proc: action verb
intransitive	Proc: intransitive verb
transitive	Proc: transitive verb
unrestricted	Proc: 'vb. trans. & intrans.'
non-middle	:Ag; if mental process, Phen:Ag
active	Proc: active verb; Ag:Su; Af.Co
—Affected	—Af
passive	Proc: passive verb (unless *be*); Af:Su; Ag:Ad (*by*)
mental process	Af: human noun; :Phen (:thing or fact)
—Phenomenon	—Phen
middle: 'active'	Proc: active verb; Phen:Co; Af:Su
middle: 'passive'	Proc: passive verb; Phen:Su; Af:Ad (*by*)
perception	Proc: verb of perception
reaction	Proc: verb of reaction
cognition	Proc: verb of cognition
verbalization	Proc: verb of verbalization; Phen: fact (only)
identification	Proc: verb of identification ('equative'); Af, Ag:Id, Ir
attribution	Proc: verb of attribution ('ascriptive'); Af:Atd; :Ag
modulated or modalized	Pred(fi) in Mo:modal auxiliary (Note: both features have alternative realizations at least one of which must be selected if the two features co-occur)
uncommitted/neutral	Pred(fi): *will, won't* (also *can, can't* in modul.)
uncommitted/oblique	Pred(fi): *would, wouldn't*
weak/neutral	Pred(fi): *can, may, may not* (modal.), *needn't* (modul.)
weak/oblique	Pred(fi): *could, might, might not* (,,), *needn't* (,,)
relative (oblique)	Pred(fi): *should, ought to, shouldn't, oughtn't*
absolute/neutral	Pred(fi): *must, can't* (modal.), *mustn't* (modul.)
absolute/oblique	Pred(fi): *must, couldn't* (modal.), *mustn't* (modul.)
non-modalized	Pred(fi) in Mo:non-modal auxiliary
indicative	Mo:Su.Pred(fi); negative: add +*n't* or +*not*
declarative	Su+Pred(fi)
with tag	:Mo₂ finally; Mo₂: Pred(fi)+Su; Su: concord pronoun
WH—	:WH initially
WH—subject	Wh:Su; Su+Pred(fi)
WH—other	Wh:Co or Ad; Pred(fi)+Su
yes/no	Pred(fi)+Su
you!	Mo: *you* or φ, *don't* ((*you*))
let's!	Mo: *let's, don't let's* or *let's not*

TABLE I—*cont.*

unmarked theme	
/declarative	Th:Su
/Wh—	Th:Wh
/yes/no	Th:Pred(fi)
marked theme	
/nominal	Th:Co
/adverbial	Th:Ad
/nominalized	Th is combination of elements as nominalization
one info. unit	clause is one tone group; :((Gi.))Ne
unmarked focus	final lexical element is tonic nucleus; ((Gi+))Ne
marked focus	other element is tonic nucleus; ((Gi+))Ne+Gi
non-contrastive	tone I (falling)
contrastive	tone 4 (falling-rising)

Key to structural formulae

:x	'x is added'
:x.y	'x and y are added'
x+y	'y follows x'
x:z	'x is z'
((z))	'z is optional'

Elements of structure

Process; Affected; Modal; Propositional; Theme; Rheme; Agent; Phenomenon; Subject; Complement; Adjunct; Identified; Identifier; Attribuand; Attribute; Predicator; Predicator (finite element in); Wh-element (i.e. interrogative word); Given; New

We are not saying, it should be made clear, that there is no distinction among all such uses of language—to approve or disapprove; to express beliefs, opinions, doubts; to include and to exclude; to ask and answer questions; to express personal feelings; to greet, chat up, take leave of; all these and many others. What we are saying is that in the structure of the adult language we can recognize—we are forced to recognize—a generalized and integrated 'interpersonal' function which underlies these and many more, in the sense that they form an interrelated set of options; a definable area of meaning potential.

These two broad macro-functions of the adult language, the ideational and the interpersonal, together determine a large part of the meaning potential of the clause. The first is at the basis of the transitivity system; the second, of the system of mood. The clause serves as the structural unit for the expression of options of these two types (cf. Fig. 4 on page 14). There is also a third macro-function, the 'textual', which I shall omit from the discussion here; this is the requirement that language should be operationally relevant—that it should have a texture, in the event, that makes the difference between a message and a mere entry in the grammar or the dictionary. This third component provides the remaining strands of meaning potential to be woven into the fabric of linguistic structure (see chapter 12).

What we recognize as 'grammar', therefore, in its traditional sense as a linguistic level (i.e. the syntax and morphology chapters in the description of a language), is the inter-functional hookup: the integration of the various functional components into a unified structural form. A clause in English is a realization of meaning potential derived from the ideational, interpersonal and textual functions. It embodies all these components at the same time. But this is not done in a discrete, segmental fashion such that we can identify one bit of the clause as expressing one function and another bit as expressing another. What we find, rather, is that the clause as a whole expresses all functions, through the total set of its structural and lexical resources. Whereas in the child's proto-grammar the functional components—in principle at least: this is a theoretical end point which may never be observable in its 'pure' form—are unintegrated, being in effect functional varieties of speech act, here they are generalized and at the same time combined into complex forms which are only indirectly related to their more specific uses. A word may express one type of meaning, its morphology another and its position in sequence another; and any element may have more than one structural role, like a chord in a fugue which participates simultaneously in more than one melodic line. This last point is illustrated by the analysis of a clause in Fig. 5 below.

Example of structural analysis of a clause:

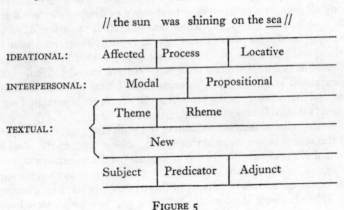

// the sun   was shining on the sea //

IDEATIONAL:	Affected	Process	Locative
INTERPERSONAL:	Modal		Propositional
TEXTUAL:	Theme	Rheme	
	New		
	Subject	Predicator	Adjunct

FIGURE 5

It is this sense in which the concept of the social function of language is being said to be central to the study of language as a system. The internal organization of language is not arbitrary but embodies a positive reflection of the functions that language has evolved to serve in the life of social man. This essentially is Malinowski's claim. As Malinowski implied, we can see this directly in the linguistic system of the young child. There the utterance has, in principle, just one structure; each element in it has therefore just one structural function, and that function is relatable to the meaning potential—to the set of options available to the child in the particular social function which the language is serving for him at the time.

In the fully developed language system of the adult, the functional basis is still discernible. The difference can be summed up by saying that here each utterance has as a rule more than one structure simultaneously—we have used the analogy of a fugue. Each element, in other words, may have more than one role and enter into more than one structure. The structure still expresses the underlying meaning potential; but because of the immense variety of social uses of language, a 'grammar' has emerged in which the options in this meaning potential are organized into a very small number of relatively discrete sets within which the speaker selects simultaneously in all uses. These sets of options can be recognized empirically; and they are found then to correspond to a few highly generalized areas of meaning that are essential to the social functioning of language—and thus intrinsic to language as a system. Since language serves a general 'ideational' function we are able to use it for all the specific purposes and situation types involving the communication of experience. Since also it serves a general 'interpersonal' function we are able to use it for all the specific forms of personal and social interaction. The third, 'textual', function is actually a prerequisite to the effective operation of the other two. It is extraordinary how much homo grammaticus expects to be able to do with his language, and even more extraordinary how often he succeeds; and in a sociolinguistic enquiry of the present kind we are interested in finding out how his success is related to (both is explained by and explains) the particular and very remarkable form taken by the complex organization of language.

3 Functions and universals of language

'Function' in Functional Theories of Language

The limitation of functional theories of language, from the point of view of linguistics, is that they have usually been purely extrinsic. They have been attempts to incorporate language into a psychological or ethnographic theory. This is entirely justifiable and desirable, but it means that the categorization of language functions which is offered in such a theory is inadequate to explain the nature of language. That is not what it is designed to do.

Let me make my own position clear on this point. In attempting to understand the organization of language I find it most helpful to work with Firth's concepts of 'system' and 'structure'—with 'system-structure theory', as it has been called. In particular, in investigating language in social contexts and settings I like to take the 'system' as the fundamental concept. A system is a set of options in a stated environment; in other words, a choice, together with a condition of entry.

It seems to me that the system-structure framework needs to be supplemented in two ways. First, it is insufficiently explicit, and needs to be underpinned by a formalized generative model. Lamb's stratification theory, with its Hjelmslevian basis, provides this, and gives a systematic account of linguistic levels that is entirely compatible with the general theory of levels developed in European linguistics. Secondly, it is insufficiently explanatory, in the sense of explaining why language has the particular form and shape it has. We cannot give anything approaching a definitive answer to the question why the human semiotic should have taken precisely this form and no other; but we can begin to look into it; and for this purpose we need a theory of linguistic functions. In principle, language is as it is because of the functions it has evolved to serve, and Prague linguistics is unique in attempting to incorporate a theory of what these functions are.

From 'The place of "Functional Sentence Perspective" in the system of linguistic description', paper read at the International Symposium on FSP, Marianske Lazne, October 1970.

Here I venture to disagree with the observation of Novák and Sgall (1968), that 'the functions concerned should be ascribed not to the language but to utterances'. In my opinion a functional theory is a theory of language, and is an essential aspect of any theory that attempts to explain the nature of language. And this is how I would approach the question of the place of Functional Sentence Perspective. The place of FSP in the system of linguistic description is determined by the fact that it is (or at least it is an aspect of) one of a small number of functional components of the language system.

In his well-known article (Daneš 1964), Daneš distinguishes three 'levels' within syntax:

(1) the level of the semantic structure of the sentence
(2) the level of the grammatical structure of the sentence
(3) the level of the organization of the utterance.

Svoboda (1968) regards these as three 'systems', semantic, grammatical and functional, each with its own syntactic elements and relations.

These are important and fundamental categories. But they are not just accidentally co-existent systems or levels of structure; they are functional components of the grammar. They are the manifestation, in the language system, of the functions of language, in the general sense in which the term has been used from the work of Bühler onwards (Bühler 1933). This being the case, however, we need to show how Bühler's categories, or else some modified version of them, are represented in the Daneš-Svoboda framework of analysis.

The Functions of Language

We have no difficulty in identifying Daneš' 'semantic level' with Bühler's 'representational function'. If one of the functions of language is to express our experience of the world that is around us and inside us, it is natural that this should be reflected in the linguistic system. At first sight, the equivalence might seem to go no further than this; but it does.

The most problematical of Daneš' categories is that of the 'level of grammatical structure'. This seems rather circular. Why should language have a level of structure whose only function is to be a level of structure? Let us look back at Bühler. He has a conative function and an expressive function. The difference between these two is significant psychologically, but linguistically it is very tenuous: is an interrogative, for example, a demand to be given information (conative), or an expression of a desire for knowledge (expressive)? It is not surprising to find that expressive and conative are not really distinct in the language system. They are combined into a single 'personal' function—or, as I would prefer to call it, to bring out its social nature, an 'interpersonal' function.

How is this represented in linguistic structure? Actually, I think, it is Daneš' 'level of grammatical structure', the 'level' whose elements are subject, predicate and the like. This is not very well named, if with Svoboda we understand 'grammatical' to mean 'purely formal'; it is a functional component like the first one—and, we may add, is equally 'semantic'. It has often been noted, for example, that the subject in English is essential to the expression of mood; and in fact the organization of clauses into some form of predicative structure has in many languages a modal function, expressing the speaker's participation in, or intrusion into, the speech event: his choice of speech role (mood) and his assessment of the validity of what he is saying (modality). This in turn is part of a more general component of meaning which includes his attitudes and comments, assertions of familiarity and distance, and the like.

Let us postulate, then, an 'experiential' component (= Bühler's 'representational', Daneš' 'semantic') and an 'interpersonal' component (= Bühler's 'conative' and 'expressive', Daneš' 'grammatical'), and insist that both are represented on equal terms in the description of language. In other words, each component has both semantic and lexicogrammatical connotations.

When it comes to the third component, Bühler has nothing to say—naturally, since he was not primarily concerned with the nature of the linguistic system. But this is also a functional component, provided we accept the notion of an enabling function that is intrinsic to language: this is what we referred to above as the function of creating text. It is this that enables language to be operational; 'text' is language in use.

The speaker's command of his *langue* includes an awareness of the difference between text and non-text—lists of words, or random sets of sentences. Normally he will assume that what he hears or reads is text, and he will go to great lengths to justify his assumption and ensure that communication is taking place. His assumption is a functional one; it rests not so much on recognizing words and structures as on recognizing the role that language is playing in the situation. And the language will be recognized as playing some role only if it is acceptable as text.

Let us refer to this as the 'textual' function of language, since it is the function of creating text—or 'texture', to use a stylistic term, which is really the same notion. This function is not in Bühler's scheme; but it is Daneš' 'level of organization of utterance', whose elements are Svoboda's 'communicative units'. Although the textual function differs from the other two in that it is intrinsic to language, and thus instrumental not autonomous, I do not think it should be regarded as restricted to *parole*, or to the utterance. It is an integral component of the language system, and represents a part of the meaning potential of this system.

FSP can be defined, in this way, as the 'textual' component in the grammar of the sentence. The study of FSP was at first directed just to the structure of sentence and clause. Subsequently, it has been extended to other units having a 'communicative' element in their structure, to various classes of the phrase—deixis in the noun phrase is an example of a text-creating element—as well as to units which, as Daneš (1960) pointed out, may have no equivalent in the grammatical hierarchy (e.g. the unit realized as one tone group in English). References to work on FSP are too numerous, and too well-known, to be cited here; there have been detailed and perspicuous descriptions, especially of English and Czech, by Czechoslovak linguists such as Travniček, Vachek, Daneš, Poldauf, Firbas, Beneš, Svoboda and others, which have given a fundamental insight into this important and otherwise rather neglected area of linguistic pattern.

Manifestation of these Functions in the Language System

Where are these functions of language manifested in the language system? Obviously, in the grammatical structure. A clause such as *the sun was shining on the sea* shows (at least) these three dimensions of grammatical structure:

	the sun	was	shining	on the sea
experiential:	Affected	Process		Locative
interpersonal:	Modal		Propositional	
textual:	Theme	Rheme		

(I take 'modal+propositional' as the more general structure from which categories like subject, predicator, object &c. can be derived.)

But since these structures are the means of expression of the basic functions of language, they relate to particular functionally defined areas of meaning. Grammatical structure may be regarded, in fact, as the means whereby the various components of meaning, deriving from the different functions of language, are integrated together. We can see that each component makes its contribution to the total structural complex.

The different functions are, quite evidently, simultaneous and compatible. We should not be misled into equating 'function of language' with 'use of language'. There are indefinitely many uses of language, which no linguistic theory has attempted to systematize; but the fact that language can serve such a variety of purposes is precisely because the language system is organized into this small set of highly generalized functional components. Whatever we are using language for, we need to make some reference to the categories of our experience; we need to take on some role in the interpersonal situation; and we need to embody these in the form of text. (I think there may also be a 'logical' component to be brought in, but this need not concern us here.) We draw on all these areas of linguistic potential at the same time.

If we describe the grammar in terms of paradigmatic sets of features or 'systems' in the Firthian sense, we find a clear indication that the grammatical system itself has a functional basis. In the English clause, for example, there is one self-contained set of interrelated systems concerned with transitivity, and another concerned with mood. But transitivity and mood are nothing other than functional components in the meaning potential of the clause. Transitivity is the grammar of processes—of actions, mental processes, relations—and the participants in these processes, and the attendant circumstances. This is the experiential component in the clause, Daneš' 'semantic'. Mood is the grammar of speech functions—the roles adopted (and those imposed on the hearer) by the speaker, and his associated attitudes. This is the interpersonal component, Daneš' 'grammatical'. And we find a third set of systems (which I referred to elsewhere under the general heading of 'theme') concerned with the grammar of messages—the status of the clause and its parts as 'units of communication'. This is the textual component of clause structure, or FSP. FSP shows up very clearly as a distinct, functionally determined set of options in the underlying grammar of the clause.

Why is Language As it Is?

We are interested in FSP because it is an integral part of the system of language, and therefore essential to the understanding of the processes of speaking, listening, reading and writing.

We take it for granted that language is a multiple coding system, organized into levels, or 'strata'. This can be explained, it is true, in terms of the problem of reduction. To oversimplify the matter, a large number of complex meanings is to be encoded in a small number of simple sounds, and this cannot be achieved without intervening levels (i.e. grammar and phonology). But this stratal structure has evolved in the context of the demands that are made on language, and the nature and organization of these intermediate levels—the nature of linguistic form, in Hjelmslev's sense—reflects the role of language in the life of man.

With the very young child, the uses of language seem to be rather discrete; and each has its own 'grammar', or 'proto-grammar' since it has no stratal organization. With my eleven-month-old son, for example, I can recognize four uses of language, with just two or three options in each. But adult use of language is such that, with minor exceptions, each utterance has to be multifunctional—while at the same time having an integrated structure. There must therefore be a level of organization of meaning: a semantic level, or in Lamb's terms 'semological stratum'. In

Hjelmslevian terms, the 'content purport' has to be separated from, and organized into, a 'content substance' as a precondition of its encoding in 'content form'.

What we are calling the functions of language may be regarded as the generalized categories of 'content substance' that the adult use of language requires. An utterance must be about something; it must express the speaker's stake in the matter; and it must be operational in its own context, either in the 'here and now' or in some second-order context created by the language. These conditions would seem to determine a significant part of the properties of the language system.

Specifically, the functional orientation of the system determines the kind of interdependence that exists within the meaning potential. Certain options are dependent on others; for example both modality and 'key' are largely dependent on mood, and all these are within the general 'interpersonal' domain. Likewise there is considerable interdependence among the options within FSP, although these are largely independent of options in the other components. Also, the functional basis of language is reflected in the nature of constituent structure, which has not merely to serve in the realization of meaning but to accommodate in a single structural realization configurations of elements deriving from different functional points of origin.

Section Two

Theory

The major theoretical notion in Halliday's linguistic work is that of *system*. In the papers brought together here, the term emerges with increasing precision and power; in chapter 8 it is both conceptually and formally the definitive term in the theory. The most helpful, and important, way to read these papers is to concentrate on the theoretical status of the term *system* in the period between 1956 and 1966. During that time the constant concern of Halliday's thinking was the establishing of a formally and conceptually adequate linguistic theory based on *choice*. This selection does not present the theory in terms of the two labels which have been used to characterize stages in the development of the theory: *Scale and category grammar*, and *systemic grammar*. This terminological division has led to an interpretation of Halliday's early work as being purely about surface structure, a formulation which he then abandoned for the semantic/functional formulation which has now gained wide acceptance and application. In section 3, the paper most closely based on the version outlined in chapter 5, namely chapter 9 'English system networks', illustrates that such a view is incorrect.

The increasing precision in the definition of the theoretical status and power of the term *system* has led to a consequent shift in the definition of the term *structure*. In chapters 4 and 5 *structure* is used in a surface manner: it provides specifications of the elements at which systems of classes operate. Chapter 8 defines *structure* as a configuration of (bundles of) functions. This non-surface interpretation is an important modification, for it allows systemic grammar to generate surface forms without the theoretically undesirable mechanisms of deletion and permutation of items of the surface structure.

The first chapter in this section, 'Grammatical categories in modern Chinese', dates from 1956. The principal terms in the grammatical description are *unit*, *element*, and *class*. Reading this paper with the benefit of hindsight, one is most impressed, first, by the lowly theoretical status of both *system* and *structure*, and second, by the fact that so many of the important categories and insights of the later work of Halliday are sketched out in this early paper. To support the first point, one can quote from the paper: '. . . the *systems of terms* operating at a particular *place in the structure* of a given unit is a *system of classes* of the unit next below . . .' (p. 36) (my italics). That is, the main organizing terms are *system* and *structure;* though their status is that of secondary categories. Similarly with Halliday's discussion of the terms *basic* and *subsidiary structure* in chapter 4. In support of the second point, one would mention e.g. the discussion of transitivity types, the recognition of an independently variable textual structure in the voice system ('The indirect secondary class dimension of voice cuts across the primary clause classes in such a way that the three terms of the voice system, neutral, passive, and ergative, have unrestricted distribution among the primary classes . . .' p. 42), as well as in the selections of *given-new*.

Structure and *system* both become major categories in chapter 5 'Categories of the theory of grammar'. Together with *class* and *unit*, they form the four major categories; they are linked by three *scales*, *rank*, *delicacy*, and *exponence*. *Unit* is, as described in chapter 4, the category set up to account for stretches of language which carry grammatical pattern. The latter presupposes likeness of events, and that is dealt with by *structure*. Structures are arrangements of elements ordered in places; each structural place therefore represents the potentiality of occurrence of a unit from the rank next below. The *class* is the grouping of terms whose common feature is their shared potentiality of occurrence in a given structural place in the unit next above in the rank scale. In the 'Categories' version, *unit*, *structure*, and *class* account for the patterned stretches, likeness of events, and grouping of like events respectively. However, this would remain a surface and structural account if it were not for the use made of *system* in the theory. It is the *system* which provides the motivated account for the occurrence of one rather than another from the number of linguistic forms. Systemic grammar is crucially concerned with the provision of motivated accounts of the significance of specific linguistic forms; it is the system, here as in the later papers, which provides the basis for such an account.

One theme which Halliday took up in his early writing, and developed in 'Categories', concerns the degree of *delicacy* to which linguistic descriptions should be pursued. His answer is that it depends on the purpose for which a description is to be used. Theoretically it should be possible to push grammatical description to such a degree of delicacy that individual utterances, which at a lower level of delicacy belong to the same syntactic type, are differentiated grammatically. At this level the description will focus primarily on distinctions between lexical items. That is, one would want to distinguish *We had cakes and ale for supper* from *We had custard and apple for dessert*. Whether or not it is possible to extend grammatical description that far remains the object of a hypothesis. In chapter 6 some evidence in support of this hypothesis is put forward; it is an interesting area, and little researched (the exception to this being the work of John Sinclair) (Sinclair *et al.* 1970).

In chapter 7 'Chain and choice in language' the theoretical possibility of organizing a linguistic theory on either one or the other of the two criteria of *chain* and *choice* is discussed overtly. The principle of *chain*, that is, syntagmatic and sequential order, leads to a description in surface structural terms; the principle of *choice*, that is systemic and non-sequential order, leads to a description in deep semantic terms. In this paper Halliday assumes that the two modes of organization are complementary, and that they might be needed in any linguistic theory.

Finally, in chapter 8 'Deep grammar: system as semantic choice' this question is answered unambiguously in favour of *system* as the criterial organizing category in a linguistic theory based on *choice*. The argument rests primarily on the realization that systemic choice determines structure: both in the sense of configurations of functions, and in the sense of surface constituent structure. The freeing of system from surface structure has as a consequence that systems are now made up of terms which are semantic features. The selection of any one feature specifies, through an accompanying realization statement, how, and by what item, the feature is to be realized in structure. Several features may have their realizations in one surface item; other features may be realized through sequence. Thus the totality of feature selections specifies both surface constituents and their sequence.

4 Grammatical categories in modern Chinese: an early sketch of the theory

The Sentence

Unit, Element and Class

The grammatical categories to be established in the description are of three types: units, elements and classes. The unit is that category to which corresponds a segment of the linguistic material about which statements are to be made, and it is proposed here to recognize five units which will be called sentence, clause, group, word and character.[1] The interrelation among the units is such that each, except the character, admits a distinction into simple and compound, the simple being that whose structure is stated as a single element while the compound is that of which the structure consists of two or more elements. Since the system of terms operating at a particular place in the structure of a given unit is a system of classes of the unit next below, the units form a hierarchy in which each may have as its structural components (that is, as forms operating at places in its structure) either one or more than one form being a term in the class system of the next. A clause having structure V is a simple clause and consists of one group; one having structure NNV is a compound clause and consists of three groups; the forms operating at V and N are terms in the system of group classes.

Elements and classes are categories set up to describe the units. The elements are structural and will be stated as symbols, using Arabic figures and letters of the Roman alphabet. In a clause whose structure is stated as ANV, A N and V are elements and occupy places in the clause structure. The classes are systemic and are stated as paradigms in interrelation with the elements; that is, as exhaustive inventories of forms classified as operating at a given place in the structure of the unit

Extract from 'Grammatical Categories in Modern Chinese' *Transactions of the Philological Society* 1956, pp. 180–202. For detailed Chinese examples, the original article should be consulted.

1. The use of the term 'character' as the name of both the unit of the script and the linguistic unit of which it is the written symbol parallels the Chinese use of the same term for both.

next above. A system of group classes such as 'verbal:transitive/intransitive' will be described in relation to the clause structure in which its terms operate: these classes are terms in the system operating at V in, for example, clause structure ANV.

A class is said to be primary when it is the unique term operating at a particular place in structure: the primary class 'verbal group' is the class name under which are brought together all forms operating at V. Other classes, including both integral subdivisions of the primary classes and systems in other dimensions cutting across the primary classes, are said to be secondary, the former direct secondary and the latter indirect secondary classes. This may be illustrated from phonology: in a syllabic structure CVC, the primary class operating at V would be the vowel, while the classes of high vowel and of palatal articulation would be ordered in secondary class systems: for example high vowel in a direct secondary system high/mid/low, palatal articulation in an indirect secondary system including other terms such as labial and not restricted to operating at V.

The Sentence

Implicit in the interrelation of elements and classes is the fact that, once the largest unit is defined and structures set up for it, the remaining units are self-defining. It is assumed that a downward direction of procedure, from the larger to the smaller unit, is methodologically acceptable without explicit justification. In the present language under description there is nothing corresponding to the full stop in a written text which will unambiguously delimit, and if necessary define, the sentence; here 'sentence' is the name given to the largest unit about which grammatical statements are to be made. The elements set up to describe the structure of the sentence represent the upper limit of systematization; these in turn determine the limits of the classes, since the class of forms operating at each place in the structure of the sentence is a class of the clause.

This does not exclude the possibility, and even necessity, of making contextual statements about some larger unit. Such statements would give meaning at another level to features accounted for in the grammatical statement, and may be required to complete an otherwise only partial systematization of the material. One could set up a unit of contextual statement features of which would determine grammatical features. Some instances of contextual determination of grammatical features are given in the text of this paper; since, however, the present analysis is grammatical, contextual features are adduced *ad hoc* for specific grammatical purposes.

Structure of the Sentence

The structure of the sentence may be described in a two-term system of elements symbolized O and X. Sentence structure is then O or O/X(. . .ⁿ)O, with the further possibility that at any O or X there may be an internal X, symbolized $\langle X \rangle$. This gives a formula $(O/X(\langle X \rangle) \ldots^n) O(\langle X \rangle)$.[1] The primary system of clause classes in sentence structure is that of free/subordinate; the class 'free' is that operating at O, the 'subordinate' at X. A sentence then consists of one free clause or of a free clause preceded by any number (in the description of a text this number would be finite) of clauses, free or subordinate; furthermore any clause, free or subordinate, may have a subordinate clause internal to it.

It is then possible to set up two direct secondary systems of clause classes in the same dimension and to state their distribution in the sentence structure:

1. At O there is a two-term system disjunctive/conjunctive, of which the disjunctive is the neutral (formally unmarked) term. Distributional probabilities are:

   (*a*) in a sequence XO where X = conditional clause (see below, 2), the probability that O = conjunctive is $\frac{1}{2}+$

   (*b*) where O is sentence-final in a compound sentence, other than when preceded by X = conditional clause, the probability that O = conjunctive is likewise $\frac{1}{2}+$

   (*c*) in a simple sentence, and where O = sentence-initial, the probability that O = conjunctive is $\frac{1}{2}-$

   (*d*) in all other structures (i.e. where O is not sentence-final nor sentence-initial nor directly preceded by X = conditional) disjunctive and conjunctive have even probability.

2. At X there is a two-term system conditional/adjectival, with distribution:

   (*a*) where X has place $\langle X \rangle$ (i.e. is internal to another clause), the probability that X = adjectival is $1-$

   (*b*) in all other structures conditional and adjectival have even probability.

The structural formula accounting for direct secondary classes is then as follows (the subscript figures denoting the number of terms in the system at each place, italicized *2* indicating uneven probability):

$$(O_2/X_2(\langle X_2 \rangle) \ldots^n) O_2(\langle X_2 \rangle),$$

1. In the structural formulae three types of bracket are used: round brackets ( ) indicate alternatives, that is elements which may or may not be present; diamond brackets $\langle \; \rangle$ indicate internal place (i.e. O$\langle$X$\rangle$ means that X is internal to O); square brackets [ ] indicate attributive elements, in the element system substantive/attributive.

with the rider that a sequence XO where X = conditional gives XO_2 while a sequence OO, or XO where X = genitival, gives OO_2, or XO_2.

Free/Subordinate and Free/Bound

The use of the term 'free' as a class name has been confined to the sentence structure, where it is opposed to 'subordinate'; but the term 'free' will be used throughout, in opposition to 'bound', to refer to that class of any unit which may operate in a simple structure; for example the word class 'free verb' is that class which operates at O in a simple group structure O, whereas the bound classes of the verb operate only in compound group structures. Since no unit has been set up greater than the sentence, having structure in which the forms operating are sentence classes, all sentences are grammatically free. It would seem desirable that ultimately the attempt should be made to set up a unit of description larger than the sentence. Such a unit might show a distribution of sentence classes, in which case it would be discussed in the grammar; alternatively a contextual unit might be shown to display a structure such that some sentences could be said to be contextually bound.

The subordinate clause is the bound term of the primary clause class system. It has been excluded from final position in the structure, though it should be assigned a probability here of o+;[1] sentence structures with final X can only be handled by the setting up of a larger contextual unit. This is exemplified by the sentence

ǰə-gə-huə čuŋ-ji -la/wuə suŋ šuəi
'this fire was ever so bright when I took the water over'

where the structure is OO (both disjunctive) and the clause order is incongruent, such that if either clause were to be marked as subordinate (conditional) it would be the latter—but it is not so marked. It may be noted that the possibility of occurrence in final position of the adjectival subordinate clause is excluded by the fact that the only form of the adjectival clause that occurs finally to a sentence is the substantive adjectival clause, which operates not in the sentence structure but in the clause structure.

The Clause

Structure of the Clause

The structure of the clause will be discussed in terms of basic and subsidiary structures. The elements set up for the basic clause structure

1. Cf. Y. R. Chao (*Mandarin Primer*, 2 Vols., Harvard University Press, 1948, p. 208, n. 23): 'A dependent clause comes after the main clause only when it is added as an afterthought.'

will be V and N; in the subsidiary structure to these will be added A and [V], [N] and [A]. Furthermore the basic structure will contain not more than one V; structures with two elements V are considered subsidiary. The systems operating in these structures are systems of group classes; the primary classes at V, N and A are respectively the verbal group, the nominal group and the adverbial group. [V], [N] and [A] are attributive elements having the same primary classes.

Basic clause structures are then combinations of V and N:

$$\text{V N NV VN NVN NNV VNN}$$

All groups are free, so that in a simple clause structure any secondary class of the respective group may operate.[1] Likewise in a compound structure any class of the respective group may operate, with the exception that in a structure VN, unless the clause has passive voice, only a transitive verbal group can operate at V; elsewhere, and in this structure with passive voice, at V transitive and intransitive verbal group have even probability. A sequence of groups 'intransitive verbal group' followed by 'nominal group' occupies a single place in the basic clause structure, either N (subsidiary structure [V]N) or (if the nominal group is of the class 'minor') V (with distribution as for intransitive verbal group). E.g.:

N: *siau+duŋsi* 'a little thing'; V: *siau yi-bəi* 'is twice as small'.

Direct Secondary Classes: Disjunctive/Conjunctive

The clause classes 'disjunctive' and 'conjunctive' are direct secondary classes of the free clause. The disjunctive is unmarked, while the conjunctive is characterized by the secondary word class 'conjunctive adverb' operating independently of the group structure. In a clause of structure V~, the conjunctive adverb precedes V; in a clause of structure NV~ or NNV~, the distribution, with probability 1—, is that the conjunctive adverb precedes N (or NN) if it is a compound word but follows N or NN (in a clause with ergative voice, precedes N or comes between NN) if it is simple.

Direct Secondary Classes: Conditional/Adjectival

The clause classes 'conditional' and 'adjectival' are direct secondary classes of the subordinate clause. The conditional clause is characterized by the secondary word class 'conditional adverb' which likewise operates independently of the group structure. There are two sub-classes of

---

1. The absence of bound group classes might be a reason for excluding the group from the unit system, thus admitting word classes as operating directly in the clause structure; the parallelism between group classes and word classes would support this. But the complexity of the description of the clause structure is considerably reduced if the intermediate unit 'group' is recognized.

conditional adverb: the 'preverbal' and the 'final'. The preverbal conditional adverb precedes V; its relation to N occurring in pre-verbal position is contextually determined: if N is contextually 'given', N precedes the conditional adverb, while if N is 'new' the order is reversed. The final conditional adverb has final position in the clause. Both subclasses may be present in one clause.

As said above, a free clause following a conditional clause is usually conjunctive. The conjunctive free clause may be said to generalize the relationship of the XO structure, while the conditional clause specifies it. The clause preceding a conjunctive clause may be subordinate or free; and the conjunctive clause itself is grammatically free (it may occur in a simple sentence structure), though it may be considered as contextually bound, presupposing a situation already in being and thus excluding 'context-initial' position.

The adjectival clause has the form of the neutral voice (or, probability $\frac{1}{2}-$, the ergative) followed by the form *di*, a word of the secondary class 'particle'. As regards the formal relation of the adjectival clause with other classes, the 'associative form' includes within itself what could be considered a special instance of the adjectival clause, while at the other end the adjectival clause is itself a special instance of the 'genitival' form (that is, the totality of forms having final *di*). Formally speaking the adjectival clause is that instance of the genitival form where the segment preceding *di* includes, or consists of, a verbal group (i.e. is a clause with structure other than N), with a limiting factor explained in the next paragraph.

Where a nominal group follows, the adjectival clause (or other genitival form) is attributive to it, and thus has the attributive value [ ] in the *clause* in which the nominal group operates, as well as operating at X in the *sentence*. In such instances an alternative form of the same structure, with probability $\frac{1}{2}-$, has *ja* or *na* at n1 in the following normal group, and no *di*. Where no nominal group follows, the adjectival clause (or other genitival form) has substantive value (always N) in the *clause* to which it is internal or adjacent but does not operate in the sentence. In the substantive adjectival clause the verbal group is likely (probability $\frac{1}{2}+$) to be preceded by *suə*, a word of class 'verbal adverb'; *suə* may occur (probability $\frac{1}{2}-$) in the attributive adjectival clause. Where in such instances the verbal group in the adjacent clause consists simply of *š* 'be', of the sub-class 'pro-verb' of the word class 'free verb', however, the resultant clause (including the genitival form) is said to have the 'associative form' and in these circumstances the genitival form is *not* classified as an adjectival clause. The associative form is the mark of the passive voice.

Voice

The indirect secondary class dimension of voice cuts across the primary clause classes in such a way that the three terms of the voice system, neutral, passive and ergative, have unrestricted distribution among the primary classes, with the exception that a passive clause does not operate at X = genitival clause. Neutral voice is unmarked, passive and ergative being marked both by distinct structures (with respect, that is, to the neutral voice) and by the presence of certain forms classified as words but operating independently of group structure.

Passive voice is marked by the associative form: the genitival form (as in a substantive adjectival clause) plus the pro-verb *š*. If there is any other element N in the clause (outside the genitival form), *š* occurs between this N and the genitival form; if not, *š* precedes the genitival form (probability 1—; regular exception is . . . *yiəu -di š* 'there's no lack of . . .'). In the associative form, on the one hand, the elements of the clause structure are contextually distributed in a system of 'given'/ 'new',[1] and on the other hand any two elements falling within one oi other category are bracketed together as one term by the genitival form. The 'given' is defined as a term already present in the context of situation, whether or not in the verbal action of a participant. In this system the term immediately following the *š* is thereby marked as new, and this is likely (probability $\frac{1}{2}+$) to be the second term (if one term only is present, it is always the new).

At this point it is useful to be able to refer distinctively to a grammatical structure which reflects a contextual structure (by matching it with maximum probability) as 'congruent'. It is not of course implied that the grammatical reflection of a contextual feature, if it can be shown, is congruent in a universal sense, but merely that this form of description is valid in particular instances on the basis of certain formal criteria. Here the congruent grammatical form is that in which given precedes new; in the congruent form, stress is facultative (that is, there is no stress system at this point), while in the incongruent form the formal mark of incongruence is the phonological reflection of the new by stress. The use of this concept here, and the choice of the phonologically unmarked member as the congruent term, are justified by the probability function taken together with the stress marking of the one form and not the other.

1. I have not used the terms 'subject' and 'predicate'; the given/new system is clearly accounting for features which have often been accounted for by subject/ predicate, but the latter terms would not generally be considered applicable e.g. to the positional system in the conjunctive adverb (see above, p. 40). The actual contextual categories reflected by the grammar in any language are particular to that language; so also may vary the devices (and even the *level* of the devices) by which such categories are reflected: compare the partly phonological reflection of contextual given/new in English.

The following table of constructed examples shows the associative form in its relation to the neutral voice structure. Note that:

(*a*) simple clauses (structure V, N only) have been omitted;

(*b*) in the associative form, structures with one contextual term only have been omitted (e.g.: VN *š mai čəz -di*);

(*c*) two forms are given, one with V = simple verbal group (*mai* transitive, *siau* intransitive), the other with V = (VN)) *gəi-wuə* transitive);

(*d*) English labels may be attached to the words which are exponents of V, N here as follows: *mai* 'sold', *siau* 'is small', *gəi* 'gave'; *wuə* 'I/me', *čəz* 'car', *ta* 'he/him', *cian* 'money'; *lai* 'has come', *ma* 'swore at', *ŋai-ma* 'got sworn at';

(*e*) in the associative form, the colon marks the break between the given and the new, while underlining indicates the incongruent position of the new.

Neutral	Associative	
	Congruent	Incongruent
NV	N:V	N:V
wuə mai	*wuə š mai di*	*š wuə mai -di*
čəz mai	*čəz š mai -di*	*š čəz mai -di*
čəz siau	*čəz š siau -di*	*š čəz siau -di*
ta gəi-wuə	*ta š gəi-wuə -di*	*š ta gəi-wuə -di*
cian gəi-wuə	*cian š gəi-wuə -di*	*š cian gəi-wuə -di*
VN	V:N	
	mai -di š wuə	
mai čəz	*mai -di š čəz*	
	siau -di š čəz	
gəi-wuə cian	*gəi-wuə di š cian*	
NVN	N:VN	N:VN
wuə mai čəz	*wuə š mai čəz -di*	*š wuə mai čəz -di*
	NV:N	
	wuə mai -di š čəz	
	N:VN	
ta gəi-wuə cian	*ta š gəi-wuə cian -di*	*š ta gəi-wuə cian -di*
	NV:N	
	ta gəi-wuə -di š cian	
NNV	NN:V	N:N:V
čəz wuə mai	*čəz wuə š mai -di*	*čəz š wuə mai -di*
	N:NV	N:NV
	čəz š wuə mai -di	*š čəz wuə mai -di*

	NN:V	N:N:V
cian ta gəi-wuə	*cian ta š gəi-wuə -di*	*cian š ta gəi-wuə -di*
	N:NV	N:NV
	cian š ta gəi-wuə -di	*š cian ta gəi-wuə -di*
VNN	VN:N	
	mai čəz -di š wuə	
	gəi-wuə cian -di š ta	

A vertical systematization gives (i) unmarked (neutral)/marked (associative), (ii) within the associative, unmarked (congruent)/marked (incongruent). Even in the neutral form there is some system of congruence, as shown by the fact that *mai čəz = čəz mai* (i.e. in both *mai* is given, *čəz* new) and not = *čəz mai* (*čəz* given, *mai* new). The horizontal systematization presents the grammatical themes on which the contextual variations are played (whereas in a description for pedagogical or translation purposes these would be presented as grammatical variations on a contextual theme); for each inversion of the elements of the grammatical structure (including, between NVN on the one hand and NNV, VNN on the other, inversion of the nominal terms (in all NVN forms *wuə* precedes *čəz*, in all others *čəz* precedes *wuə*), so that N_aVN_b becomes N_bN_aV, VN_bN_a) there are possible variations of the given/new structure.

That the name 'voice' should be given to one or another dimension along which this material is systematized is suggested by its characteristic of inversion of the terms coupled with a formal change in the elements of structure; on the same grounds the marked term in such a system may be named 'passive'. There are various possible groupings: if inversion is to be the main criterion, then NVN would be neutral and others passive, but this permits no classification of the two-element structures and cuts across the formal distinctness of the associative form. (It would be possible to talk of inversion with two-element structures on the criterion of contextual equivalence: *mai čəz : čəz mai :: lai čəz : čəz lai* but :: *ma wuə : wuə ŋai-ma* (not : *wuə ma*); in the neutral form NV cannot always be unambiguously replaced by VN, so that *ma -di š wuə* may be the contextual equivalent of either VN *ma wuə* or NV *wuə ma*. It seems preferable to consider the associative form as such as the mark of passive voice, all other structures (with the exception of the ergative; see next paragraph) forming the neutral term in the voice system.

There is one further form characterized by inversion of the clause structure with the addition of a grammatical marker: to this I have given the name 'ergative' in view of its singling out of the verbal element as new by opposition to all nominal elements. The ergative voice always has structure NV or NNV; where two N are present their order is that of the neutral form NVN (that is, N_aN_bV), and not that of neutral or passive NNV which have N_bN_aV. The form *ba* (word class prepositive verb) precedes the immediately pre-verbal N. As with the passive, there is an incongruent form with either N marked as new by stress.

It may be remarked here that the polysystemic form of the description may justifiably be represented as a simplification and not a complication of the material. In language primers this polysystematization appears when an identical form is classified under a number of different heads; but the question whether, for example, *š* 'be' is 'one word' or half a dozen 'different words' in Chinese does not arise if one says of a linguistic form that it operates at certain places in certain structures. Such a treatment is possible with a multi-dimensional description according to which a form may be systematized (that is, identified as a term in a grammatical system) along a number of different dimensions, sometimes for different purposes. For example, for pedagogical purposes where the language of description is English it is useful to isolate one form of the passive (as here described), the incongruent NNV form, and classify it with the ergative into a two-term marked voice system, because of the existence of a particular 'agentive' form (with 'by') of the English passive, at the same time grouping the same NNV form (as it were at right angles) with the other associative forms into a separate system comparable on contextual criteria with one system in the field of English intonation grammar, where a certain intonation form marks the category of the new. This is not to imply that there is direct translatability between any one term in the English systems and any one term in the Chinese systems; it means that the *systems* are identified contextually (*not* grammatically) as being comparable in the two languages, and that this identification permits the monosystemic statement of the contextual conditions under which particular terms in the systems of the two languages may operate. Since languages differ in their grammatical reflection of contextual categories (both as regards whether or not and as regards in what priority they reflect them), there is not to be expected a one-to-one translation correspondence of grammatical terms.

Aspect

The terms in the aspect system are neutral, perfective and imperfective. Neutral is as always formally unmarked; the marked terms are characterized by the presence of certain forms (of the word class 'particle') directly following the verbal group. Perfective clauses have *lə* or *guə* (the occurrence of both together has probability $o+$), of which *lə* marks a term in a succession (whether or not the final term is indicated modally; a clause with *lə* in neutral mood has probability $\frac{1}{2}+$ of being not sentence final), *guə* an isolated term (conceptually a term in a series of which the second and final term is the present). Imperfective clauses have $\acute{j}$, which likewise has probability $\frac{1}{2}+$ of being not sentence-final in a clause of neutral mood. The grouping of these forms into a single system is suggested by their being mutually exclusive (probability o of occurrence in combination); the names chosen for the system and for its terms have been current for some time in the description of this, or more often some overlapping, system.

Associated with the aspect system is a system of polarity with marked aspect, including both negative polarity and the 'reflex' positive form. The marks of negative polarity and of the reflex positive form, as given in the next paragraph, are respectively *bu* and *š*; these operate, however, only in the neutral aspect, and corresponding forms in the marked aspects are as follows:

Polarity: Aspect:	Neutral	Negative	Reflex positive
Neutral	V	*bu* V	*š* V
Perfective	V *lə*	*məi* V	*š* V *lə* or *yiəu* V (*lə*)
	V *guə*	*məi* V *guə*	*š* V *guə* or *yiəu* V (*guə*)
Imperfective	V *ǰ*	*buzai* V (*ǰ*)	*zai* V (*ǰ*)

Constructed examples with structure VN would give:

mai čəz	*bu+mai čəz*	*š+mai čəz*
mai-lə čəz	*məi+mai čəz*	*š+mai-lə čəz* or *yiəu+mai (-lə) čəz*
mai-guə čəz	*məi+mai-guə čəz*	*š+mai-guə čəz* or *yiəu+mai (-guə) čəz*
mai-ǰ čəz	*buzai+mai (-ǰ) čəz*	*zai+mai (-ǰ) čəz*

Polarity

The terms of the system of polarity are neutral, negative and interrogative, all of which have unrestricted distribution among the primary classes with the exception that an interrogative clause never occurs at X = conditional clause. The neutral term is unmarked; the negative has *bu* in a clause with neutral aspect, *məi* with perfective and *buzai* with imperfective (word class 'verbal adverb'). There exists by the side of the negative term a type of neutral polarity which may be considered as a marked positive, formed by a sort of reflex from the negative; in this form to *bu* and *məi* corresponds *š* (to *məi* sometimes *yiəu*, probability $\frac{1}{2}-$), while to *buzai* corresponds *zai*. It may be remarked that the form *š* operates in three similar but distinct structures: (i) word class free verb, sub-class pro-verb, always with *di*, in passive voice; (ii) word class verbal adverb, always preceding V, in the reflex positive form of neutral polarity; (iii) word class free verb, sub-class (*c*), as V_1 in the double-V structure. Examples of these are:

(i) *ta mai -di š čəz*; (ii) *ta š+ mai čəz*; (iii) *š ta mai čəz*. If the form operating at V is a compound verbal group with postpositive verb, the negative adverb in neutral aspect precedes the postpositive verb; otherwise it precedes the verbal group (with probability o+ of following the auxiliary verb).

Interrogative polarity is characterized by the repetition of the group, or of an element within the group, operating at V, the appropriate negative adverb preceding the repeated term and the whole complex having the value of element V; if the repeated term is a verbal group with postpositive verb the negative adverb has position appropriate to such a group. In a passive clause it is always *š* that is repeated; the combination of interrogative polarity with ergative voice has probability $\frac{1}{2}-$.

For translation purposes it is useful to regard neutral polarity as a synthesis of affirmative and imperative; descriptively this arises as a system only at one point, where there is a two-term system imperative/affirmative. This arises only in a clause neutral in voice and aspect with structure V or NV; the imperative is unmarked and has the form of neutral polarity with an attributive verb, while the affirmative has the form of double-V. Examples are:

(imperative) *(ni) kuai+lai*; (affirmative) *ni lai-də+kuai*

Mood

The three terms of the modal system are neutral, aspectival and polar mood, of which the marked terms (the two latter) operate only with value O in the sentence structure, and that only (probability 1—) in sentence-final position (with the exception that polar mood occurs with probability $\frac{1}{2}-$ at X = conditional clause). Marked modal clauses are characterized by a system of forms of the word class of particle in clause-final position. Aspectival mood is associated with the dimension of aspect and is marked by the forms *la*, *laiǰ* and *na*, occurring either with neutral aspect or in certain combinations with marked aspect, as follows:

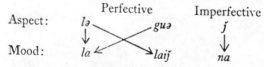

(including possibility of combination with the corresponding negative forms of marked aspect). Conceptually the modal forms may be thought of as the modal or subjective equivalents of marked aspect: they are contextualized as it were at one degree of abstraction, stressing the participation of the speaker rather than the totality of the situation. It is for this reason that modal *la* in a negative clause (neutral or perfective) usually admits English translation equivalent 'no longer' or 'not, after all': the negative of 'the situation has arisen that . . .' is 'the situation has arisen that . . . not . . .'. Aspect *lə* and modal *la* are phonologically overlapping (in syllabic transcription *lə* is *lə/liau*, *la* is *la/lə*); where there is positional ambiguity (that is, in a clause with final V) there is only one perfective term, unmarked as to aspect or mood, though the unambiguous forms *la*, *liau* exist by means of which one or the other may be specified.[1]

For pedagogical purposes it is useful to synthesize this modal system with the aspect system, regarding *lə* and *la* as perfective (respectively non-final and final, that is occurring the one in non-sentence-final clauses, the other in sentence-final clauses, with probability $\frac{1}{2}+$), *ǰ+/-na* as imperfective (*na* in sentence-final clauses only) and *guə*, *laiǰ* as a separate two-term system characterized as: *guə*, 'past in present,' *laiǰ* 'present in past'. For comparison with Early New Chinese, as exemplified in the language of the Chinese translation of the 'Secret History of the Mongols', one can set up for the latter the following system: (i) perfective: *le* (non-final/final), (ii) imperfective: *ǰo*, (iii) tense (non-aspectival): *lai/yieulai/yieu/yie*; with this one could compare Modern Pekingese (i) *lə(/la)*, (ii) *ǰ(/na)*, (iii) *guə/laiǰ*. For comparison with Cantonese, one can set up for the latter: (i) aspect: *zo/guo* (perfective), *gan* (imperfective), (ii) mood: *la/lak/lok*, etc.; and compare with these Modern Pekingese (i) *lə/guə, ǰ*, (ii) *la/laiǰ, na* and other modal forms.

Polar mood is associated with the dimension of polarity and marked by the forms *bu*, *məiyiəu*, *ma*, *ni*, *ba* and *ŋa*. These combine with the terms of the polarity system as follows: neutral polarity may have any of them, negative polarity only *ma*, *ni*, *ba* and *ŋa*, and interrogative only *ni* and *ŋa*. Since *məiyiəu* is the regular clause-final form of the negative pro-verb *məi/məiyiəu*, which is lexically identifiable with negative verbal adverb *məi*, *bu* and *məiyiəu* may be regarded as corresponding to negative polarity, *ma*, *ni*, *ba* and *ŋa* to interrogative; but in fact all (except *ni* and *ŋa*) exclude interrogative nominal or adverbial forms from the clause (*šəma*, *zəmayiaŋ* etc.). One then has the combinations:

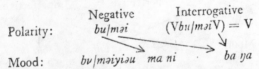

A clause with neutral or negative polarity is marked as a yes-or-no question, with varying degrees of modality, by *ma*, *ni*, *ba* and *ŋa*, and (with marked aspect) *bu* and *məiyiəu*; questions already so marked, by

1. Chao, op. cit., p. 41: '. . . when the two suffixes come into juxtaposition, they are telescoped into one.'

interrogative polarity or other interrogative forms, may have modal *ni* or *ŋa*.

The classification of modality through contextually specified examples (with if necessary class names such as *ma*: 'indignant affirmation') is useful pedagogically; and the combination of mood (with *ma*, *ni* and *ŋa*) and conditional clause (being the low probability occurrence of marked mood at X in the sentence structure) provides a formal link for such classification. Aspectival and polar mood may combine in one clause, the aspectival particle preceding the polar (but *na*, *ni* have probability o of combination); *na* and *ni* are phonologically overlapping (as *na/nə* and *ni/nə*), such that the form *nə* occurs as a synthesis of aspectival and polar mood: for example:

> *ǰəŋ-ǰ mantəu nə, wuə bu+gan-duŋ na-gə-huə*
> 'I daren't disturb the fire while I'm steaming bread'

All words marking mood (like those marking aspect and the repeated term in interrogative polarity—*bu* and *məi* in negative polarity have a stress/unstress system) are unstressed.

Adverbial Structures

In addition to the basic clause structures, which are combinations of one element V with one or more element N, three subsidiary forms of clause structure may be recognized. The first of these has the additional element A, the primary class corresponding to which is the adverbial group. The element A occurs in the subsidiary structures AV($\sim$) (including NAV($\sim$)) ANV($\sim$) and ($\sim$)VA, including combinations of these with more than one A (e.g. ANVA). In immediately pre-verbal position (AV, NAV etc.) there is a two-term system with even probability at A of endocentric and exocentric adverbial group; elsewhere the probabilities are uneven, such that at A preceding preverbal N the endocentric group has probability $\frac{1}{2}+$ while at A in final position the exocentric group has probability $1-$. The occurrence of structure AN$\sim$ or NA$\sim$ where A = endocentric group is determined by the contextual system of given/new, the given as always preceding (e.g. *miŋtian wuə* ... answers 'what are you doing to-morrow?', *wuə miŋtian* ... answers 'when are you ... ?'); the occurrence of structure ($\sim$)AV or ($\sim$)VA where A = exocentric group, while partially determined in the same way, is further restricted in that certain forms of the exocentric adverbial group (identified by the occurrence of certain forms operating at v3, e.g. *gəi*) have probability $\frac{1}{2}+$ ($1-$ in ergative voice) of *following* a verbal group if the latter is simple, for example:

> *kəyi ba-biyin-guəi zai-bisəyin-di+yi-ləi*
> 'you can classify the nasals with the plosives'

Only the adverbial group operates at A; some of the adverbial word classes do not operate in the group (and therefore never occur at A) but independently in the clause structure, either at [A] or as marking certain clause classes.

Attributive Structures

Attributive structures are subsidiary clause structures incorporating the element [ ]. This is in fact a single element, but since the operative forms are classes of the group, and may be described in relation to the system of group classes set up for the elements V, N and A, it is helpful to state attributive possibilities in relation to elements [V], [N] and [A], noting the occurrence of classes of the respective primary groups in the various attributive structures.

The following attributive structures may then be recognized:

$$[V]V \qquad\qquad [A]V$$
$$[V]N \qquad [N]N \qquad [A]N$$

In [V]V, only the intransitive verbal group can operate at [V], and then only a simple group. For pedagogical purposes it is useful to set up a restricted system in which the form [V]V is opposed to a double-V structure of type (1), the former being imperative, the latter affirmative. In [V]N, attribution may or may not be marked by *di* preceding N. If it is, the attributive form is considered to be an attributive adjectival clause with value at two levels, at X in the sentence and at [ ] (or [V]) in the clause; this form never has passive voice. Without *di*, the attributive form is restricted as in [V]V, to simple intransitive verbal group. Since such a group when attributive to N may still have *di*, a separate two-term system is formed by [V]N/[V]*di*N where [V] = simple intransitive verbal group, of which the latter is the marked attributive form.[1]

In [N]N, only the major nominal group can operate at [N]. N may or may not be preceded by *di*; if it is, [N] may be simple or compound nominal group; the question of whether or not a compound nominal group may operate at [N] without *di* depends on the analysis of a clause such as *ʃə-gə-řən*(+) *šəŋyin da* 'this man has a loud voice'. If *ʃə-gə-řən* is attributive (and the fact that in some such clauses[2] an alternative form without *di* is not possible does not preclude the analysis of this as [N]N), then [N] includes the possibility of a compound group; alternatively, however, all such clauses could be described as NNV, this

---

1. Kao Ming-k'ai, *Han-yü yü-fa lun*, Shanghai, Kaiming, 1948, p. 154, instances *duan+ku* 'shorts', *duan-di+ku* 'short trousers'; this is comparable with the variation of position of the attributive adjective relative to the noun in Romance languages.

2. e.g. Chao, op. cit., p. 35. '*Woo daw. luh sheng* (*wuə*(+)*daulu šəŋ*) "I, the roads are unfamiliar—I don't know my way here".'

being the only instance of V = intransitive group in NNV with neutral voice. The same system of presence or absence of *di* operates as at [V]N.

The forms operating at [A], unlike those at [V] and [N], are not forms of the corresponding (here adverbial) group but secondary classes of words of the adverb class, the verbal adverb in [A]V, the nominal adverb in [A]N. Attributive forms at [A] have probability only o+ (as contrasted with even probability for [V] and [N]) of occurring internally to a group, immediately preceding element O (classes free verb and free noun).

Double-V Structures

Except in interrogative polarity, where the complex of verbal group plus negative plus repeated verbal group has the value of a single element V, V excludes more than one verbal group. There are, however, two distinct clause structures containing two elements V.

1. Structure ($\sim$)VV, with the form (word class post-positive verb) *də* occurring between the two V. V_1 is transitive (probability $\frac{1}{2}+$; it may be intransitive with certain forms at V_2, e.g. *ləŋ -də lihai* 'terribly cold'); V_2 is simple and intransitive. The whole form is affirmative (as opposed to imperative with [V]) but may have negative and interrogative polarity (i.e. is not 'positive'); the negative adverb precedes V_2 and in interrogative polarity only V_2 is repeated. The form has probability 1— of being neutral in aspect and voice. Alternatively the form could be analysed (i) as two distinct clauses, the first subordinate— but a single clause structure appears preferable in view of the affirmative/imperative system; or (ii) as a single compound verbal group—but it does not operate with the negative/reflex positive system of the latter, having (not v: o3/ɔbu3/odə3 but) negative V -*də bu*+V.

2. Structure ($\sim$)V(N)V($\sim$), with probability $\frac{1}{2}+$ that N is present. Here it is convenient to recognize 2(a) and 2(b). In 2(a) V_2 is unrestricted, but there is a sub-class of free verbs (sub-class (c)) occurring in the verbal group operating at V_1. In 2(b) both V_1 and V_2 are unrestricted, and V_1 is always directly followed by *də* (since VN*də* is excluded, where V_1 is followed by N it must be repeated, and this is considered to mark a separate clause: e.g. *ta šuə huа/šuə -də wuəmən du+bu+duŋ* 'he spoke in such a way that none of us understood'). The form could alternatively be analysed as two distinct clauses, the first subordinate (a special instance of either conditional or adjectival clause, cf. 1 above)— but this would involve either the assignment of *də* to a different word class outside the verbal group or the recognition of a postpositive verb as marking a subordinate clause. 2(a) and 2(b) may combine in one clause, giving in fact a treble-V structure: e.g. *ta šuə -də məiyiəu řən duŋ* 'he spoke in such a way that no one understood'.

5 Categories of the theory of grammar

Starting Point

It will perhaps be helpful if the point of departure is first made clear. The following is a summary of what is taken as 'given' for the purposes of this paper.

1.1 One part of general linguistic theory is a theory of how language works. It is from this that the methods of descriptive linguistics are derived.

1.2 The relevant theory consists of a scheme of interrelated categories which are set up to account for the data, and a set of scales of abstraction which relate the categories to the data and to each other. The data to be accounted for are observed language events, observed as spoken or as codified in writing, any corpus of which, when used as material for linguistic description, is a 'text'.

1.3 Description consists in relating the text to the categories of the theory. The methods by which this is done involve a number of processes of abstraction, varying in kind and variable in degree. It is the theory that determines the relation of these processes of abstraction to each other and to the theory. The set of these abstractions, constituting the body of descriptive method, might be regarded as a 'calculus', since its function is to relate the theory to the data. It is important to distinguish between calculus (description) and theory; also between description and the set of generalizations and hypotheses by which the theory was arrived at in the first place. The latter precede the theory and are not susceptible of 'rigorization'; though we may distinguish the logical stages of observation-generalization-hypothesization-theory, keeping Hjelmslev's distinction between 'hypothesis' and 'theory' (Hjelmslev 1947). Here we are concerned with the stages, once the theory is formulated, of theory-description-text.

1.4 The theory requires that linguistic events should be accounted for at a number of different levels: this is found to be necessary because of the difference in kind of the processes of abstraction involved.

Extract from 'Categories of the theory of grammar' *Word* 17.3, 1961, sections 1–7.

1.5 The primary levels are 'form', 'substance' and 'context'. The substance is the material of language: 'phonic' (audible noises) or 'graphic' (visible marks). The form is the organization of the substance into meaningful events: 'meaning' is a concept, and a technical term, of the theory (see below, *1.8*). The context is the relation of the form to non-linguistic features of the situations in which language operates, and to linguistic features other than those of the item under attention: these being together 'extratextual' features.

1.6 The complete framework of levels requires certain further subdivisions and additions, and is as follows:

  (a) Substance may be either 'phonic' or 'graphic'.
  (b) If substance is phonic, it is related to form by 'phonology'.
  (c) If substance is graphic, it is related to form by 'orthography' (or 'graphology'), either
    (i) if the script is lexical, then directly, or
    (ii) if the script is phonological, then via phonology.
  (d) Form is in fact two related levels, 'grammar' and 'lexis'.
  (e) Context is in fact (like phonology) an 'interlevel', relating form to extratextual features.

1.7 The study of phonic substance belongs to a distinct but related body of theory, that of general phonetics. Since phonology relates form and phonic substance, it is the place where linguistics and phonetics interpenetrate. Linguistics and phonetics together make up 'the linguistic sciences'.

1.8 Language has 'formal meaning' and 'contextual meaning'. Formal meaning is the 'information' of information theory, though (i) it can be stated without being quantified and was in fact formulated in linguistics independently of the development of information theory as a means of quantifying it, and (ii) formal meaning in lexis cannot be quantified until a method is found for measuring the information of non-finite ('open') sets (see below, *2.1* and chapter 6). The formal meaning of an item is its operation in the network of formal relations.

1.9 Contextual meaning, which is an extension of the popular—and traditional linguistic—notion of meaning, is quite distinct from formal meaning and has nothing whatever to do with 'information'. The contextual meaning of an item is its relation to extratextual features; but this is not a direct relation of the item as such, but of the item in its place in linguistic form: contextual meaning is therefore logically dependent on formal meaning.

1.10 It follows from *1.8* and *1.9* that, in description, formal criteria are crucial, taking precedence over contextual criteria; and that the statement of formal meaning logically precedes the statement of contextual meaning.

1.11 Finally, it is necessary to distinguish not only between theory and description but also between description and presentation. Presentation, the way the linguist expounds the description, varies with purpose, and relative merit is judged by reference to the specific purpose intended. Description depends on the theory; theoretical validity is demanded, and relative merit is judged by reference to comprehensiveness and delicacy. Theoretical validity implies making maximum use of the theory (see below, *2.3* and *6.2*). It is not necessary to add a separate criterion of 'simplicity', since this is no use unless defined; and it would then turn out to be a property of a maximally grammatical description, since complication equals a weakening of the power of the theory and hence less grammaticalness.

Grammar

2.1 Grammar is that level of linguistic form at which operate closed systems. Since a system is by definition closed, the use of the term 'closed' here is a mnemonic device; but since 'system' alone will be used as the name of one of the four fundamental grammatical categories (see below, *6*) it is useful to retain 'closed system' when referring to the system as the crucial criterion for distinguishing grammar from lexis.

A closed system is a set of terms with these characteristics:

(a) The number of terms is finite: they can be listed as A B C D, and all other items E . . . are outside the system.
(b) Each term is exclusive of the others: a given term A cannot be identical with B or C or D.
(c) If a new term is added to the system this changes the meaning of all the others.

The reference is, of course, to formal meaning : it is form that is under discussion. It may always happen that the addition of a new term changes the contextual meaning of at least one of the others, since terms that are formally mutually exclusive are likely to carry contextual distinctions; but this is not a property of a system. The 'addition' of a new term is not of course considered as a process (though historical change is one type of instance of it): it may be displayed in any comparison of two related systems. For example, two possible systems of first and second person pronouns used by different speakers of Italian (quoted in oblique disjunct form; I = 'interior to social group', E 'exterior . . .'):

I	me	me
I+	noi	noi
2I	te	te
2I+	voi	
2E	lei	voi
2E+	loro	

(The distinctions made in written Italian are ignored, since they would not affect the point.) The difference in formal meaning is a function of the different number of terms: in system one *me* excludes five others, in system two only three. In contextual meaning only terms of the 2 group are affected.

Any part of linguistic form which is not concerned with the operation of closed systems belongs to the level of lexis. The distinction between closed system patterns and open set patterns in language is in fact a cline; but the theory has to treat them as two distinct types of pattern requiring different categories. For this reason general linguistic theory must here provide both a theory of grammar and a theory of lexis, and also a means of relating the two. A description depending on general linguistic theory will need to separate the descriptions of the two levels both from each other and from the description of their interrelations. This paper is primarily concerned with the theory of grammar, though reference will be made to lexis at various points.

2.2 The fundamental categories for the theory of grammar are four: 'unit', 'structure', 'class', and 'system'. These are categories of the highest order of abstraction: they are established, and interrelated, in the theory. If one asks: 'Why these four, and not three, or five, or another four?', the answer must be: because language is like that— because these four, and no others, are needed to account for the data: that is, to account for all grammatical patterns that emerge by generalization from the data. As the primary categories of the theory, they make possible a coherent account of what grammar is and of its place in language, and a comprehensive description of the grammars of languages, neither of which is possible without them.

Each of the four is specifically related to, and logically derivable from, each of the others. There is no relation of precedence or logical priority among them. They are all mutually defining: as with theoretical categories in general, 'definition' in the lexicographical sense is impossible, since no one category is defined until all the others are, in the totality of the theory. The order chosen here for exposition is therefore simply that which seemed the easiest: namely the order in which they are listed above.

The relation of these categories to each other and to the data involve three distinct scales of abstraction, those of 'rank', 'exponence', and 'delicacy'; these are considered separately (see below, 7) but have also to be referred to in connection with the categories. In discussing these I have used the terms 'hierarchy', 'taxonomy', and 'cline' as general scale types. A hierarchy is taken to mean a system of terms related along a single dimension which must be one involving some form of logical precedence (such as inclusion). A taxonomy is taken to mean a special type of hierarchy, one with two additional characteristics: (i) there is a constant relation of each term to the term immediately following it, and a constant reciprocal relation of each to that immediately preceding it; and (ii) degree is significant, so that the place in order of each one of the terms, stable as the distance in number of steps from either end, is a defining characteristic of that term. A cline resembles a hierarchy in that it involves relation along a single dimension; but instead of being made up of a number of discrete terms a cline is a continuum carrying potentially infinite gradation.

2.3 In this view of linguistics description is, as already emphasized, a body of method derived from theory, and not a set of procedures. This has one important consequence. If description is procedural, the only way of evaluating a given description is by reference to the procedures themselves: a good description is one that has carried out the right procedures in the right order, but for any more delicate evaluation external criteria have to be invoked. Moreover every language has to be treated as if it was unknown, otherwise procedural rules will be violated; so the linguist has to throw away half his evidence and a good few of his tools.

A theory on the other hand provides a means for evaluating descriptions without reference to the order in which the facts are accounted for. The linguist makes use of all he knows and there is no priority of dependence among the various parts of the description. The best description is then that which, comprehensiveness presupposed, is maximally grammatical: that is, makes maximum use of the theory to account for a maximum amount of the data. Simplicity has then to be invoked only when it is necessary to decide between fewer systems with more terms and more systems with fewer terms: and since both information theory and linguistic intuition favour the latter even this preference might be built in to the theory. The theory thus leads to 'polysystemic'-ness in description—both syntagmatically and paradigmatically. Syntagmatic polysystemic statement follows from the linking of classes and systems to places in structure. Paradigmatically, the 'simplicity' referred to here follows from the requirement of making maximum use of the category of 'system' by polysystemic or 'multidimensional' statement in grammar. (See chapter 4 of this book, pages 42–45.)

Unit

3.1 Language is patterned activity. At the formal level, the patterns are patterns of meaningful organization: certain regularities are exhibited over certain stretches of language activity. An essential feature of the stretches over which formal patterns operate is that they are of varying extent. Abstracting out those of lexis, where the selection is from open sets, we find that the remaining, closed system, patterns are associated with stretches that not only are of differing extent but also appear as it were one inside the other, in a sort of one-dimensional Chinese box arrangement. Since language activity takes place in time, the simplest formulation of this dimension is that it is the dimension of time, or, for written language, of linear space: the two can then be generalized as 'progression' and the relation between two items in progression is one of 'sequence'.

But there is a danger here. It is obvious that absolute measurements of linear progression belong to language substance (where one may be interested in the number of seconds, or possibly even the number of inches, occupied by an utterance). What is less obvious is that the whole dimension of progression in fact belongs to substance, and that the stretches which carry grammatical patterns—or rather the members of that abstract category that we set up to account for these stretches— have to be ranged on a dimension of which linear progression is only a manifestation in substance: a dimension we may call 'order'. 'Manifes- tation' (in substance) and 'realization' (in form) are introduced here to represent different degrees along the scale of exponence (see below, 7.3). In this paper I have used 'exponent' as indicating relative position on the exponence scale (a formal item as exponent of a formal category, and a feature of substance as exponent of a formal category or item); this departs from the practice of those who restrict the term 'exponent' to absolute exponents in substance. As used here, 'formal item' is a techni- cal term for the endpoint of the exponence relation ('most exponential' point) in form: the lexical item 'cat', the word 'cat' as member of the word class of noun, the morpheme '-ing' (as class member operating at the place of an element) in word structure, etc.; it is thus already an abstraction from substance and will be stated orthographically or phono- logically. In this formulation, exponence is the only relation by which formal category, formal item and feature of substance are linked on a single scale: hence the need for a single term to indicate relative position on the scale. Two defined positions on this scale can then be dis- tinguished as 'realization' and 'manifestation'.

By implication, this allows that in any given instance sequence may not manifest order, or that order may have other manifestations; even if this never happens, the distinction is necessary until such time as it is shown that the theory does not need to make provision for its happening. In fact it does happen: sequence is a variable, and must be replaced in the theory by the more abstract dimension of order.

3.2 The category set up to account for the stretches that carry gram- matical patterns is the 'unit'. The units of grammar form a hierarchy that is a taxonomy. To talk about any hierarchy, we need a conver- sational scale; the most appropriate here might seem that of size, going from 'largest' to 'smallest'; on the other hand size is difficult to represent in tables and diagrams, and may also trap one into thinking in substantial terms, and a vertical scale, from 'highest' to 'lowest', has advantages here. For the moment we may use both, eventually preferring the latter. The relation among the units, then, is that, going from top (largest) to bottom (smallest), each 'consists of' one, or of more than one, of the unit next below (next smaller). The scale on which the units are in fact ranged in the theory needs a name, and may be called 'rank'.

'Consists of', like 'unit' and 'rank', also belongs to the theory: its realization in form varies between and within languages, and is stated of course in description. The possiblities are sequence, inclusion and conflation. Thus if in a given instance a unit of one rank consists of two units of rank next below, these may appear in form as one following, interrupting, or overlaying the other.

Three further points about the rank relation need to be clarified. First, the theory allows for downward 'rank shift': the transfer of a (formal realization of a) given unit to a lower rank. Second, it does not allow for upward rank shift. Third, only whole units can enter into higher units. Taken together these three mean that a unit can include, in what it consists of, a unit of rank higher or equal to itself but not a unit of rank more than one degree lower than itself; and not, in any case, a part of any unit. The two latter restrictions represent an important addition to the power of the 'unit' as a theoretical category. As Chomsky has said (*Syntactic Structures*, pp. 23–4), 'the assumption that languages are infinite is made in order to simplify the description of these languages . . . If a grammar does not have recursive devices it will be prohibitively complex'.

3.3 The number of units in the hierarchy is a feature of the description. It varies from language to language, but is fixed by the description for each language, or rather for each describendum or 'état de langue'. The possibility of there being only one is excluded by the theory, since a hierarchy cannot be composed of one member. It is however theoretically possible to conceive of a language having only two, and an artificial language could be constructed on these lines (whereas it would not be possible to construct an artificial language having only one unit). English grammar, as far as it has been studied to date, seems to require five, though further, statistical, work on grammar might yield at least one more. So, for the description of English:

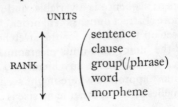

```
                    UNITS

                  ⎛ sentence
                  ⎜ clause
          RANK    ⎜ group(/phrase)
                  ⎜ word
                  ⎝ morpheme
```

3.4 The theory requires that each unit should be fully identifiable in description. This means that, if the description is textual, every item of the text is accounted for at all ranks, through the various links of the 'exponence' chain which involve, of course, the remaining theoretical categories. If the description is exemplificatory, exactly the same is implied, except that the description proceeds from category to exponent instead of from exponent to category.

It will be clear from the discussion in the next sections that there can be no question of independent identification of the exponents of the different units, since criteria of any given unit always involve reference to others, and therefore indirectly to all the others. A clause can only be identified as a clause if a sentence can be identified as a sentence and a group as a group, and so on up and down the line. For this reason description is not and can never be unidirectional: it is essential to 'shunt', and 'shunting' is a descriptive method that is imposed on description by theory.

Structure

4.1 The unit being the category of pattern-carrier, what is the nature of the patterns it carries? In terms once again of language as activity, and therefore in linear progression, the patterns take the form of the repetition of like events. Likeness, at whatever degree of abstraction, is of course a cline, ranging from 'having everything in common' to 'having nothing in common'. The commonplace that no two events are ever identical, that the same thing can never happen twice, is of no relevance whatever to linguistics; as soon as description starts, however little the generalization involved, absolute identity is a necessary hypothesis, which is then built into the theory, as one endpoint of the likeness cline. Likeness, including absolute identity, is of course redefined for each level and each category.

In grammar the category set up to account for likeness between events in successivity is the 'structure'. If the relation between events in successivity is 'syntagmatic', the structure is the highest abstraction of patterns of syntagmatic relations. The scale used for talking about it, and for its graphic display, will most naturally be the orthographic scale: to those of us brought up on the roman alphabet this happens to run horizontally from left to right, which is enough reason for adopting this version of the scale. But, as in the case of the unit, it must be stressed that linear progression itself is a feature of substance. A structure is made up of 'elements' which are graphically represented as being in linear progression; but the theoretical relation among them is one of 'order'. Order may, but does not necessarily, have as its realization 'sequence', the formal relation carried by linear progression; sequence is at a lower degree of abstraction than order and is one possible formal exponent of it. Since sequence is a variable, and may or may not be an exponent of structure, we find differences in sequence without difference in structure (cf. below, *4.3*), or difference in structure without difference in sequence. I am indebted to J. M. Sinclair for a recent conversational example of the latter: orthographically, 'The man came (,) from the Gas Board'. Phonologically (relevant units: 'tone group', bounded by //, and 'foot', by / ; these are unit boundaries and have nothing to do with juncture): what was said was (tonic syllable underlined):

// ɪ the / <u>man</u> / came // ɪ / from the / <u>Gas</u> / Board //

Grammatically, one clause, structure SP; exponent of P 'came', of S 'the man ... from the Gas Board', being a nominal group, structure MH+Q. (For explanation of structural symbols see below, *4.3*.) What might have been said was

// ɪ the / man / came from the / <u>Gas</u> / Board //

Grammatically, one clause, structure SPA; exponents, S 'the man', P 'came', A 'from the Gas Board'. The two are different in grammatical structure, and this difference has its exponent in phonic substance which can be stated phonologically. (That the phonological patterns, and the distinction between them, abstracted from the substance along one dimension correspond regularly (though not one/one) with the grammatical patterns, and the distinction between them, abstracted along another dimension from the same substance can be shown by the construction of other partially like clauses.) But though the difference in structure has its manifestation in substance (there can of course be ambiguity in substance, as in Hockett's 'old men and women', 'Two Models'), in form the difference is not realized in sequence. In sequence, 'from the Gas Board' occupies the same place in both instances; in order, S and A stand in different relations to P, and 'from the Gas Board' is exponent of (part of) S in the one case and of (the whole of) A in the other.

Sequence is presumably always manifested in phonic substance as linear progression; the distinction is then one of exponence, 'sequence' being the name for that formal relation between formal items of which linear progression is the manifestation in phonic substance.

4.2 A structure is thus an arrangement of elements ordered in 'places'. Places are distinguished by order alone: a structure XXX consists of three places. Different elements, on the other hand, are distinguished by some relation other than that of order: a structure XYZ consists of three elements which are (and must be, to form a structure) place-ordered, though they can be listed (X, Y, Z) as an inventory of elements making up the particular structure. A structure is always a structure of a given unit. Each unit may display a range of possible structures, and the only theoretical restriction is that each unit must carry at least one structure that consists of more than one place.

Each place and each element in the structure of a given unit is defined with reference to the unit next below. Each place is the place of operation of one member of the unit next below, considered as one occurrence. Each element represents the potentiality of operation of a member of one grouping of members of the unit next below, considered as one item-grouping. It follows from this that the lowest unit has no structure; if it carried structure, there would be another unit below it.

4.3 In description, structures are stated as linear arrangements of symbols, each symbol (occurrence) standing for one place and each different symbol (item) standing for one element. Since elements of structure 'exist' only at this degree of abstraction, the relation 'stands for' means simply 'is shorthand for', like that of an initial: ' "U" stands for "United" '. In a few cases traditional names exist which can usefully serve as names for elements of structure, with the initial letter as the descriptive symbol. In the statement of English clause structure, for example, four elements are needed, for which the widely accepted terms 'subject', 'predicator', 'complement', and 'adjunct' are appropriate. These yield four distinct symbols, so that S, P, C, A would be the inventory of elements of English clause structure. All clause structures can then be stated as combinations of these four in different places: SAPA, ASP, SPC, ASPCC, etc. For one type of group we have the names 'modifier', 'head', 'qualifier', giving an inventory M, H, Q: here, if the total range of possible structures is H, MH, HQ, MHQ, these possibilities can be stated in a single formula, where parentheses indicate 'may or may not be present', as (M) H (Q). This formulaic presentation is useful as a generalized statement of an inventory of possible structures: a list H, MH, HQ, HMQ can be generalized as (M)H(Q). This particular instance is an oversimplification, since there may be more than one exponent of M and Q: the formula would then read $(M \ldots^n)H(Q \ldots^n)$, where $\ldots^n$ allows infinite progression.

In other cases, no names come ready to hand; names can be imported or coined, or arbitrary symbols chosen—colours, for example, have advantages over letters in presentation, though there are not enough of them and they have to be re-defined in description for each unit. It is tempting sometimes to derive the symbols from the name given to the grouping of members of the unit next below which operates at the given element (as if one were to put V instead of P because what operates at P is the verbal group); but it is important to avoid identifying this grouping, which belongs to a different category as well as a different rank, with the element itself—therefore if this method is to be used at all it must be used all the time and a statement made to cover it. The real point is to avoid taking two distinct theoretical steps at once. As said below (5), the relation of 'class' to 'structure' is such that a class of a given unit stands in one/one relation to an element of structure of the unit next above: thus, the exponent of the element P in the structure of the unit 'clause' is the class 'verbal' of the unit 'group'. We could—provided we did so consistently—replace the symbol P here by V, thus conflating two statements. But not only are there descriptive reasons for not doing so (cf. below, 5.4); it is theoretically invalid, since two sets of relations are involved (element of clause structure to unit 'clause', class of group to unit 'group'), and if the two steps are taken at once the crucial relation of structure to class on the rank scale is obscured.

There are some instances where an element of structure is identified as such solely by reference to formal sequence: where the element is defined by place stated as absolute or relative position in sequence. It is useful to indicate that here sequence is so to speak built in to structure, and this can be shown by an arrow placed over the symbols for the elements concerned. For example, in English clause structure it is a crucial criterion of the element S that it precedes P in sequence: structures can be stated as $\overrightarrow{SPCA}$, $\overline{S}A\overrightarrow{PA}$, $A\overrightarrow{SP}$, etc. If, instead, an inventory of elements is stated first, the arrow can be added (where it really belongs) in the inventory: $\overrightarrow{S, P}$, C, A. It is then no longer required in the statement of structures, since it is presupposed.

This displays the contrast between this situation, where S is crucially defined by position relative to P, and realized sequences of elements which are not however defined by sequence, which may be indicated by simple linearity of the symbols. In a Latin clause of structure SOP (O = object), sequence plays no part in the definition of the elements: so no arrow. But rearrangements of the elements, to give SPO, OSP, etc., can be usefully employed to state the more delicate distinctions between

puer puellam amat, *puellam puer amat*, etc. In English, where $\overrightarrow{SP}$ sequence is crucial to the definition of S (though various arrangements of C and A are possible), more delicate grammatical distinctions, such as those carried by intonation, must be shown secondarily.

4.4 In the consideration of the places and elements of structure of each unit, which of course vary from language to language and from unit to unit within a language, a new scale enters, that of 'delicacy'. This is depth of detail, and is a cline running from a fixed point at one end (least delicate, or 'primary') to that undefined but theoretically crucial point (probably statistically definable) where distinctions are so fine that they cease to be distinctions at all, like a river followed up from the mouth, each of whose tributaries ends in a moorland bog. Primary structures are those which distinguish the minimum number of elements necessary to account comprehensively for the operation in the structure of the given unit of members of the unit next below: necessary, that is, for the identification of every item at all ranks. (M)H(Q), and the various possible combinations of S, P, C, A are primary structures: one cannot account for all words in group structure, or all groups in clause structure, with fewer than these elements or places.

Subsequent more delicate differentiations are then stated as 'secondary' structures. These are still structures of the same unit, not of the unit next below; they take account of finer distinctions recognizable at the same rank. For example the following two exponents of the (class) nominal (of the unit) group:

all the ten houses on the riverside

and

the finest old houses on the riverside

have the same primary structure M . . . HQ (or MMMHQ). But a more delicate statement of M, still at group rank, shows distinct secondary structures, the first example having D_aD_bN, the second D_bNE. Rank and delicacy are different scales of abstraction: primary group structures differ in rank from primary clause structures, but are at the same degree of delicacy; while primary and secondary clause structures differ in delicacy but not in rank.

As the description increases in delicacy the network of grammatical relations becomes more complex. The interaction of criteria makes the relation between categories, and between category and exponent, increasingly one of 'more/less' rather than 'either/or'. It becomes necessary to weight criteria and to make statements in terms of probabilities. With more delicate secondary structures, different combinations of elements, and their relation to groupings of the unit next below, have to be stated as more and less probably. The concept of 'most delicate grammar', and its relation to lexis, is discussed below (see 6.3); but the 'more/less' relation itself, far from being an unexpected complication in grammar, is in fact a basic feature of language and is treated as such by the theory. It is not simply that all grammar can be stated in probability terms, based on frequency counts in texts: this is due to the nature of a text as a sample. But the very fact that we can recognize primary and secondary structures—that there is a scale of delicacy at all—shows that the nature of language is not to operate with relations of 'always this and never that'. Grammatical theory takes this into account by introducing a special scale, that of delicacy, to handle the improbability of certainty; this frees the rest of the theory from what would otherwise be the weakening effect of this feature of language. The category of structure, for example, is the more powerful because it can be used to state the patterns of a given unit comprehensively at the primary degree without the assumption that it has accounted for all the facts.

Class

5.1 The structure is set up to account for likeness between events of the same rank, and it does so by referring them to the rank next below. To one place in structure corresponds one occurrence of the unit next below, and at each element operates one grouping of members of the unit next below. This means that there will be certain groupings of members of each unit identified by restriction on their operation in structure. The fact that it is not true that anything can go anywhere in the structure of the unit above itself is another aspect of linguistic patterning, and the category set up to account for it is the 'class'.

The class is that grouping of members of a given unit which is defined by operation in the structure of the unit next above. It accounts for a 'paradigmatic' relation, being a grouping of items 'at risk' under certain conditions. It is related primarily to elements of structure: the first degree of classification yields classes which stand in one/one relation to elements of primary structures, and these we may call 'primary classes'.

5.2 Class, like structure, is variable in delicacy. Clearly, in the first place, more delicate classes are the product of more delicate structures: in fact, 'secondary' classes are derived from structure in two ways. Firstly the same element at different places in structure may yield distinct secondary classes. If a given unit has primary structures XY, XYZ, YZ, and XYZY, the primary classes of the unit next below are 'class operating at X' 'class operating at Y' and 'class operating at Z'. If however there is a further restriction such that in XYZY, which will now be (secondarily) rewritten XY_aZY_b, only a section of the members of the class at Y can operate at Y_a and only another section (not necessarily mutually exclusive) at Y_b, this yields as secondary classes 'class operating at Y_a' and 'class operating at Y_b'.

Secondly, with increased delicacy the elements of primary structure will be differentiated into secondary elements. A primary structure generalized as X ... nYZ of which XXXXYZ is an instance, shows a generalized relation of X to (say) Y; but there may be internal relations within X ... n such that XXXX is rewritten pqrs. These will yield secondary classes 'class operating at p', 'class operating at q', etc.

In the second place, more delicate classes appear whenever a restriction is found which differentiates among the members of a primary class. There may be a relation of mutual determination, or 'concord', between two classes; each divides into two sections such that a member of one section of one class is always accompanied by a member of one section of the other class. Thus if the primary class at X is 1 and that at Y is 2, a structure XY must have as its exponent either $1.1+2.1$ or $1.2+2.2$. Secondary classes arrived at in this way in description may be referred to distinctively as 'sub-classes', to indicate that they are derived by differentiation from primary classes without reference to secondary structures; but it is important to state that there is no theoretical difference here. The relation between structure and class is a two-way relation, and there is no question of 'discovering' one 'before' the other. In any given instance there may be descriptive reasons for stating the one without the other; but all structures presuppose classes and all classes presuppose structures.

5.3 What is theoretically determined is the relation between structure and class on the one hand and unit on the other. Class, like structure, is linked to unit: a class is always a class of (members of) a given unit: and the class-structure relation is constant—a class is always defined with reference to the structure of the unit next above, and structure with reference to classes of the unit next below. A class is not a grouping of members of a given unit which are alike in their own structure. In other words, by reference to the rank scale, classes are derived 'from above' (or 'downwards') and not 'from below' (or 'upwards').

The distinction between downward and upward movement on the rank scale is important in grammar, but it is a mistake to raise it to the status of a choice between different theories, which it is not. The 'formal/functional' dichotomy is one of those which linguistics is better rid of; it is misleading to say even that classes are functionally determined, since they are set up with reference to the form of the unit next above—the whole description is both formal and functional at the same time, and 'function' is merely an aspect of the form. The distinction does however need a name, and this seems the best use for the terms 'syntax' and 'morphology'. Traditionally these terms have usually referred to 'grammar above the word' (syntax) and 'grammar below the word' (morphology); but this distinction has no theoretical status. It has a place in the description of certain languages, 'inflexional' languages which tend to display one kind of grammatical relation above the word ('free' items predominating) and another below the word ('bound' items predominating). But it seems worthwhile making use of 'syntax' and 'morphology' in the theory, to refer to direction on the rank scale. 'Syntax' is then the downward relation, 'morphology' the upward one; and both go all the way. We can then say, simply, classes are syntactical and not morphological.

5.4 In the description the term 'class' covers primary and secondary classes. It is often unnecessary to specify; but it is useful to state primary classes first, since these form the link between elements of structure and more delicate classes. More delicate classes derived from secondary structures are referable both as exponents to secondary structures and as subdivisions (same degree of exponence, but more delicate) to primary classes. Diagrammatically:

SCALE OF DELICACY

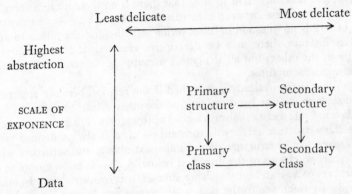

For the different classes of each unit, many names are available, especially at word rank—though it is precisely the long history of terms like 'verb' and 'noun' which reinforces their need for rigorous redefinition in the theory. In other cases names can often be found, especially where structural restrictions permit class identification between units: if certain word classes only (or predominantly) operate in one class of group and others only in another, one can talk of 'verbal group' and 'verb' (= 'verb word'), 'nominal group' and 'noun (word)' and so on. At the same time it is safer not to allow complete terminological identity between units: 'verb' alone should not serve as the name both for a class of group and for a class of word.

In the use of symbols for classes, figures have the advantage of avoiding confusion with elements of structure. This is not only theoretically desirable, because of their different status; it has descriptive value in that the theoretical one/one relation between elements and classes allows for instances where two different elements of structure, standing in different relation to each other or to a third, yield primary classes the membership of which is coextensive: these then form a single primary class derivable simultaneously from two elements of structure.[1]

If letters are used for elements of structure, and figures for classes, the relation between the two can be demonstrated by the use of a colour code.

1. Or nearly coextensive: the criteria for the setting up of one primary class or two are descriptive. For example, in English clause structure S and C are different elements standing in different relation to P. There is a high degree of overlap between their exponents: one primary class (class 'nominal' of unit 'group') can be set up as exponent of both S and C. The lack of exact coextensiveness will be stated by secondary elements and classes, to account for (for example) the occurrence of 'the old hall', 'the old town', 'the old town hall', 'this hall / town / town hall is old', 'this is a hall / town / town hall', and the non-occurrence of 'this old is a hall', 'this is an old', or 'this hall is town'.

System

6.*1* Up to this point the theory has accounted for three aspects of formal patterning: the varying stretches that carry patterns, the ordered repetition of like events that makes up the patterns and the grouping of like events by their occurrence in patterns. What remains to be accounted for is the occurrence of one rather than another from among a number of like events.

The category set up for this purpose is the 'system'. This falls under the general definition of system given above (*2.1*). But this does not yet state its place in grammatical theory, its relation to the other fundamental categories.

The class is a grouping of items identified by operation in structure: that is, what enters into grammatical relations of structure is not the item itself considered as a formal realization but the class, which is not a list of formal items but an abstraction from them. By increase in delicacy, the primary class is broken down into secondary classes of the same rank. This set of secondary classes now stands in the relation of exponent to an element of primary structure of the unit next above.

This gives a system of classes. If class 1 is the primary class (say of the group) operating at X in (clause) structure, and this has secondary classes 1.1, 1.2, and 1.3, then 1.1, 1.2 and 1.3 form a system of classes operating at X. X is now shown to presuppose a choice—a choice that is implied by the nature of the class (as a grouping of items) but that is displayed first still in the abstraction, by reference to the category of class itself. Diagrammatically (axes as in *5.4*, above):

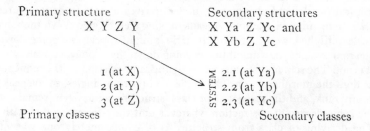

Primary structure
X Y Z Y

Secondary structures
X Ya Z Yc and
X Yb Z Yc

1 (at X)
2 (at Y)
3 (at Z)
Primary classes

SYSTEM 2.1 (at Ya)
2.2 (at Yb)
2.3 (at Yc)
Secondary classes

6.*2* Systems of secondary classes thus allow the description to remain at a high degree of abstraction while displaying at each step, each increase in delicacy, a more finely differentiated range of choice. This is the value of the concept of 'sub-class' (above *5.2*), since wherever a choice among a finite number of mutually exclusive possibilities is found to occur within a class one can recognize a system whose terms have the nature and degree of abstraction of the 'class': their relation to secondary elements of structure is implied but need not be stated.

Thus the system provides what is, in the order in which the categories are presented here, the final requisite for the linking of the categories to the data. Through the system, in one of two ways, the description can now account for the formal exponents, the items identified in linguistic form—and through them is linked, by description at other levels, to the ultimate exponents in substance. But there is a crucial point here. Any category can be linked directly to its exponents: a given formal item can be at one and the same time, and in the same sense, an exponent of a unit, a structure, an element of structure, a class, and a term in a system. So, for example, the formal item 'were driven' may be exponent of: (i) the unit 'group', (ii) the element P in structure, (iii) the class 'verbal', and (iv) the term passive in a system of secondary classes. All these statements are interdependent: the link of exponent to each theoretical category depends on its link to all the others and on their own inter-relations in the theory. Thus the unit 'group' is linked to the structure of the 'clause'; the class 'verbal' is a class of the unit 'group' and is linked to the elements of structure of the clause; the system 'voice' has as terms classes of the verbal group; these classes have their own structures, etc. At the same time the aim of grammar is to stay in grammar: to account for as much as can possibly be accounted for grammatically, by reference to the categories of grammatical theory. This, since it implies maximum generalization and abstraction, means that one proceeds from category to exponent by the longest route that is compatible with never going over the same step twice.

Here it is important to avoid theoretical confusion between the scales of exponence and rank. Since the relation of class to structure is syn-tactical (as defined above, 5.3), if one derives classes from structures then 'remaining in grammar' means moving step by step down the rank scale until the lowest unit is reached. So it might appear as if going down the rank scale is the same thing as going down the exponence scale. But it is not. The sentence stands in exactly the same relation to its exponents as does the morpheme; one can move over (at right angles, so to speak) at any rank, and the categories of class, structure, and system remain at the same degree of abstraction whatever unit they are associated with. The deriving of class from structure is of course merely one way of stating a theoretical relation which could equally be viewed from the other end; in this case 'remaining in grammar' would mean going up the rank scale and it would appear (equally erroneously) that it was only at the rank of the sentence that one reached the exponents.

6.3 There comes a point, however, when one is forced out to the ex-ponents; and this happens in one of two ways. In the first case the description yields a system in which the formal exponents themselves operate as terms. Here we have gone all the way in grammar; the formal items are grammatically contrastive (and do not belong in the dictionary). In the second case the description yields a class where no further breakdown by grammatical categories is possible, a class whose exponents make up an open set. Here we must leave grammar; the relations between the exponents must be accounted for as lexical relations.

Neither of these endpoints of grammar is restricted to the rank of any one unit. The exit to lexis tends to be associated predominantly—but probably never uniquely—with one unit, which for this reason is called in description the 'word'. The system of exponents also tends to operate at the lower end of the rank scale; but this, although predictable as economy of resources, is not a theoretical restriction: the rank distribution of formal exponents in systems is a descriptive feature which, in a five-unit description, may be expected to involve at any rate the three lower units.

The theoretical place of the move from grammar to lexis is therefore not a feature of rank but one of delicacy, except in the sense that the description will always try a move down the rank scale as a possible way of extending its power ('remaining in grammar'). But wherever the lexical item is greater than a morpheme, its further analysis by grammar into morphemes will leave its lexical relations unaccounted for. For example, in 'the train left ten minutes late, but made it up', *made up* is a discontinuous verbal group analysed as two words, one (*made*) of two morphemes, the other simple; but it enters into an open set *qua* lexical item *make up*, which itself is here assigned to no grammatical unit. It is defined theoretically as the place where increase in delicacy yields no further systems; this means that in description it is constantly shifting as delicacy increases. The grammarian's dream is (and must be, such is the nature of grammar) of constant territorial expansion. He would like to turn the whole of linguistic form into grammar, hoping to show that lexis can be defined as 'most delicate grammar'. The exit to lexis would then be closed, and all exponents ranged in systems. No description has yet been made so delicate that we can test whether there really comes a place where increased delicacy yields no further systems: relations at this degree of delicacy can only be stated statistically, and serious statistical work in grammar has hardly begun. It may well be that the nature of language is such that this 'most delicate grammar' will evaporate in distinctions which are so slenderly statistical that the system has, in effect, been replaced by the open set. For the moment it seems better to treat lexical relations, where even the identification of the items concerned by grammatical means is extremely complex, as on a different level, and to require a different theory to account for them.

6.4 A brief illustration, from English grammar, of the four fundamental categories. The exponent of the element S in primary clause structure is the primary class 'nominal' of the unit 'group'. The primary structure of the nominal group is $(M \ldots^n)H(Q \ldots^n)$. The primary classes of the unit 'word' operating at H and M are respectively the noun and the pre-noun. The element M can be broken down into secondary structures composed of any combination of the elements D, N, E in that order, whose exponents are the secondary classes 'deictic', 'numerative', and 'adjective' of the word. Deictics include a number of systems whose terms are the formal exponents themselves, with further secondary classes separating, for example, 'all/both/such/half' (class 1, at D_a) from 'a/the/some etc.' (class 2, at D_b) and various sub-classes involving concord. Adjectives likewise include a number of secondary classes, but in most of these the exponents form open sets, and for further treatment of these grammar hands over to lexis.

Rank, Exponence, and Delicacy

7.1 In relating the categories to each other and to their exponents, the theory needs to operate with three scales of abstraction, the scales of rank, exponence, and delicacy.

7.2 The scale of rank has been discussed with reference to the unit, the basic category which operates on this scale. The syntactic ('downward') determination of classes is a feature of the theory, so that with respect to the category of class the rank scale appears as one of logical precedence running from highest to lowest unit. But this precedence applies to class criteria only, so that even in the theory it is not a one-way relation: the theory itself embodies 'shunting' (moving up and down the rank scale) as crucial to the interrelation of the categories. In description, all statements presuppose shunting; the description of the sentence cannot be complete until the description of the morpheme is complete, and vice versa. In presentation, of course, procedure varies according to purpose and scope: downward presentation seems easier to make clear, but this may well be overriden—for example if grammar is an adjunct to lexical description, as sometimes in the statistical study of lexis.

Rank is distinct both from exponence and from delicacy. A shift in one never by itself entails a shift in either of the others. The reason why rank is often confused with other scales is that there are cases where a shift in rank does accompany a shift in something else; but this is always by virtue of the logical relations among the categories involved. The fact that by moving from structure to class, which is (or can be) a move on the exponence scale, one also moves one step down the rank scale, is due to the specific relation between the categories of 'class' and 'structure', and not to any inherent interdetermination between exponence and rank. The descriptive relevance of keeping the scales distinct is that it is important to be able to display what happens if one shifts on one scale, keeping the other two constant. One may want to compare primary and secondary structures of the same (class of the same) unit: shift in delicacy only. One may want to compare classes of one unit with classes of the unit next below: shift in rank only. Or one may want to state and exemplify the classes of a given unit: shift in exponence only.

7.3 Exponence is the scale which relates the categories of the theory, which are categories of the highest degree of abstraction, to the data. In Firth's words:

The term *exponent* has been introduced to refer to the phonetic and phonological 'shape' of words or parts of words which are generalized in the categories . . . The consideration of graphic exponents is a companion study to phonological and phonetic analysis . . . The phonetic description of exponents which may be cumulative or discontinuous or both, should provide a direct justification of the analysis. It may happen that the exponents of some phonological categories may serve also for syntactical categories. But the exponents of many grammatical categories may require *ad hoc* or direct phonetic description . . . The exponents of the phonological elements of structure and of the . . . terms of systems are to be abstracted from the phonic material . . . The exponents of elements of structure and of terms in systems are always consistent and cannot be mutually contradictory. (Firth 1957a, pp. 15–16)

Since the categories stand in different relations to the data, it might seem necessary to recognize four different scales of exponence, one leading from each category. In fact, however, exponence can be regarded as a single scale.

In the first place, each category can be linked directly by exponence to the formal item: it is in fact a requirement of the theory that any descriptive category should be able to be so linked. This may be stated by way of exemplification, as when we say ' "the old man" is (an example of) an exponent of S in clause structure'. This is however not a description of the element S, since by relating it to its exponent at a stage when it was not necessary to do so we should have lost generality. So instead of throwing up the grammatical sponge and moving out to lexis while this is still avoidable, the description takes successive steps down the exponence scale, changing rank where necessary, until (at the degree of delicacy chosen) it is brought unavoidably face to face with the formal item.

In the second place, therefore, the step by step move from any one category to the data can proceed via any or all of the other categories. This is then a move down the exponence scale, and at each step, given that delicacy is constant, one category is replaced by another (either with or without change of rank, according to which category is replaced by which). While therefore the categories are distinct, they are interrelated in such a way that the relation of exponence has the status of a single scale.

7.4 Delicacy is the scale of differentiation, or depth in detail. It is a cline, whose limit at one end is the primary degree in the categories of structure and class. In well-described languages, such as English, any extension in delicacy beyond what is already known requires either or both of large-scale textual studies with frequency counts and complex secondary classification based on multiple criteria, criteria which often cut across each other and may have to be variably weighted. And, as suggested above, a point will perhaps be reached where probabilities are so even as to cease to be significant and classes so delicately differentiated that the description will have to decide on crucial criteria and ignore the others, thus setting its own limits.

Delicacy is distinct from rank and the limit of delicacy applies at the rank of all units, for example differentiation of clause structures and of classes of the group. At one stage, therefore, it becomes a limit on the grammatical differentiation of items which then remain to be lexically differentiated: it sets an endpoint to grammar where lexis takes over. Here the scales of delicacy and exponence meet. The endpoint set to grammar on the exponence scale is where abstraction ceases: one has to move from abstract category to exponential item. That set on the delicacy scale is where differentiation ceases: the set of exponents of each class, and of each element of structure, permits no further, more delicate groupings. If the formal items are still not ranged in systems, the implication in either case is that further relations among them are lexical.

Whether or not grammatical delicacy can reach a point where there is one/one category-exponent relation (where each element of structure, and each class, has only one formal item as exponent), when all formal relations, including those among what are now treated as lexical items, can be accounted for by the grammatical categories and stated grammatically—in other words, whether or not, ultimately, all linguistic form is grammar, we do not know. At present, lexical items must be treated separately, and lexical relations established in their own right. These lexical relations do not depend on grammatical categories [1] (so they are not yet 'most delicate grammar') and they have their own dimensions of abstraction (so not yet 'most exponential grammar'). There must, therefore, be a theory of lexis, to account for that part of linguistic form which grammar cannot handle.

[1]. That is, have not yet been shown to be dependent on grammatical categories, and must therefore be postulated to be independent until shown to be otherwise: on the general theoretical principle that heterogeneity is to be assumed until disproved by correlation. Recent work by McIntosh suggests that lexical relations may, in some cases, be better described by reference to grammatical restrictions of variable extent; if so, this will affect both the theory of lexis and the relations between the levels of lexis and grammar

6 Lexical relations

Let us consider an example. The sentence *he put forward a strong argument for it* is acceptable in English; *strong* is a member of that set of items which can be juxtaposed with *argument*, a set which also includes *powerful*. *Strong* does not always stand in this same relation to *powerful*: *he drives a strong car* is, at least relatively, unacceptable, as is *this tea's too powerful*. To put it another way, *a strong car* and *powerful tea* will either be rejected as ungrammatical (or unlexical) or shown to be in some sort of marked contrast with *a powerful car* and *strong tea;* in either case the paradigmatic relation of *strong* to *powerful* is not a constant but depends on the syntagmatic relation into which each enters, here with *argument, car* or *tea*.

Grammatically, unless these are regarded as different structures, which seems unlikely, they will be accounted for in a way which, whatever the particular form of statement the model employs, will amount to saying that, first, *strong* and *powerful* are members of a class that enters into a certain structural relation with a class of which *argument* is a member; second, *powerful* (but not *strong*) is a member of a class entering into this relation with a class of which *car* is a member; and third, *strong* (but not *powerful*) is a member of a class entering into this relation with a class of which *tea* is a member. It would be hoped that such classes would reappear elsewhere in the grammar defined on other criteria. *Argument, car* and *tea* will, for example, already have been distinguished on other grounds on the lines of 'abstract', 'concrete inanimate' and 'mass'; but these groupings are not applicable here, since we can have *a strong table* and *powerful whisky*, while *a strong device* is at least questionable.

The same *patterns* do reappear: *he argued strongly, I don't deny the strength of his argument, his argument was strengthened by other factors. Strongly* and *strength* are paralleled by *powerfully* and *power, strengthened* by *made more powerful*. The same restrictions have to be stated, to

Extract from 'Lexis as a linguistic level' in Bazell et al. *In Memory of J. R. Firth*, London: Longman, 1966, pp. 150–61.

account for *the power* (but not *the strength*) *of his car* and *the strength* (but not *the power*) *of her tea*. But these involve different structures; elsewhere in the grammar *strong*, *strongly*, *strength* and *strengthened* have been recognized as different items and assigned to different classes, so that *the strong of his argument* has been excluded on equal terms with *the strong of his car*. *Strong* and *powerful*, on the other hand, have been assigned to the same class, so that we should expect to find *a powerful car* paralleled by *a strong car*. The classes set up to account for the patterns under discussion either will cut across the primary dimension of grammatical classification or will need to be restated for each primary class.

But the added complexity involved in either of these solutions does not seem to be matched by a gain in descriptive power, since for the patterns in question the differences of (primary) class and of structure are irrelevant. *Strong*, *strongly*, *strength* and *strengthened* can all be regarded for this present purpose as the same item; and *a strong argument*, *he argues strongly*, *the strength of his argument* and *his argument was strengthened* all as instances of one and the same syntagmatic relation. What is abstracted is an item *strong*, having the scatter *strong*, *strongly*, *strength*, *strengthened*, which collocates with items *argue* (*argument*) and *tea;* and an item *power* (*powerful*, *powerfully*) which collocates with *argue* and *car*. It can be predicted that, if *a high-powered car* is acceptable, this will be matched by *a high-powered argument* but not by *high-powered tea*. It might also be predicted, though with less assurance, that *a weak argument* and *weak tea* are acceptable, but that a *weak car* is not.

As far as the collocational relation of *strong* and *argue* is concerned, it is not merely the particular grammatical relation into which these items enter that is irrelevant; it may also be irrelevant whether they enter into any grammatical relation with each other or not. They may be in different sentences, for example: *I wasn't altogether convinced by his argument. He had some strong points but they could all be met.* Clearly there are limits of relevance to be set to a collocational span of this kind; but the question here is whether such limits can usefully be defined grammatically, and it is not easy to see how they can.

The items *strong* and *power* will enter into the same set as defined by their occurrence in collocation with *argue;* but they will also enter into different sets as defined by other collocations. There is of course no procedural priority as between the identification of the items and the identification of the paradigmatic and syntagmatic relations into which they enter: 'item', 'set' and 'collocation' are mutually defining. But they are definable without reference to grammatical restrictions; or, if that is begging the question, without reference to restrictions stated elsewhere in the grammar. This is not to say that there is no interrelation between structural and collocational patterns, as indeed there certainly is; but if, as is suggested, their interdependence can be regarded as mutual rather than as one-way, it will be more clearly displayed by a form of statement which first shows grammatical and lexical restrictions separately and then brings them together. If therefore one speaks of a lexical level, there is no question of asserting the 'independence' of such a level, whatever this might mean; what is implied is the internal consistency of the statements and their referability to a stated model.

Here I wish to consider some of the properties of this type of pattern in language, and some of the problems of accounting for it. Clearly lexical patterns are referable in the first place to the two basic axes, the syntagmatic and the paradigmatic. One way of handling grammatical relations on these two axes is by reference to the theoretical categories of 'structure' and 'system' with the 'class' definable as that which enters into the relations so defined. In lexis these concepts need to be modified, and distinct categories are needed for which therefore different terms are desirable.

First, in place of the highly abstract relation of structure, in which the value of an element depends on complex factors in no sense reducible to simple sequence, lexis seems to require the recognition merely of linear co-occurrence together with some measure of significant proximity, either a scale or at least a cut-off point. It is this syntagmatic relation which is referred to as 'collocation'. The implication that degree of proximity is here the only variable does not of course imply how this is to be measured; moreover it clearly relates only to statements internal to the lexical level: in lexicogrammatical statements collocational restrictions intersect with structural ones. Similarly in place of the 'system' which, with its known and stated set of terms in choice relation, lends itself to a deterministic model, lexis requires the open-ended 'set', assignment to which is best regarded as probabilistic. Thus while a model which is only deterministic can explain so much of the grammar of a language that its added power makes it entirely appropriate for certain of the purposes of a descriptive grammar, it is doubtful whether such a model would give any real insight into lexis. Collocation and lexical set are mutually defining as are structure and system: the set is the grouping of members with like privilege of occurrence in collocation.

Second, in grammar a 'bridge' category is required between element of structure and term in system on the one hand and formal item on the other; this is the class. In lexis no such intermediate category is required: the item is directly referable to the categories of collocation and set. This is simply another way of saying that in lexis we are concerned with a very simple set of relations into which enter a large number of items, which must therefore be differentiated *qua* items, whereas in grammar we are concerned with very complex and variable relations in which the primary differentiation is among the relations themselves: it is only secondarily that we differentiate among the items, and we begin by 'abstracting out' this difference. In other words there is a definable sense in which 'more abstraction' is involved in grammar than is possible in lexis.

Third, the lexical item is not necessarily coextensive on either axis with the item, or rather with any of the items, identified and accounted for in the grammar. For example, on the paradigmatic axis, in *she made up her face* one can identify a lexical item *make up*(1) whose scatter and collocational range are also illustrated in *your complexion needs a different makeup*. This contrasts with the lexical item *make up*(2) in *she made up her team* and *your committee needs a different makeup*. That the distinction is necessary is shown by the ambiguity of *she made up the cast, she was responsible for the makeup of the cast*. Grammatically, the primary distinction is that between *made up* and *makeup;* this distinction of course involves a great many factors, but it also relates to many other items which are distinguishable, by class membership, in the same way. If the grammar is at the same time to handle the distinction between *make up*(1) and *make up*(2) it must recognize a new and independent dimension of class membership on the basis of relations to which the previous dimension is irrelevant. Any one example can of course be handled by *ad hoc* grammatical devices: here for instance the potentialities of *make up*(2) in intransitive structures are more restricted. But such clearly grammatical distinctions, even when present, are so restricted in their range of validity that the generalizing power of a grammatical model is of little value as compared with the cost, in increased complexity, of the cross-classifications involved.

It may be worth citing a further example of a similar kind. We can distinguish grammatically, but not lexically, between *they want the pilot to take off* (= 'so that they can take off') and (= 'they desire him to do so'): these are not necessarily distinguished by intonation, although the unmarked tone selections are different. On the other hand it is easier to distinguish lexically than grammatically between *he took two days off* (= 'he did not work') and (= 'reduced the time available'). In *the take-off of the president* (= 'his becoming airborne') and (= 'the imitation of the president') the distinction can usefully be made both in grammar and in lexis.

On the syntagmatic axis, it may be useful to recognize a lexical item which has no defined status in the grammar and is not identified as morpheme, word or group. For example, in *he let me in the other day for a lot of extra work*, one could handle *let in for* as a single discontinuous item in the grammar; but this complexity is avoided if one is prepared to recognize a lexical item *let in for* without demanding that it should carry any grammatical status. Similarly the ambiguity in *he came out with a beautiful model* may be explained, instead of by giving two different grammatical descriptions, by identifying two distinct lexical items, *come* and *come out with* (and of course two different lexical items *model*).

It is not suggested of course that such non-coextensiveness between the items of grammar and those of lexis is the norm, but merely that for certain purposes it is useful to have a descriptive model of language that allows for it. At the same time the above considerations suggest that the lexical component requires not, as it were, a second 'runthrough' of the model designed for the grammar but rather a specifically lexical model with distinct, though analogous, categories and forms of statement.

Nor is it suggested that the set of patterns recognized as language form is neatly divided into two types, the grammatical and the lexical. A model for the description of language form may recognize only one kind of pattern and attempt to subsume all formal relations within it: some grammatical models, as has been noted, envisage that it is the grammar's task to distinguish *strong* from *powerful* as well as to distinguish *a* from *the* and 'past' from 'present'; while a lexicographical model in which *a* and *the*, as well as *strong* and *powerful*, are entered in the dictionary and described by means of citations could be regarded as in a similar way attempting to subsume grammar under lexis. Even where the model recognizes two distinct kinds of pattern, these still represent different properties of the total phenomenon of language, not properties of different parts of the phenomenon; all formal items enter into patterns of both kinds. They are grammatical items when described grammatically, as entering (via classes) into closed systems and ordered structures, and lexical items when described lexically, as entering into open sets and linear collocations. So in *a strong cup of tea* the grammar recognizes (leaving aside its higher rank status, for example as a single formal item expounding the unit 'group') five items of rank 'word' assignable to classes, which in turn expound elements in structures and terms in systems; and the lexis recognizes potentially five lexical items assignable to sets.

But, to take a further step, the formal items themselves vary in respect of which of the two kinds of pattern, the grammatical or the lexical, is more significant for the explanation of restrictions on their occurrence *qua* items. The items *a* and *of* are structurally restricted, and are uniquely specified by the grammar in a very few steps in delicacy; collocationally on the other hand they are largely unrestricted. For the item *strong*, however, the grammar can specify uniquely a class (sub-class of the 'adjective') of which it is a member, but not the item itself within this class; it has no structural restrictions to distinguish it from other members of the class (and if the members of its 'scatter' *strong, strength* etc. turn out to operate collocationally as a single item then this conflated item is not even specifiable *qua* class member); collocationally however it is restricted, and it is this which allows its specification as a unique item. There might then appear to be a scale on which items could be ranged from 'most grammatical' to 'most lexical', the position of an item on the scale correlating with its overall frequency ranking. But these are three distinct variables, and there is no reason to assume a correlation of 'most grammatical' with either 'least lexical' or 'most frequent'. The 'most grammatical' item is one which is optimally specifiable grammatically: this can be thought of as 'reducible to a one-member class by the minimum number of steps in delicacy'. Such an item may or may not be 'least lexical' in the sense that there is no collocational environment in which its probability of occurrence deviates significantly from its unconditioned probability.

In a lexical analysis it is the lexical restriction which is under focus: the extent to which an item is specified by its collocational environment. This therefore takes into account the frequency of the item in a stated environment relative to its total frequency of occurrence. While *a* and *of* are unlikely to occur in any collocationally generalizable environment with a probability significantly different from their overall unconditioned probabilities, there will be environments such that *strong* occurs with a probability greater than chance. This can be regarded, in turn, as the ability of *strong* to 'predict' its own environment. In extreme cases, *fro* and *spick* may never occur except in environments including respectively *to* and *span* (the fact that *to and fro* accounts for only a tiny proportion of the occurrences of *to*, while *spick and span* may account for all occurrences of *span*, is immaterial to the specification of *fro* and *spick*); here it is likely that, for this very reason, *to and fro* and *spick and span* are to be regarded as single lexical items.

It is the similarity of their collocational restriction which enables us to consider grouping lexical items into lexical sets. The criterion for the definition of the lexical set is thus the syntactic (downward) criterion of potentiality of occurrence. Just as the grammatical system (of classes, including one-item classes) is defined by reference to structure, so the lexical set (of items) can be defined by reference to collocation. Since *all* items *can* be described lexically, the relation of collocation could be regarded as being, like that of structure, chain-exhausting, and a lexical analysis programme might well begin by treating it in this way; but this is not a necessary condition of collocation, and if closed-system items turn out, as may be predicted, to be collocationally neutral these items could at some stage be eliminated by a 'deletion-list' provided either by cross-reference to the grammar or, better, as a result of the lexical analysis itself. Once such 'fully grammatical' items are deleted, collocation is no longer a chain-exhausting relation.

Moreover while grammatical structures are hierarchically ordered, so that one can recognize a scale of 'rank' each of whose members is a chain-exhausting unit (text items being then fully accounted for in sentence structure and again in clause structure and so on), it does not seem useful to postulate such an ordered hierarchy for lexis. Lexical items may indeed enter into a sort of rank relation: it is likely, for example, that on collocational criteria we would want to regard *stone*, *grindstone* and *nose to the grindstone* each as a separate lexical item, and though triads of this kind may be rare it looks as though we need the categories of 'simple' and 'compound', and perhaps also 'phrasal', lexical item, in addition to 'collocational span', as units for a lexical description. Since the only 'structural' relation in lexis is one of simple co-occurrence, these represent a single serial relation: the item *stone* enters (say) into the collocation *grindstone*, which then does not itself collocate like the sum of its parts but enters as an item into (say) the collocation *nose to the grindstone*, which likewise does not collocate like the sum of its parts but enters as an item into (say) the collocation *he's too lazy to keep his nose to the grindstone*. The first stage of such compounding yields a morphological (upward) grouping of items, the 'lexical series' which, like its analogue in grammar, may or may not coincide with the syntactic grouping recognized as a 'set': *oaktree ashtree planetree beechtree* presumably do operate in the same set, while *inkstand bandstand hallstand grandstand* almost certainly do not. The series is formed of compound items having one constituent item in common; this item, here *tree* and *stand*, is the 'morphologically unmarked' member of the series and, likewise, if the series forms a set it may or may not be the 'syntactically unmarked' member of the set. Equivalence or non-equivalence between series and set is an interesting feature of lexical typology: one would predict that in Chinese, for example, practically all such series do form sets (with an unmarked member), whereas in Malay and English they very often do not.

The lexical item itself is of course the 'type' in a type-token (item-occurrence) relation, and this relation is again best regarded as specific to lexis. The type-token relation can be made dependent on class membership: just as in grammar two occurrences assigned to different primary classes, such as *ride* (verb) and *ride* (noun), can be regarded as different (grammatical) items, so in lexis two occurrences assigned to different primary sets can be regarded as different lexical items. This can then be used to define homonymity: if the two occurrences of *model* in the example above are shown to differ according to criteria which would assign them to different sets then they represent two homonymous items. It is not to be assumed, of course, that grammatically distinguished items such as *ride* (verb) and *ride* (noun) may not also operate as distinct lexical items, as indeed they may; merely that if they turn out to belong to the same set they will on that criterion be said to constitute a single lexical item, as also will *strong*, *strength*, *strongly* and *strengthen*, and perhaps also (if they can be suitably delimited) non-cognate 'scatters' such as *town* and *urban*. This would provide a basis for deciding how many lexical items are represented by 'expressions' such as *form*, *stand* and *term*.

If we say that the criterion for the assignment of items to sets is collocational, this means to say items showing a certain degree of likeness in their collocational patterning are assigned to the same set. This 'likeness' may be thought of in the following terms. If we consider n occurrences of a given (potential) item, calling this item the 'node', and examine its 'collocates' up to m places on either side, giving a 'span' of $2m$, the $2mn$ occurrences of collocates will show a certain frequency of distribution. For example, if for 2,000 occurrences of *sun* we list the three preceding and three following lexical items, the 12,000 occurrences of its collocates might show a distribution beginning with *bright*, *hot*, *shine*, *light*, *lie*, *come out* and ending with a large number of items each occurring only once. The same number of occurrences of *moon* might show *bright*, *full*, *new*, *light*, *night*, *shine* as the most frequent collocates.

On the basis of their high probability of occurrence (relative to their overall frequency) in collocation with the single item *sun*, the items *bright*, *hot*, *shine*, *light*, *lie*, *come out* constitute a weak provisional set; this resembles the weak provisional class recognizable in the grammar on the basis of a single 'item-bound' substitution frame—although in lexis it is relatively less weak because of the lower ceiling of generality: lexis is more item-bound than grammar. If we intersect these with the high frequency collocates of *moon* we get a set, whose members include *bright*, *shine*, and *light*, with slightly greater generality. That is to say, *bright*, *shine* and *light* are being grouped together because they display a similar potentiality of occurrence, this being now defined as potentiality of occurrence in the environment of *sun* and in that of *moon*. The process can be repeated with each item in turn taken as the node; that is, as the environment for the occurrence of other items. The set will finally be delimited, on the basis of an appropriate measure of likeness, in such a way that its members are those items showing likeness in their total patterning in respect of all those environments in which they occur with significant frequency.

This is of course very much oversimplified; it is an outline of a suggested approach, not of a method of analysis. As Sinclair has shown (Sinclair 1966), however, methods of analysis can be developed along these lines. Many other factors are involved, such as the length of the span, the significance of distance from the node and of relative position in sequence, the possibility of multiple nodes and the like. One point should be mentioned here: this is the importance of undertaking lexico-grammatical as well as lexical analysis. It is not known how far collo-cational patterns are dependent on the structural relations into which the items enter. For example, if a *cosy discussion* is unlikely, by comparison with *a cosy chat* and *a friendly discussion*, is it the simple co-occurrence of the items that is unlikely, or their occurrence in this particular structure? All that has been said above has implied an approach in which grammatical relations are not taken into account, and reasons have been given for the suggestion that certain aspects of linguistic patterning will only emerge from a study of this kind. But it is essential also to examine collocational patterns in their grammatical environments, and to compare the descriptions given by the two methods, lexical and lexicogrammatical. This then avoids prejudging the answer to the question whether or not, and if so to what extent, the notion of 'lexicalness', as distinct from 'lexicogrammaticalness', is a meaningful one.[1]

An investigation on the lines suggested requires the study of very large samples of text. The occurrence of an item in a collocational environment can only be discussed in terms of probability; and, although cut-off points will need to be determined for the purpose of presenting the results, the interest lies in the degree of 'lexicalness' of different collocations (of items and of sets), all of which are clearly regarded as 'lexical'. Moreover the native speaker's knowledge of his language will not take the form of his accepting or rejecting a given collocation: he will react to something as more acceptable or less acceptable on a scale of acceptability. Likely collocations could be elicited by an inquiry in which the subject was asked to list the twenty lexical items which he would most expect to find in collocation with a given node; but the number of such studies that would be required to cover even the most frequent lexical items in the language is very large indeed. Textually, some twenty million running words, or 1,500–2,000 hours of conversation, would perhaps provide enough occurrences to yield interesting results. The difficulty is that, since lexical patterns are of low generality, they appear only as properties of very large samples; and small-scale studies, though useful for testing the methods, give little indication of the nature of the final results.

It is hard to see, however, how the results could fail to be of interest

---

1. The implication is, in effect, that 'wellformedness' is best regarded as 'lexicogrammaticalness', and that a departure from wellformedness, may be ungrammatical, unlexical or unlexicogrammatical. That the last two are distinct is suggested by such examples as *sandy hair*, *sandy gold* and *sandy desk*: *sandy desk* is unlexical, in that this collocation is unlikely to occur in any grammatical environment, whereas *sandy gold* is merely unlexicogrammatical: there is nothing improbable about *golden sand*. An analogous distinction is observable in clichés; in *shabby treatment* the mutual expectancy is purely lexical, and is paralleled in *they treated him shabbily*, *a shabby way to treat him* and so on, whereas the collocation *faint praise* is restricted to this structure, in the sense that it will not occur with similar probability under other grammatical conditions.

and significance for linguistic studies. Their contribution to our knowledge of language in general, and of one language in particular, may
perhaps be discussed in relation to the use of the term 'semantics'. If
lexis is equated with semantics, the implication is that lexical patterns
can only be described either externally (that is, as relations between
language and non-language, whether approached denotatively or contextually) or lexicogrammatically (that is, in dependence on grammatical
patterns). This restriction leaves two gaps in our understanding of
language: the internal relations of lexis, and the external relations of
grammar—that is, lexis (lexical form), and grammatical semantics. But
linguistics is concerned with relations of both types, both internal (formal, within language) and external (contextual or 'semantic', between
language and non-language); and all linguistic items and categories,
whether operating in closed contrasts, like *the* and *a*, or 'past' and
'present', or in open ones, like *strong* and *powerful*, enter into both.
Moreover, as Firth stressed, both these types of relation are 'meaningful': it is part of the meaning of 'past' that it contrasts with 'present',
and it is part of the meaning of *strong* that it collocates with *tea*. The
fact that the labels for grammatical categories are chosen on semantic
grounds should not be taken to imply that they represent an adequate
substitute for a grammatical semantics; but equally the existence of
traditional methods in lexical semantics does not mean that lexical items
display no internal, formal patterns of their own.

A thesaurus of English based on formal criteria, giving collocationally
defined lexical sets with citations to indicate the defining environments,
would be a valuable complement to Roget's brilliant work of intuitive
semantic classification in which lexical items are arranged 'according to
the *ideas* which they express'. But even such a thing as a table of the
most frequent collocates of specific items, with information about their
probabilities, unconditioned and lexically and grammatically con-
ditioned, would be of considerable value for those applications of linguistics in which the interest lies not so much in what the native speaker
knows about his language as in what he does with it. These include
studies of register and of literary style, of children's language, the
language of aphasics and many others. In literary studies in particular
such concepts as the ability of a lexical item to 'predict' its own environment and the cohesive power of lexical relations are of great potential
interest. Lexical information is also relevant to foreign language teaching; many errors are best explained collocationally, and items can be
first introduced in their habitual environments.[1] A further possible field
of application is information retrieval.

1. Some examples of collocational errors made by foreign learners: festive
animals, circumspect beasts, attired with culture, funny art, barren meadows,
merry admiration, the situation of my stockings was a nightmare, lying astray,

Only a detailed study of the facts can show in what ways and to what extent the introduction of formal criteria into the study of lexis, as implied by the recognition of a 'lexical level', are of value to any particular applications of linguistics. But there seem to be adequate reasons for expecting the results to be interesting; and if they are, this is yet another indication of the great insight into the nature of language that is so characteristic of J. R. Firth's contribution to linguistic studies.

---

fashionable airliner, modern cosy flights, economical experience, delightfully stressed, serious stupid people, shining values, a wobbly burden, light possibility, luxurious man, whose skin was bleeding, driving a bicycle, old and disturbed bits of brick wall, a comprehensive traffic jam, her throat became sad, my head is puzzled, people touched with assurance, thoughts are under a strain, a sheer new super car.

7 Chain and choice in language

Class, System and Structure

It is the class that enters into relations of structure and of system in language. A structure is an ordered arrangement of elements in chain relation, such as the English clause structure 'predicator+complement' (e.g. *fetch the ink*). While (in this instance) the ultimate exponent of the element 'predicator' is *fetch* and that of the element 'complement' is *the ink*, the direct exponents of these elements are respectively the class 'verbal group' and the class 'nominal group'. Similarly: a system is a limited ('closed') set of terms in choice relation, such as the English system of 'number' (e.g. *boy/boys*). While (in this instance) the ultimate exponents of the terms in the system are *boy* and *boys*, the direct exponents of these terms are the class 'singular nominal group' and the class 'plural nominal group'. It is useful to be able to distinguish classes derived in these two ways: they can be referred to respectively as 'chain classes' (those relating to structure) and 'choice classes' (those relating to system).

Difficulty is sometimes caused here by the need to recognize one-member classes. These do not really constitute a problem, being no different, *qua* classes, from the others; but the tendency to refer to them sometimes as category (by class name) and sometimes as item (by naming the unique member) may obscure the fact that the exponence relation (that is, the relation of item to category) is unaffected by the fact that class membership is limited to one item. For example, in English the definite article *the* forms a one-member class; if we are describing the particular choice, in English grammar, that is exemplified in *the man* and *a man* it does not matter whether we state the terms in the system as *the/a* or as 'definite article' / 'indefinite article' (or other more appropriate class name): it is the *class* that enters into the relation of choice. It may be noted in passing that the one-member class has a particular significance in linguistic theory: if grammar is taken to be

Extract from 'Class in relation to the axes of chain and choice in language'
Linguistics 2, 1963, pp. 5–15.

that part of linguistic form in which choices are 'closed', by contrast with lexis (vocabulary) in which they are 'open', then any item which can be shown to be the unique member of its class is fully and unambiguously identified in the grammar.[1] Thus *the* can be shown to be grammatically distinct from all other items in the English language; whereas the grammar has no means of distinguishing, say, *haddock* from *halibut*, and this distinction must be accounted for in some form of lexical statement.

It is a commonplace of linguistics that on the chain axis, that involving relations of structure, the value of sequence is variable. That is to say, the sequence in which items occur may or may not be a crucial property of the structure in question. It is important to realize, however, that this 'may or may not be' is something of an oversimplification. To take an example, in the English clause 'John saw Mary yesterday' the sequence is clearly crucial in one respect: *John* is subject and *Mary* complement; whereas in the clause 'Mary saw John yesterday' *Mary* is subject and *John* complement. The adjunct *yesterday*, however, remains adjunct even if put at the beginning: 'yesterday John saw Mary'. Now if there was no difference in meaning between 'John saw Mary yesterday' and 'yesterday John saw Mary', we should be justified in saying that this particular feature of the sequence had no significance: it made no difference whatever to the structure. This, however, is manifestly not true: there is a difference in meaning, and although it does not seem so important as that between 'John saw Mary' and 'Mary saw John', it certainly cannot be ignored.

This problem can be handled through the concept of 'delicacy'. The difference between 'John saw Mary yesterday' and 'yesterday John saw Mary' is still a difference of structure; but it is a more 'delicate' distinction than that between 'John saw Mary' and 'Mary saw John'. It is perhaps doubtful whether there are any instances in language where a difference in sequence makes no difference whatever to the meaning, and therefore does not need to be recognized as expounding a distinct structure, though we should allow for such cases in the theory. But when we say that sequence 'may or may not be' significant for structure, what we mean is that it may be significant at varying degrees of delicacy, down to a point where a distinction becomes so delicate that we do not know what to say about it; in such cases we may have to be prepared to treat the particular feature of sequence as being nonsignificant.

1. Another way of drawing the same distinction between grammar and lexis is to say that grammar is 'deterministic' by contrast with lexis which is 'probabilistic'; in the sense that in grammar one can distinguish what is possible from what is impossible (before assigning probabilities, if one wishes, to what is possible), whereas in lexis one can only distinguish between what is more and what is less probable.

This has important implications for the category of 'class'. For each grammatical unit (i.e. sentence, clause and so on) in each language we can recognize 'primary' (least delicate) elements of structure; for the clause in English, for example, the elements subject, predicator, complement and adjunct. From these we derive our primary classes: these are the sets of items of lower rank that enter into the primary structures with the value of the elements concerned. Thus the class corresponding to predicator is 'verbal group', that to both subject and complement is 'nominal group', and that corresponding to adjunct is 'adverbial group'. Where the sets of items operating as two or more elements of structure show more than a certain degree of overlap, as in the case of subject and complement—most items that can be subject can also be complement, and vice versa—these are conflated into a single primary class: thus the nominal group is the primary class expounding both subject and complement in English clause structure.

Primary classes are always chain classes. That is to say, the first step (on the scale of delicacy) is to state the classes derived from the primary elements of structure. When we take the class further in delicacy, however, and recognize secondary classes, some of these more delicate classes are chain classes and others are choice classes. It is clear that primary classes cannot be choice classes, since we cannot account for a choice until we have established that place in structure where the choice is made: for example, the choice classes 'singular nominal group' and 'plural nominal group' are meaningful only in relation to the primary (chain) class 'nominal group' which defines the context of the choice.

For examples of secondary classes of both types we may take an element of structure of the English nominal group, the element 'deictic'. The class of word defined as operating with this value is the class sometimes known as 'determiner'. This includes some forty items that are fully grammatical (i.e. reducible to one-member classes by successive steps in delicacy; *the this that which whose my its a any some either each other same certain* etc.), together with other items forming an open set (i.e. that cannot be so reduced; *John's*, etc., including compound ones as in '*the railway company's* property').

This class of determiner may be variously subdivided along both axes. On the one hand, there are certain sets whose members can occur in combination, as in '*all my other* friends'; there are in fact three such secondary groupings, the members occurring respectively in first, second and third place in a maximum sequence. This gives three secondary chain classes which may be called 'predeterminer' (e.g. *all*), 'determiner' (e.g. *my*) and 'postdeterminer' (e.g. *other*). Within each of these three classes, choices are made. There are many ways of describing these, according to what are taken to be the principal dimensions. The determiner, for example, may be 'specific' / 'non-specific' (*my*/*every*); 'selective' / 'non-selective' (*my*/*the*); and, as a further subdivision of the class formed by the intersection of 'specific' and 'selective', it may be 'possessive' / 'demonstrative' (*my*/*this*). These and various other systems eventually yield, by their subdivisions and intersections, one-member classes: thus *my* can be uniquely classified as 'determiner: specific, possessive: personal: first person'.

Secondary classes regularly cut across each other. The systems of 'specification' and 'selection', for example, form a matrix as follows:

	Specific		Non-specific
Selective	this/these that/those	which what	both all every each no neither
Non-selective	my your our their his/her its John's (etc.)	whose	
	the		a some any either another

It is not uncommon to find a large number of such intersecting classes, which may be very difficult to sort out; the above is only one of many possible ways of approaching the classification of the English determiners. But the patterns they display are typical in their complexity: a given class breaks down by simple subdivision into a system of more delicate classes, but the same original class will also subdivide in a number of different ways, so that many dimensions of classification intersect with one another. Any given item, to be fully identified, may require to be simultaneously classified on all such dimensions. In this way it can be assigned to a 'microclass', this representing its value in respect of all the properties which have been found relevant to the way it patterns in the language. There will be, of course, a very large number of such micro-classes: for example, in a computational study of English 'phrasal verbs' (items like *take up*, *put on*) which is being carried out at the moment, 557 such items were found to yield 125 microclasses.

8 Deep grammar: system as semantic choice

In the representation of syntagmatic relations in language, we can distinguish between a linear sequence of classes, such as 'adjective followed by noun', and a non-linear configuration of functions, such as 'modifier-head relation' or simply 'modification'. Both of these have been referred to as 'structure', although this term has also been extended to cover paradigmatic as well as syntagmatic relations. For Hjelmslev, for whom 'structure' was not a technical term (see e.g. Hjelmslev 1947) 'the structural approach to language . . . (is) conceived as a purely relational approach to the language pattern' (1947; quoted in Firth, 1951: 74–5); among others who have emphasized the relational aspect of such studies are Firth (1957a; 17, ff, 1951: 227–8; cf. Robins, 1953; Palmer, 1964a), Tesnière (cf. Robins, 1961: 81 ff.) and Pike (cf. Long-acre, 1964: 16). Chomsky's (1964: 32) distinction, using Hockett's terms, between 'surface structure' and 'deep structure', while also extending beyond syntagmatic relations, is extremely valuable and widely accepted: the surface structure of a sentence is defined as 'a proper bracketing of the linear, temporally given sequence of elements, with the paired brackets labelled by category names', while the deep structure, which is 'in general not identical with its surface structure', is 'a much more abstract representation of grammatical relations and syntactic organization'.

A representation involving the concepts of CLASS and SEQUENCE may thus be said to be a representation of surface structure. Here the ordering, if each pair of brackets is said to enclose an 'ordered set' of classes, is interpreted in the usual sense of the word, as linear successivity, or sequence. Such an interpretation does not preclude discontinuity or fusion of constituents, nor is it affected by the depth of the bracketing imposed: both the more copious bracketing of IC-type representations and the much sparser bracketing of, for example, a tagmemic analysis can adequately specify the relation of sequence in a surface structure.

Extract from 'Some notes on "deep" grammar' *Journal of Linguistics* 2.1, 1966, pp. 57–67.

The labelling attached to the entities specified as entering into this relation of sequence may then be 'class'-type labelling and interpreted as
such, 'the class "adjective" ' being the set whose members are *good*,
bad, . . .; although functional labels have also been introduced: for
example Nida (1966) states generalized syntagmatic relations, such as
hypotaxis, within the framework of an IC analysis.

If the representation of syntagmatic relations is merely in terms of
this type of surface structure, sequence is then the only determinable
relation. A considerable amount of bracketing may be introduced in
order to give as much information as is possible, within this limitation,
about the syntactic relations involved. Class labels do not by themselves
reduce the bracketing required, since classes do not fully specify syntactic function. Such labels may be conventionally interpreted as functional, but if so their correct interpretation depends on their association
with a designated pair of brackets; for example 'adjective' is to be interpreted as 'modifier' when attached to a particular node in the tree.
This adds considerably to the syntactic information; but if the tree itself
represents sequence at the surface its application is limited (cf. Palmer,
1964a).

It has always been realized that the concepts of class and sequence
alone were inadequate for the representation of syntagmatic relations in
language. Indeed the development of modern structuralism may be seen
as having taken place in the context of a tradition in which it was the
more surface elements that had remained least explicit. Relational terms
like 'subject' and 'predicate' have always co-existed with class names
such as 'noun' and 'verb'; while the definition of the classes has rested
at least in part on syntactic criteria, so that the designation of an item
by its class name indicates something of its potentiality of syntactic
function. Classes were not thought of as specifying actual syntactic functions within a given sentence, since the theory also recognized the deeper
syntactic relations into which the classes entered; the attempt to combine morphological with syntactic criteria in the definition of the classes
(since morphological 'types' have to be accounted for somewhere), while
it may lead to difficulties, is entirely explicable within such a framework.

While the underlying syntagmatic relations have been recognized as
non-linear, or at least as not manifested in the linear sequence of the
linguistic items, their representation, as Palmer (1964a: 125) points out,
has usually involved some form of linear notation. Since there is also a
level of abstraction at which the relevant syntagmatic relation is one of
sequence, it may be important to recognize that two different kinds of
representation are involved. In this sense class and sequence are inherently surface concepts, specifying the items of the language and their
arrangement; this is no less true of syntactically defined than of morphologically defined classes, the former being merely sets of items identified

as relevant to the deeper representation. For terminological simplicity we might perhaps here follow one tradition in referring to an arrangement of classes in sequence as a SYNTAGM, reserving the term STRUCTURE for a configuration of functions. If then function-type labels such as 'modifier' are introduced, whether as such or as conventional interpretations of class-type labels, they will not be located in the syntagm, since their defining environments is not stated in terms of (its) sequence. This holds true even if in a given language (say) a modifier-head structure is always realized as a syntagm of adjective followed by noun; a structure is not defined by its realizations.

The ordering that is ascribed to structure may be thought of in dependency terms, or in constituency terms as an underlying sequence which does not (necessarily) correspond to syntagmic sequence, or as mere co-occurrence or absence of ordering. In all cases it is of a different nature from syntagmic sequence, in that the components are functions, not sets of items. If (with Lamb) we use · to represent configuration, this being interpreted as 'unordered with respect to syntagmic sequence, whether or not any other form of ordering is considered to be present', then a structural representation may take the form m·h, or interchangeably h·m (modifier-head); this contrasts with a syntagmic representation of the form adj^n (adjective followed by noun). Representation such as m^h and adj·n would then appear as mixed types, where deep (structural) labels are attached to a surface (syntagmic) relation, or vice versa. These might be given conventional interpretations, perhaps for example m^h as 'modifier-head structure with realization by sequence alone' (i.e. where modifier and head are realized by the same class), adj·n as 'modifier-head structure with realization by class alone' (i.e. where the classes may occur in either sequence); but these would be merely a shorthand for combining two types of representation.

While many other formulations are possible, the recognition in some form or other of two distinct types of representation, linked by some form of 'realization' relation,[1] is relevant to the understanding of syntagmatic patterns, and the distinction can be made and discussed solely in terms of relations on the syntagmatic axis. Clearly however it is relevant also to relations on the paradigmatic axis. It may be helpful to relate this point to the distinctions made by Hjelmslev and by Firth. In Hjelmslev's terms, linguistic function embraces both relation and correlation; relation is syntagmatic, within the semiotic process, or the text, while correlation is paradigmatic, within the semiotic system, or the language. While his view of the relation between the two axes was

1. I use Lamb's term 'realization' instead of the earlier 'exponence'. Lamb's term is more widely known; it also corresponds closely to my own use, whereas as Palmer (1964b) pointed out my use of 'exponence' differed materially from that of Firth. (See quotation from Firth on page 71 [Ed.].)

somewhat different from that of Hjelmslev, Firth likewise makes a terminological distinction, referring (1957a: 17) to syntagmatic relations as relations of structure and to paradigmatic relations as relations of system.

Provided there is at least some syntactic element in the definition of the classes concerned, even a syntagmic, class-sequence representation already gives some information about the paradigmatic relations into which an item enters, but to a very limited extent. This limitation is again inherent in the nature of the class-sequence concept: paradigmatic 'relatedness' depends on a functionally defined environment. Two entities can only be said to contrast if they have a functional environment in common, and this environment is generally specified in terms of syntagmatic function; it presupposes therefore a representation of structure— that is, of 'deep' syntagmatic relations. The structural representation thus specifies the environment both for sets of paradigmatic relations and for further networks of syntagmatic relations, those within the lower-order constituents; for example the function of 'subject', itself specified syntagmatically in clause structure, defines an environment both for the syntagmatic relation of modifier-head and for the paradigmatic relation of singular/plural. For paradigmatic relations in the highest unit there is no functionally defined environment in this sense, so that if the sentence is said to be 'either declarative or interrogative' this either/or relation rests on other grounds: the sentence as a primitive term, or some postulated higher unit not yet structurally described; the appeal to contextually defined sentence functions such as 'statement' and 'question' is not one of these, this being rather a way of saying that declarative and interrogative have no environment in common.

The paradigmatic contrasts associated with a given defined environment may be thought of as being accounted for either in a single representation of 'deep' grammar, in which are incorporated both syntagmatic and paradigmatic function, or in a separate form of statement, distinct from, but related via the specification of the environment to, the statement of syntagmatic relations. Firth's concept of the system embodies the second approach. The 'system' may be glossed informally as a ' "deep" paradigm', a paradigm dependent on functional environment; in a sense, and mutatis mutandis, the relation of system to paradigm is analogous to that of structure to syntagm as these terms were used above. One could think of 'paradigmeme' as a possible tagmemic term. In Hjelmslev the 'system', likewise a paradigmatic concept, is defined as a 'correlational hierarchy', the underlying notion being that of commutation (Hjelmslev 1947). A system is thus a representation of relations on the paradigmatic axis, a set of features contrastive in a given environment. Function in the system is defined by the total configuration, for example 'past' by reference to 'present' and 'future' in a three-term tense system, as structural function is defined by reference to the total structural configuration, for example 'modifier' by reference to 'head'.

If paradigmatic relations are represented separately in this way, this implies that the full grammatical description of a linguistic item should contain both a structural and a systemic component. It may be useful therefore to consider the notion of a 'systemic description' as one form of representation of a linguistic item, the assumption being that it complements but does not replace its structural description. The systemic description would be a representation of the item in terms of a set of features, each feature being in contrast with a stated set of one or more other features: being, in Firth's terms, a 'term in a system'. This is exactly the sort of characterization that has been familiar for a long time in the form of 'this clause in interrogative, finite, present tense, . . .', given that we are told somewhere in the grammar not merely what other tenses, moods, etc. are found in the language but also which of them could have occurred in this particular clause all other features being kept constant.

There is however one modification of a traditional 'systemic description' of this kind which may need to be considered. This concerns the ordering of the features listed. In the traditional version they are unordered; but if the grammar specifies not only the relevant systems but also their interrelations with one another, in particular their hierarchization on what I have called elsewhere (Halliday 5: 272, 14: 18)[1] the 'scale of delicacy', then partial ordering is introduced. Any pair of systems, such that a feature in one may co-occur with a feature in the other in a systemic description, may be hierarchical or simultaneous; if two systems are hierarchically ordered, features assigned to these systems are ordered likewise. So for example the system whose terms are declarative/interrogative would be hierarchically ordered with respect to the system indicative/imperative, in that selection of either of the features declarative and interrogative implies selection of indicative. If this is taken together with another system, unpredicated theme/predicated theme, likewise dependent on indicative, then the item *John has seen the play* may be represented in respect of these features as:

(indicative: (declarative/unpredicated theme))

where: indicates hierarchy and / simultaneity. Then *it's John who has seen the play* contrasts with it in respect of one feature:

(indicative: (declarative/predicated theme))

and *is it John who has seen the play* in respect of two features:

(indicative: (interrogative/predicated theme))

1. See Appendix II, pp. 238–39

The systemic description would represent a selection from among the possibilities recognized by the grammar. As far as these examples are concerned the grammar would show that in a given environment selection is made between indicative and imperative; and if indicative is selected, there is also simultaneous selection between declarative and interrogative and between unpredicated theme and predicated theme, the two latter selections being independent of one another. Any item thus contrasts with others in respect of such features and combinations of features as the ordering of the systems permits.

For any set of systems associated with a given environment it is possible to construct a system network in which each system, other than those simultaneous at the point of origin, is hierarchically ordered with respect to at least one other system. This includes the possibility of complex dependence, where a system is dependent on more than one other system. Except in cases of disjunct complex dependence, where a system is dependent on either of two others, a feature determined by others in this way, such as 'indicative' in the examples above, would be recoverable from the grammar by reference to the rest of the description. An example of a system network would be the following, which is extracted and modified from a network representing the English clause.

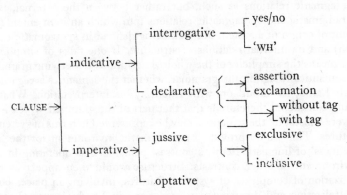

The point of origin is specified syntagmatically, so that all features are associated with a syntagmatic environment; at the same time the system network provides a paradigmatic environment for each one of the features, specifying both its contrastive status and its possibilities of combination.

It is not the aim here to present in detail the properties of a systemic description, but rather to discuss it in general terms. Systemic description may be thought of as complementary to structural description, the one concerned with paradigmatic and the other with syntagmatic relations. On the other hand it might be useful to consider some possible consequences of regarding systemic description as the underlying form of representation, if it turned out that the structural description could be shown to be derivable from it. In that case structure would be fully predictable, and the form of a structural representation could be considered in the light of this. It goes without saying that the concept of an explicit grammar implied by this formulation derives primarily from the work of Chomsky, and that steps taken in this direction on the basis of any grammatical notions are made possible by his fundamental contribution. Nevertheless my specific debt is to Lamb, whose formalization of stratification theory is based on general notions closely akin to those which I had adopted in my own work. The present paper, however, attempts no more than an informal discussion of the question of a grammatical description in terms of features, here based on the notion of a feature as one of a set of contrastive 'terms in system'.

Presenting the systemic description of a linguistic item as the underlying grammatical representation of that item would seem to imply that its paradigmatic relation to other items of the language was in some way its more fundamental property, from which its internal (syntagmatic) structure is considered to be derived. This would seem to be Hjelmslev's view, in his discussion of system and process (Hjelmslev 1947). But the priority which is implied is not one between paradigmatic and syntagmatic relations as such, but rather between the external, both paradigmatic and syntagmatic, relations into which an item enters (the point of origin of a system network being defined in syntagmatic function) and its internal relations of structure. If one talks of simplicity, this means the simplicity of the whole description; underlying grammar is 'semantically significant' grammar, whether the semantics is regarded, with Lamb, as 'input' or, with Chomsky, as interpretation. What is being considered therefore is that that part of the grammar which is as it were 'closest to' the semantics may be represented in terms of systemic features. This would provide a paradigmatic environment for the 'relatedness' of linguistic items, a contrast being seen as operating in the environment of other contrasts. Structure would then appear as the realization of complexes of systemic features, involving in places both neutralization and diversification as defined in Lamb's terms (Lamb, 1964a: 64).

If the structural representation is not required to account for paradigmatic relations, the question of how 'deep' it needs to be is determinable by reference to other considerations: it should give an adequate account of syntagmatic relations, and permit the explicit realization of the systemic description in terms, ultimately, of a sequence of classes. This may be illustrated from the example *it's John who has seen the play*. Leaving aside variation that is immaterial to the discussion, there would seem to be three possible representations of its structure:

(1) *it* subject, *is* predicator, *John who has seen the play* complement

(2) *it . . . who has seen the play* subject, *is* predicator, *John* complement

(3) *it's John who* subject, *has seen* predicator, *the play* complement

(1) would presumably be an attempt merely to state the simplest sequence of classes in the syntagm, although it could be shown to be unsatisfactory even on class-distributional grounds. (2) is distributionally acceptable and would account adequately for the syntagmatic relations; but it fails to account for the paradigmatic relations in that it does not show the 'relatedness' of this clause to *John has seen the play*, etc. If the structural description is required to show the paradigmatic as well as the syntagmatic relations of the grammar we need some representation such as (3) in which *John* is the subject. This leads to complexity in the realization, since a nominalization of the form *it's John who* seems to add no new insight elsewhere in the grammar. A more serious difficulty arises in relation to the element 'subject' in English, which is a complex element within which it is possible to distinguish three components, or features; each of these may contrast independently of the other two, although there is a general, and generalizable, tendency to co-variation among them.

The three contrasts can be seen independently in (i) *John has seen the play*, with tonic on *play*, versus, respectively, (ii) *the play has been seen by John* (subject as actor versus subject as goal); (iii) *the play John has seen* (= 'the play, John has seen, but . . .', subject as theme versus subject non-thematic); (iv) *John has seen the play* (with *John* tonic; subject as 'given' versus subject as 'new'). Each of these three is related paradigmatically to the original item, and each of them contrasts with it in respect of one feature only. By a further contrast, that of 'unpredicated theme' versus 'predicated theme', (iv) is related to (v) *it's John who has seen the play* with *John* tonic. Thus despite the difference in constituent structure (v) differs from (iv) in respect of only one feature. Such patterns, where different complexes of (paradigmatic) features may be combined in what is syntagmatically one and the same element of structure, here the 'subject', involve some complexity for a structural description; if they were handled in systemic terms, the structure need represent only their realization in syntagmatic relations. We could then adopt a form of structural representation such as (2) above.

The examples cited might be regarded as irrelevant on the grounds that they do not involve cognitive distinctions and therefore belong to the realm of stylistic variation. But this is to assume that it is the task of a grammatical theory to differentiate between these different types of distinction. Such problems seem to me to fall more properly within the domain of a semantic theory, where the selection of a particular variable, such as paraphrase, as a basis for the classification of distinctions is not arbitrary as it seems to be in the grammar. This is not to deny that the speakers of a language recognize some distinctions as 'more important' than others, and that this may depend at least in part on a concept of paraphrase. The hierarchization of systems in delicacy, in a system network, does seem to reflect some notion of the relative importance of the systems involved; this is an instance of the convergence of semantic and distributional criteria referred to by Lyons in his important discussion of semantics and grammar (1963: chapter 2). Even if a clear answer can always be given to the question 'is *a* a paraphrase of *b* or not?', or to other questions where this is irrelevant (e.g. in the distinction between *John has seen the play* with *John* tonic and with *play* tonic, which answer different questions), the place of a given distinction in the grammar would, as I see it, depend on its environment in terms of other distinctions, this presupposing also its syntagmatic environment, rather than on a classification of its semantic function.

To return to the discussion, another relevant factor here would be the desire to incorporate into the grammar phonological realizations of grammatical features, particularly (in English) those of intonation and rhythm. Such features may be assigned a place in a syntagmatic representation, either as superfixes in a syntagm or as elements in a structure; but the assignment of, say, a pitch contour as a constituent to a specified place in a structural representation, while it may be necessitated by the realization requirements, seems in other respects rather arbitrary. Intonation, in English, provides instances of both neutralization and diversification; one and the same feature may be realized in some environments by a structural pattern and in others by intonation, and a given intonation pattern may realize different features in different environments. In other words, intonation is not predictable from its structural environment. It can however be shown to be predictable in the grammar if it is regarded as a form of the realization of systemic features, at the same degree of abstraction (same stage of representation) as the structural elements but without constituent status.

Intonation however is merely a special, if clear, case of a more general point, namely that if a representation in terms other than of constituent structure is adopted for the statement of paradigmatic relations, and is then made to determine the constituent structure, then provided the structural description adequately handles the syntagmatic relations there is no need for everything to be accounted for at a constituent stage of representation. This is most obviously relevant to phonological features of the prosodic type, but could be extended also to items identified as being markers of, rather than elements in, syntactic relations.

The crucial factor in the designation of any feature as present in the grammar would thus be its assignment to a place in the systemic network. A putative feature which could not be shown to contrast independently with one or more others at some point would not be a distinct feature; each feature that is recognized is thus a term in a system, which system is located in hierarchical and simultaneous relation to other systems. The location is 'polysystemic': the recognition of a system, and the assignment of a feature to it, depends on the potentiality of contrast in the stated environment. For example, there might seem to be a pro-portionality in English such that *he can go* is to *can he go* as *he is wonder-ing if he can go* is to *he is wondering can he go*; but the related features are different in the two cases: that is, the two syntagmatic environments determine different sets of paradigmatic relations. The ordering of the systems in delicacy would thus be important in the identification of the systemic features.

It would be necessary also to specify the syntagmatic environment, in order to define the point of origin of a system network. This can be done in terms of the notion of rank, where the initial identification and labelling of certain stages in a constituent hierarchy in such general terms would provide a starting-point for the delimitation of different more specific environments. The designation of rank, in other words, is a possible first step in the specification of what Haas (1966: 125) calls 'functional relations', relevant here in that it makes possible the assign-ment of a system to a place determined solely by constituent status (e.g. all clauses) and allows further specification of the environment to be in terms of features: a feature x may be associated with constituents having the features y and z rather than with constituents having a given syn-tagmatic function. The possibility of contrast between active and passive in the clause depends on other features of the clause, not on its function in the sentence.

In stratificational terms, rank defines an inner series of strata, or sub-strata, within the outer grammatical stratum, with each rank charac-terized by a different network of systems. While many, though by no means all, features would be present at more than one rank, with conse-quent pre-selection at certain points, an important distinction is to be made here between pre-selection, where the choice of a feature at one rank determines the choice of a feature at a lower rank but the two operate in different paradigmatic environments, and the realization of a feature at a lower rank than that in which it has its environment. The latter includes such familiar instances as the realization in the structure of the word of a choice, such as that of number, associated with the group. There seems no reason to assume a necessary relationship be-tween the rank at which a feature has its environment and that in whose constituent structure it is realized.

The relevance of the concept of rank in this connection would thus be that it is as it were neutral between system and structure. While clearly a constituency notion, reflecting here the speaker's awareness of the hierarchic organization of linguistic items, it imposes a minimum of bracketing and in this way facilitates the interrelating of paradigmatic and syntagmatic modes of representation. The discussion of 'systemic description' here has been in terms of a rank-type constituent structure, since this would be one way of defining a point of origin for a system network: each system, like each structure, would be assigned to a given rank as its most generalized functional environment. It is not implied that a description in terms of features would necessitate a rank-type constituent structure, but rather that the status of constituents in the grammar would need to be brought into the discussion.

Palmer (1964a: 130) wrote: 'Perhaps we need a pre-grammatical statement in which order is utterly divorced from sequence'. In this paper I am following up Palmer's conclusion by asking whether such a statement could be thought of as a representation of the 'deep' grammar. If deep grammar is equated with deep structure, in the sense of being thought of as relations of the constituency type, it may be difficult to avoid connotations of sequence and to solve some of the problems Palmer raised. If the underlying 'order' is thought of as systemic, the more abstract representation of grammatical relations carries no implication of sequence. Sequence can be stated by reference to these, a 'linguistic element whose exponent is sequence' having a status no different from that of others. Such a description is in a sense of the WP type, with word replaced by unit, or constituent, and paradigm by system. It is not suggested that paradigmatic relations are somehow 'more important' than syntagmatic ones; but merely that a description in terms of features, if it can be made explicit, may help in bringing the 'unidimensional time sequence' of language into relation with its deeper patterns of organization.

Section Three

Descriptions

The theoretical background of systemic grammar has been outlined in the previous section. It would, however, be quite wrong to imply that in the work of Halliday there is a clear split between theory and description of language. One of the fundamental assumptions of his theory is that language is as it is because it serves to realize specific demands, and forms, of social organization. So a description of an area of English grammar is at the same time a description of instances of specific functions of language and of realizations of social forms and relations. Theory and description are quite inseparable in Halliday's practice.

The papers in this section illustrate this close connection. And because of this too, the theory in the form it has had since about 1966 is illustrated through descriptive exemplifications. The three functional components, the *ideational, textual* and *interpersonal* components, are exemplified in chapters 11, 12 and 13, respectively. The first paper in this section, 'English system networks', shows the close relation between description and theory particularly well. It is based, roughly speaking, on the paper 'Categories of the Theory of Grammar'. But whereas in that paper *system* is one of four major grammatical categories, here, in the description of English, *system* emerges as the pivotal grammatical category. The terms in the systems are semantic features; and these are accompanied by realization statements. The two together provide a full and adequate account not only of the *semantic potential* of the language, but also of its possible surface forms. It was written between May and August 1964; the theoretical consequences drawn from this description form the substance of the chapter 'Deep grammar: system as semantic choice', published in 1966.

Chapter 11 'Types of process' is an example of the grammar of the ideational function of language, namely the grammar of transitivity. Transitivity types in the English clause are discussed in terms of systemic features indicating process types. This analysis has advantages over the two other possibilities most often found in the description of English clauses: analysis in terms either of participant roles, or in terms of verb classes. The former tends to lead to a multiplication of categories, and to a lack of overlap between the underlying participants and their realization in the surface structure. The latter comes up against the well known fact that English verbs notoriously belong to a number of verb classes. Chapter 13 'Modality and modulation in English' explores an area of English which has received scant attention in modern linguistic theories. It encompasses both the speaker's attitude and relation to the message he intends to communicate, and that speaker's communication of his perceived social place vis-a-vis his addressee. Statements about both these facets of English have of course been made by grammarians and by sociolinguists; however, this paper represents the first significant attempt to incorporate such statements into a coherent grammatical framework. The same is true of chapter 12 'Theme and information'. Here Halliday discusses the textual function of language, the grammar of *theme*. The issue centres on the syntactic potential of any language to make utterances appropriate to surrounding text. Halliday deals with this under three headings: (1) *thematization*, that is, the significance of the sequential order of constituents in an English clause; (2) *information*, that is, the structure of speech qua *new* and *given* information; and (3) *identification*, which deals with the potential of the language to present constituents of a clause in an identifying relation. (Where the English clause *John read the book* is related through options in the system of *identification* to the identifying clause *What John read was the book*).

In all of Halliday's writing on language one is constantly aware of the sound of language, not at all a usual experience in reading modern linguistic descriptions. In this section this is especially true of chapters 9, 12, 13 and above all, overtly, in chapter 14 'Intonation and meaning'. Halliday presents an account of intonation which is completely integrated into the grammatical framework: one of the very few attempts at this. He also provides a systemic account of the meaning potential which is inherent in the intonation system in English. These two features of his account of intonation in English make it unique.

Q English system networks

This chapter on English System Networks (ESN) is a description of English, and can be profitably read in conjunction with the descriptive chapters which follow. The latter are discursive statements about English, and it might be easier to read these first: say, Types of process, and then the transitivity system network on page 110. This would be a fairly easy way into reading networks. The descriptions in Section Three were written over a period of six years, so that they are not identical; they differ in detail at times, and in some cases slight shifts in Halliday's theoretical stance have brought descriptive changes. But ESN is also a formal description in systemic terms, and illustrates the theoretical relation between 'deep' systemic feature description and 'surface' structural realization.

TABLE I

Tonality: Distribution of utterance into tone groups (location of tone group boundaries)

Tonicity: Distribution of tone group into tonic and pretonic (location of tonic foot)

Tone (primary; pitch movement on tonic)

1	fall	\	5	rise-fall	⋀	
2	high rise	/	13	fall plus low rise	\ ⏝	
3	low rise	⏝	55	rise-fall plus low rise	⋀ ⏝	
4	fall-rise	⋁				

Tone (secondary)

	Pretonic			*Tonic*
1	1 even (level, falling, rising)	⎫	1+	high fall
	−1 uneven ('bouncing')	⎬ ×	1	mid fall
	...1 suspended ('listing')	⎭	1−	low fall
2	2 high (level, falling, rising)	⎫ ×	2	high rise
	−2 low (level, rising)	⎭	2	high fall—high rise
3			3	low rise
			3	mid level—low rise
4			4	high fall–rise
			4	low fall–rise
5			5	high rise–fall
			5	low rise–fall

Symbols

//	tone group boundary (always also foot boundary)	__	tonic syllable
		.	silent ictus
/	foot boundary	...	pause

Tone, primary and secondary, is shown by Arabic figures, alone or with diacritics, placed immediately after the tone group boundary marker.

This paper, previously unpublished, was written between May and August 1964 and formed the substance of a course on the description of English given by Halliday at Indiana University during that time.

TABLE II

Tonicity: location of 'information focus'
  tonic = final lexical item (neutral)
  tonic = pre-final item or final grammatical item (contrastive)

Tone (assuming tonality neutral):
  Place of clause in sentence structure: final main 1, non-final
    co-ordinate 3, non-final subordinate 4.

Declarative clauses
reservation: 1 unreserved, <u>4</u> reserved
involvement: 1 neutral, 3 uninvolved, 5 involved
agreement: 1 neutral, <u>3</u> confirmatory, 2 contradictory
information: 1 one information point, 13 two information points
'key': 1 neutral, 1 + strong, 1 — mild

Interrogative clauses, WH- type
'key': 1 neutral, 2 (with final tonic) mild
relation to previous utterance: 1 unrelated, 2 (with WH-tonic) echo

Interrogative clauses, yes/no type
'key': 2 neutral, 1 strong
involvement: 2 neutral, 3 uninvolved, 5 involved
place in alternative question: 2 first alternative, 1 second
    alternative
specification of point of query: 2 unspecified, <u>2</u> specified

Imperative clauses
'key' (positive): 1 neutral, <u>3</u> moderate, 13 mild
'key' (negative): <u>3</u> neutral, 1 strong, 13 mild
force: 1 neutral, <u>4</u> compromising, 5 insistent
function: 1 &c. command, 2 question

'Moodless' clauses (also as declarative)
function: 1 answer &c., 2 question, 3 warning, 5 exclamation

In the section under 'tone', the headings (e.g. 'reservation') indicate the
nature of the choice, the entries under each heading representing the
terms in the choice with their appropriate tone. Thus '1 unreserved, <u>4</u>
reserved' means 'in this choice tone <u>4</u> indicates reservation, by contrast
with tone 1 which indicates no reservation'. Secondary tones are indicated
where relevant.

SYSTEMS OF TONE

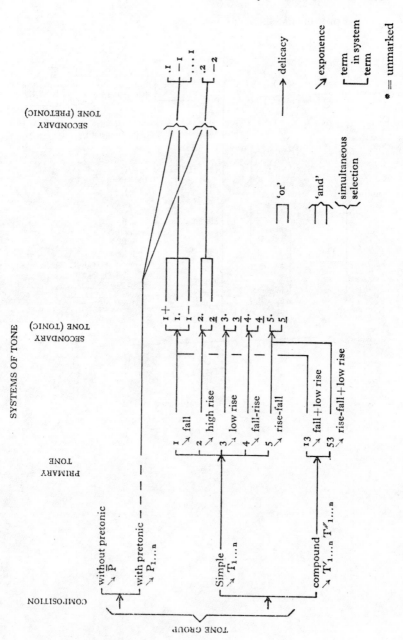

104 Descriptions

SYSTEMS OF THE CLAUSE (1)

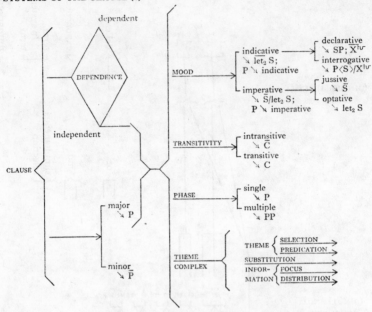

SYSTEMS OF THE CLAUSE (2): DECLARATIVE CLAUSE

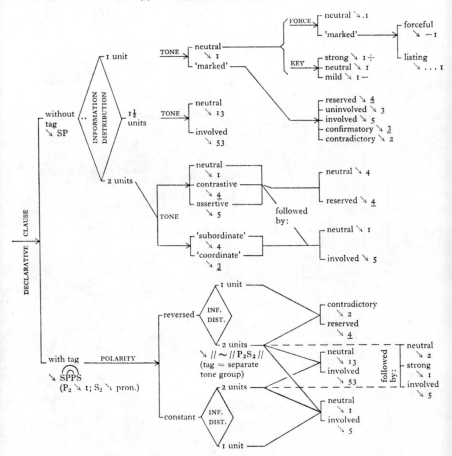

SYSTEMS OF THE CLAUSE (3): INTERROGATIVE I

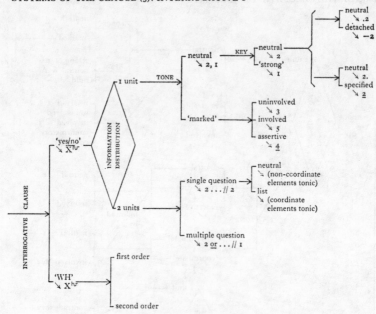

SYSTEMS OF THE CLAUSE (4): INTERROGATIVE II

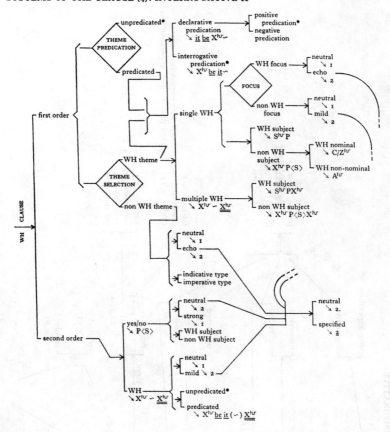

SYSTEMS OF THE CLAUSE (5): IMPERATIVE

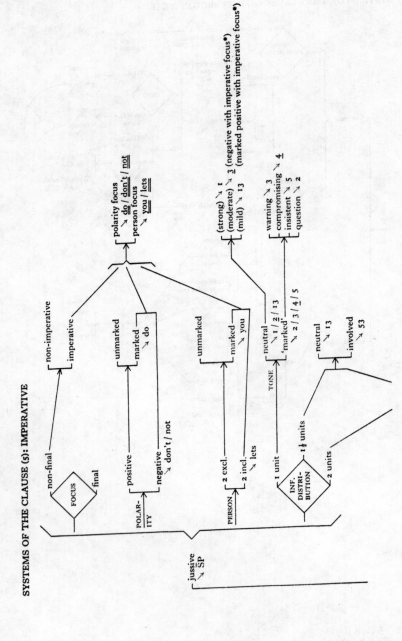

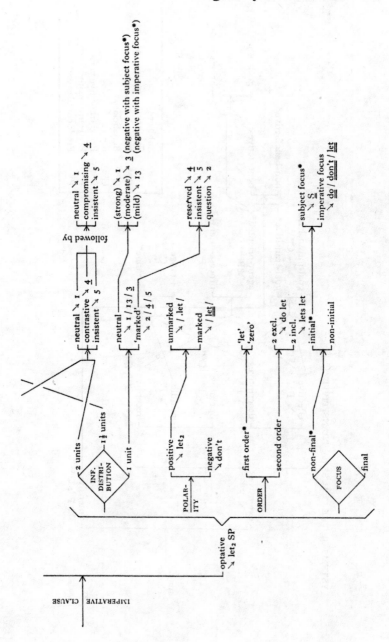

SYSTEMS OF THE CLAUSE (6): TRANSITIVITY

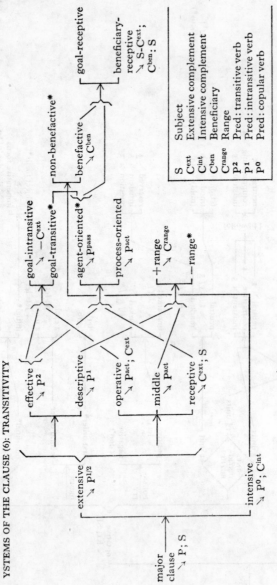

extensive: (effective/operative: (goal-intransitive))
    John threw; Mary washed (sc. the clothes)

extensive: (effective/operative: (goal-transitive: non-benefactive))
    John threw the ball; Mary washed the clothes

extensive: (effective/operative: (goal-transitive: benefactive))
    John gave the dog a bone; Mary washed the boys their clothes

extensive: (effective/middle)
    Mary washed (sc. herself)

extensive: (effective/receptive: (agent-oriented: non-benefactive))
    the ball was thrown; the clothes were washed

extensive: (effective/receptive: (agent-oriented: benefactive: (goal-receptive)))
    the bone was given the dog

extensive: (effective/receptive: (agent-oriented: benefactive: (beneficiary-receptive)))
    the dog was given the bone

extensive: (effective/receptive: (process-oriented))
    the books sold; the clothes washed

extensive: (descriptive/operative)
    the sergeant marched the prisoners

extensive: (descriptive/middle: (+range))
    Peter jumped the wall

extensive: (descriptive/middle: (-range))
    Peter jumped; the prisoners marched

extensive: (descriptive/receptive)
    the prisoners were marched

intensive: non-benefactive
    Mary seemed happy; Mary made a good wife

intensive: benefactive
    Mary made John a good wife

SYSTEMS OF THE CLAUSE (7): THEME

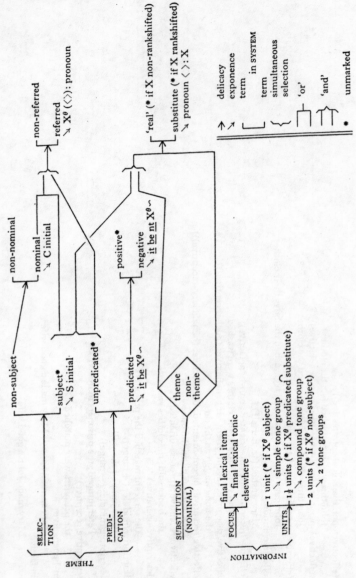

Examples of tone-expounded systems in declarative clause (from spontaneous conversation)

//1 this of course de/pends on the / country where they / live //

//— 1 . and / this is a / bit / hard //

//— 1 . it's / rather / interesting //

//. . . 1 . it's grade / one / two / three to / nine //

//. . . 1 . of / vitamins and / sugars and / salts and . . .

//1+ . in fact the / smaller ones / eat the / bigger ones //

//1+ . well / yes they're e/normously / long //

//1— . I'm / not / sure that it's / worth it //

//1 . and there was a / photograph of a / rabbit //1 quivering his / ears a //1— lovely / white / rabbit and //1— he was

a / little man / sitting behind the / rabbit //

//4 . oh / mine / aren't / parasites //

//4 no worse than / anyone / else //

//3 six / foot //3 I don't / know //

//3 . they / just find a / comfortable /¡place in your / gut and they //3 stick their / hooks in and //1 stay there //

//5 he was a / very / famous / man //

//5 . it's / very / interesting //

//—3 that's / right //

//—3 . yes it's / not the / first thing //

Examples contd.

||2 yes they / do ||

||— 2 I don't / know ||

||13 . that's the / trouble with / growing bac/teria in / culture ||

||13 . they / change peri/odically ||

||53 . they / do in / some uni/versities ||

||53 . and it / helps / them ||

||4 . in the / case of the / British ex/am I ||/1 don't know / whether it / does ||

||4 . they / may have ||/1+ pushed the / standard / up ||

||3 . fascinatingly e/nough I mean the //1 facts seem to be / fairly / true ||

||4 oh the ma/terial was //5 excellent ||

||2 . you're not / serious //2 are you ||

||4 . no there / was a / Russian in the / first one //2 wasn't there ||

||1 . and in fact / most of the / zoo department were / there //2 weren't they ||

||5 . I'm / sure they do //2 don't they ||

||1 Cambridge / always / was //1 wasn't it ||

||5 oh / no that's / very em/barassing //1 isn't it ||

||1 used to be the / habit in / China //2 did it ||

FIRST ORDER WH CLAUSE SYSTEMS

Key to Examples:

	Option o	Option I
1 THEME	WH: o	non-WH: I
2 NO. OF WH ELEMENTS	single: o	multiple: I
3 SINGLE WH: FOCUS	non WH: o	WH: I
4 NON-WH FOCUS: TONE	neutral: o	mild: I
5 WH FOCUS: TONE	neutral: o	echo: I
6 TONE 2	neutral: o	specif.: I
7 SUBJ.	non WH: o	WH: I
8 NON-WH SUBJ.	nom.: o	non-nom: I
9 PREDIC.	unpred.: o	predic: I
10 PREDICAT.: MOOD	interrog.: o	declar.: I

Selection matrix (systems 1–10):

Example	1	2	3	4	5	6	7	8	9	10
1	o	o	I	—	o	—	I	—	o	—
2	o	o	I	—	I	o	I	—	o	—
3	o	o	I	—	o	—	I	—	I	o
4	o	o	I	—	I	o	I	—	I	o
5	o	o	I	—	I	o	I	—	I	I
6	o	o	I	—	o	—	o	o	o	—
7	o	o	I	—	I	I	o	o	o	—
8	o	o	I	—	I	o	o	o	I	o
9	o	o	I	—	I	o	o	I	o	—

Examples

//I who said / that//
//2 who said / that//
//I who was it / said that//
//2 who was it / said that//
//2 . it was / who said / that//
//I who did you / see//
//2 who did you / see//
//2 who was it you / saw//
//2 where did he / go//

||2 where was it he / went //
||1 who said / that //
||2 who said / that //
||1 who was it / said / that //
||2 who was it / said / that //
||1 who did you / see //
||1 who was it you / saw //
||2 where did he / go //
||1 where / was it he / went //
||1 who wants / what //
||2 who's / going to sit / where //
||1 which shall I / put / where //
||1 John said / what //
||2 John said / what //
||1 I put it / where //
||2 John put / what there //

SECOND ORDER WH CLAUSE SYSTEMS

Key to Examples

1 QUESTION TYPE	2 YES/NO TYPE: SUBJECT	3 YES/NO TYPE: TONE	4 PREDICATION	5 WH TYPE: TONE	6 TONE 2
yes/no: o WH: I	non WH: o WH: I	neutral: o strong: I	unpredicated: o predicated: I	neutral: o mild: I	neutral: o specified: I

				2	3	4	5	6
o	I	I	o	o	—	—	o
o	I	I	I	o	—	—	—
o	o	o	o	o	—	—	I
o	o	I	I	o	—	—	—
I	—	—	—	o	o	I	—
I	—	—	—	I	o	—	—
I	—	—	—	o	o	—	—
I	—	—	—	o	I	I	I
I	—	—	—	o	I	I	o
I	—	—	—	I	I	I	o

Examples

	2 . did / who do it	
	1 . did / who do it	
	2 did he do / what	
	1 did he go / where	
	1 who said / what	
	1 who was it / said / what	
	1 what did / who say	
	2 where did / who go	
	2 who went / where	
	2 where was it / who went		!

IMPERATIVE SYSTEMS: JUSSIVE

Key to Examples

1 FOCUS	2 NON-FINAL FOCUS	3 POLARITY	4 POSITIVE POLARITY	5 PERSON	6 2 EXCLUS. PERSON	7 IMPERATIVE FOCUS	8 TONE	9 INFORMATION DISTRIBUTION
final: o	imperative: o	posit.: o	unmarked: o	2 excl.: o	unmarked: o	polarity: o	unmarked: o	unmarked: o
non-final: ɪ	non-imp.: ɪ	negat.: ɪ	marked: ɪ	2 incl.: ɪ	marked: ɪ	person: ɪ	marked: ɪ	marked: ɪ

Example	1	2	3	4	5	6	7	8	9
ɪ	o	ɪ	o	o	o	ɪ	—	—	o
ɪ	o	ɪ	o	o	o	ɪ	—	—	o
ɪ	o	ɪ	o	o	ɪ	—	—	—	o
ɪ	o	o	ɪ	ɪ	—	—	—	o	o
ɪ	o	o	ɪ	ɪ	—	—	—	—	o
ɪ	o	o	o	ɪ	o	o	ɪ	o	o
ɪ	o	o	ɪ	o	o	o	ɪ	o	o
ɪ	o	ɪ	ɪ	ɪ	ɪ	ɪ	ɪ	o	o
ɪ	o	o	o	ɪ	—	—	—	—	o

Examples

//ɪ ask / John //
//ɪ you ask / John //
//ɪ you ask / John //
//ɪ let's ask / John //
//ɪ let's ask / John //
//ɪ do ask / John //
//ɪ3 do ask / John //
//ɪ you / do ask / John //
//ɪ do let's ask / John //

	//13 do let's ask / John //	//3 don't ask / John //	//13 don't ask / John //	//4 don't / you ask / John //	//1 don't / let's ask / John //	//1 let's / not ask / John //	//13 don't let's ask / John //	//13 let's not ask / John //	//1 you / ask / John //	//5 don't let's / ask John //	//53 . let's / ask / John //	//1 you ask //4 John //
	o	o	o	o	o	o	o	o	o	o	⊢	⊢
	o	o	o	⊢	o	o	o	o	o	⊢				
	o					⊢	⊢	o	o	⊢								
			o	o	⊢										⊢					⊢
	⊢	o	o	o	⊢	⊢	⊢	⊢	o	⊢	⊢	o
	⊢																		o			o	o
	o	⊢	⊢	⊢	⊢	⊢	⊢	⊢	o	⊢	o	o
	o			o	o	o	o	o	o	o	⊢	⊢				
	⊢	o	⊢	⊢	⊢	⊢	⊢	⊢	⊢	⊢	o		

THEME SYSTEMS: EXAMPLES

Key to Examples

	1	2	3	4	5	6	7	8	9
	THEME SELECTION		THEME REFERENCE	THEME PREDICATION		SUBSTITUTION		INFORMATION FOCUS	INFORMATION DISTRIBUTION
	subject/ non-subj.	(non-subj.) non-nom./ nominal	non-ref./ referred	unpred./ predic.	(predic.) positive/ negative	theme 'real'/ substitute	non-theme 'real'/ substitute	final/ non-final	1 unit/ 1½ units/ 2 units
	subj.: o	non-nom.: o	non-ref.: o	unpredic.: o	positive: o	real: o	real: o	final: o	1 unit: oo
	non-subj.: 1	nominal: 1	referred: 1	predic.: 1	negative: 1	substitute: 1	substitute: 1	non-final: 1	1½ units: oi
									2 units: 1o

Examples

	1	2	3	4	5	6	7	8	9
||1 John / saw the / play / yesterday ||	o	—	o	o	—	o	o	o	oo
||13 John / saw the / play / yesterday ||	1	—	o	o	—	o	o	o	oi
||4 John || / I saw the / play / yesterday ||	o	—	o	o	—	o	o	1	1o
||1 John / saw the / play / yesterday ||	o	—	o	1	o	o	o	o	oo
||1 John / saw the / play / yesterday ||	o	—	o	1	1	o	o	o	oo
||13 John / saw it / yesterday the / play ||	1	—	o	o	—	1	o	o	oi
||13 . he / saw the / play / yesterday / John ||	1	—	o	o	—	o	1	o	oi

Phrase									
//4̲ . it / wasn't / John that / saw the / play / yesterday //	0	|	0	1	1	0	0	1	00
//13 . it was / John that / saw the / play / yesterday̲ //	0	|	0	1	1	0	0	1	01
//4̲ . it / wasn't the / play̲ John / saw / yesterday //	1	1	0	1	0	0	0	1	00
//13 . it was the / play John / saw / yesterday̲ //	1	1	0	1	1	0	0	1	01
//4̲ John he //1 saw the / play / yesterday //	0	|	1	0	0	0	0	0	10
//1 yesterday / John / saw the / play̲ //	1	0	0	0	|	0	0	0	00
//4̲ yesterday //1 John / saw the / play̲ //	1	0	0	0	|	0	0	0	10
//1 . the / play / John saw / yesterday //	1	1	0	0	|	0	0	0	00
//4̲ . the / play //1 John saw / yesterday̲ //	1	1	0	0	|	0	0	0	10
//4̲ . it / wasn't / yesterday̲ John / saw the / play //	1	0	0	1	1	0	0	1	00

Examples of theme and information systems (from spontaneous conversation)

in the first month one was too ill to move

adjudicator I thought they were called

the sound that went floating out on the air I didn't know I had it in me

aged legal gentlemen all like pipes

the metal container somehow it turns your coffee rather sour

Britain it's all roads

it's inhaling that's harmful

it's the side that has possession is at an advantage

it was that part I didn't enjoy

it's rather good coffee this

it was quite fascinating to see her

it does interest me how memory works

imagining some suffering is worse than experiencing it oneself

// this of course de/pends on the / country where they / live //

// . I / thought / cats always / ate them //

// how / long do these / changes / take //

// . that's / why it's so / awful to / have to get / rid of it //

// . it / looked rather / odd having those / needles //

// . no / I saw the / first one //

// . but / in A/merica they // layer / things //

// all the / dialect forms are // marked / wrong //

Paradigm examples corresponding to those on preceding page

H.P.—10

yesterday I saw John
John I saw yesterday
John I saw him yesterday
I saw John yesterday
John yesterday he saw me
John he saw me yesterday

it was John that saw me yesterday
it was John saw me yesterday
it was John I saw yesterday

he saw me yesterday John
it was strange to see John
it was strange how I saw John
seeing John was strange

// . I / saw / John / yesterday //
// I saw / John / yesterday //

// . I / saw / John //

// . I / saw / John //
// . it was / strange to / see / John //
// . it was / strange / seeing / John //
// I saw / John / yesterday //

// yesterday I // saw / John //
// I saw / John // yesterday //

SYSTEMS OF THE VERBAL GROUP (1)

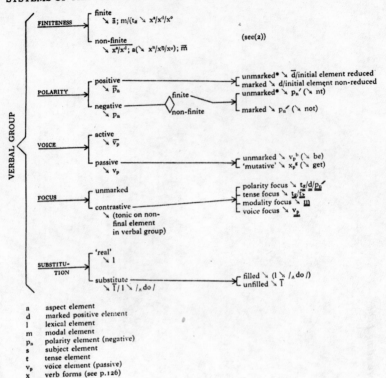

a   aspect element
d   marked positive element
l   lexical element
m   modal element
p_n polarity element (negative)
s   subject element
t   tense element
v_p voice element (passive)
x   verb forms (see p.126)

SYSTEMS OF THE VERBAL GROUP (2)

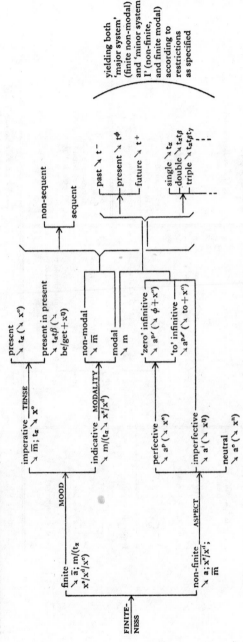

VERBAL GROUP

Major system:

$$t_\alpha \rightarrow \begin{cases} t_\alpha - \nearrow \phi + x^d \\ t_\alpha \phi \nearrow \phi + x^s \\ t_\alpha + \nearrow \text{ will} + x^o \text{ (shall)} \end{cases}$$

$$p_a \rightarrow \begin{cases} p_a{'} \nearrow x_1 + nt \\ p_a \nearrow x_1 + not \end{cases}$$

$d \nearrow do + x^o$

Imperative system:

$$s \rightarrow \begin{cases} s^{excl} \nearrow \text{ you} \\ s^{incl} \nearrow \text{ lets} \end{cases}$$

$(t_\alpha, d; p_a \text{ as major})$

All systems:

$$t_\beta \rightarrow \begin{cases} t_\beta - \nearrow \text{ have} + x^n \\ t_\beta \phi \nearrow \text{ be} + x^0 \\ t_\beta + \nearrow \text{ be going to / about} + x^o \end{cases}$$

Minor system (modal/non-finite):

$$t_\alpha \rightarrow \begin{cases} t_\alpha - \nearrow \text{ have} + x^n \\ t_\alpha \phi \nearrow (+m) \phi + x^o \quad (-m) \phi \\ t_\alpha + \nearrow \text{ be going to} + x^o \text{ about} \end{cases}$$

p_a: $(+m)$ ... $(-m)$ $\begin{cases} p_n{'} \nearrow x_1 + nt \\ p_a \nearrow x_1 + not \end{cases}$

$$a \rightarrow \begin{cases} a^{p'} \nearrow a^{p'} \phi + x^o \\ a^p \nearrow to + x^o \\ a^1 \nearrow \phi + x^o, t + \text{ about} \\ a^o \nearrow \phi + (v_p \phi +) 1^n \end{cases}$$

$$m \rightarrow \begin{cases} m^{1-} \nearrow \text{ could was to} \\ m^1 \phi \nearrow \text{ can is to} \\ m^o \text{ could would should may might must used to ought to need dare)} + x^o \end{cases}$$

Minor system (sequent):

$$t_\alpha \rightarrow \begin{cases} t_\alpha - \nearrow \text{ had} + x^n \\ t_\alpha \phi \nearrow \phi + x^d \\ t_\alpha + \nearrow \text{ would (should)} + x^o \end{cases}$$

(Sequent modals:

can → could
is to → was to
may → might
(must → ought to))

$(p_n, d \text{ as major})$

t^- past tense
t^ϕ present tense
t^+ future tense
t_α primary tense
$t_\beta(..\epsilon)$ secondary tense

$$x \rightarrow \begin{cases} x^s \nearrow \text{ am is are has have take(s)} \\ x^d \nearrow \text{ was were had took} \\ x^o \nearrow \text{ be have take} \\ x^0 \nearrow \text{ being having taking} \\ x^n \nearrow \text{ been taken} \end{cases}$$

x = immediately following element other than p_a
x_1 = first element in vbl gp.

$$v_p \rightarrow \begin{cases} v_p{}^b \nearrow be + 1^n \\ v_p{}^6 \nearrow get + 1^n \end{cases}$$

$1 \nearrow$ (lexical verb)

VERBAL GROUP (1) — TENSE

t_ε	t_δ	t_γ	t_β	t_α	
				past	1
				present	2
				future	3
			past in	past	4
				present	5
				future	6
			present in	past	7
				present	8
				future	9
			future in	past	10
				present	11
				future	12
		past in	future in	past	13
				present	14
				future	15
		present in	past in	past	16
				present	17
				future	18
		present in	future in	past	19
				present	20
				future	21
		future in	past in	past	22
				present	23
				future	24
	past in	future in	past in	past	25
				present	26
				future	27
	present in	past in	future in	past	28
				present	29
				future	30
	present in	future in	past in	past	31
				present	32
				future	33
present in	part in	future in	past in	past	34
				present	35
				future	36

VERBAL GROUP (2)   TENSE (MAJOR SYSTEM)

1 took/did take
2 takes/does take
3 will take

4 had taken
5 has taken
6 will have taken

7 was taking
8 is taking
9 will be taking

10 was going to take
11 is going to take
12 will be going to take

13 was going to have taken
14 is going to have taken
15 will be going to have taken

16 had been taking
17 has been taking
18 will have been taking

19 was going to be taking
20 is going to be taking
21 will be going to be taking

22 had been going to take
23 has been going to take
24 will have been going to take

25 had been going to have taken
26 has been going to have taken
27 will have been going to have taken

28 was going to have been taking
29 is going to have been taking
30 will be going to have been taking

31 had been going to be taking
32 has been going to be taking
33 will have been going to be taking

34 had been going to have been taking
35 has been going to have been taking
36 will have been going to have been taking

VERBAL GROUP (3) TENSE (MINOR SYSTEM: MODAL/ NON-FINITE)

I to take, taking; can take   (= 2)

II to have taken, having taken; can have taken   (= 1, 4, 5)

III to be taking, being taking;* can be taking   (8 =)

IV to be, being; can be+going / about to take   (= 3, 11, 12)

V to be, being; can be+going / about to have taken (= 6, 14, 15)

VI to have, having; can have+been taking   (= 7, 16, 17)

VII to be, being; can be+going / about to be taking (= 9, 20, 21)

VIII to have, having; can have+been going / about to take
                                                             (= 10, 12, 23)

IX to have, having; can have+been going / about to have taken
                                                             (= 13, 25, 26)

X to be, being; can be+going / about to have been taking
                                                             (= 18, 29, 30)

XI to have, having; can have+been going / about to be taking
                                                             (= 19, 31, 32)

XII to have, having; can have+been going / about to have been
       taking   (= 28, 34, 35)

Note: 24, 27, 33, 36 have no equivalents in this system.

* The form *being taking* is now (predictably!) attested in regular use.

VERBAL GROUP (4)

TENSE (MINOR SYSTEM:
SEQUENT)

1 had taken
2 took
3 would take
4 (1)
5 (1)
6 would have taken
7 had been taking
8 was taking
9 would be taking
10 had been going to take
11 was going to take
12 would be going to take
13 had been going to have taken
14 was going to have taken
15 would be going to have taken
16 (7)
17 (7)
18 would have been taking
19 had been going to be taking
20 was going to be taking
21 would be going to be taking
22 (10)
23 (10)
24 would have been going to take
25 (13)
26 (13)
27 would have been going to have taken
28 had been going to have been taking
29 was going to have been taking
30 would be going to have been taking
31 (19)
32 (19)
33 would have been going to be taking
34 (28)
35 (28)
36 would have been going to have been taking

NOMINAL GROUP (1): PRINCIPAL SYSTEMS

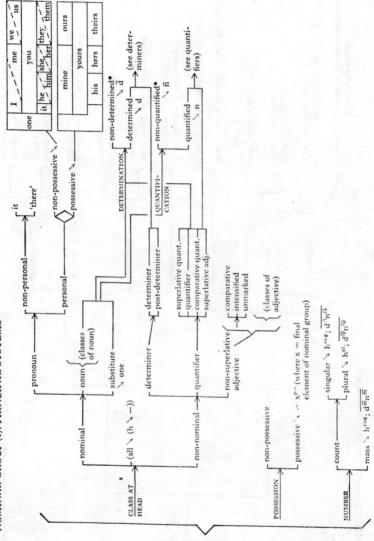

NOMINAL GROUP (2): DETERMINERS

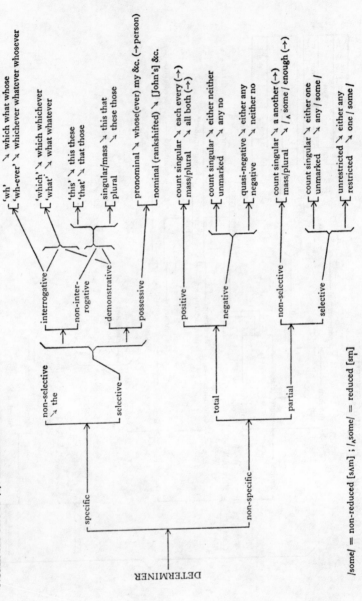

|some| = non-reduced [sʌm] ; |ₐsome| = reduced [sm̩]

NOMINAL GROUP (3): DETERMINERS (contd.)

Specific : selective

	Interrogative		Non-interrogative	
Demonstrative	which	what	this	that
	whichever	whatever	these	those
Possessive	whose		my our his her	your its her their one's
	whosever			
	[which person's] &c.		[John's] [my father's] &c.	

Non-specific : total : negative

	Quasi-negative	Negative	Count singular
	either	neither	
	any	no	Unmarked

partial : selective

	Unrestricted	Restricted
	either	one
	any	/ some /

PRE-DETERMINERS

predeterminers ⌐ pre-specific ↗ all both half
          └ preceding 'a' ↗ half such

rankshifted
quantifiers ↗ many of, a lot of, more of, two of, two-thirds of &c.

POST-DETERMINERS

complete   entire   whole   other   some   such
certain   customary   different   expected   famous   given   habitual   likely   necessary   normal
ordinary   original   particular   possible   predicted   probable   respective   special   usual
various   well-known

NOMINAL GROUP (4): QUANTIFIERS

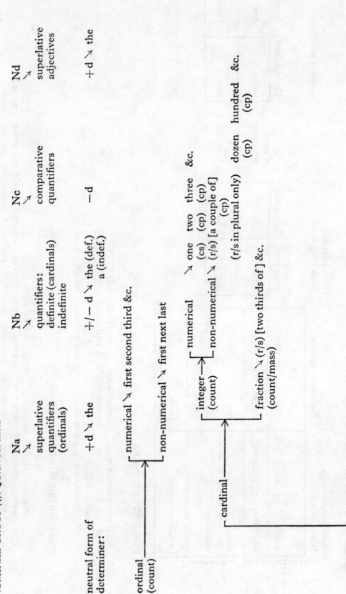

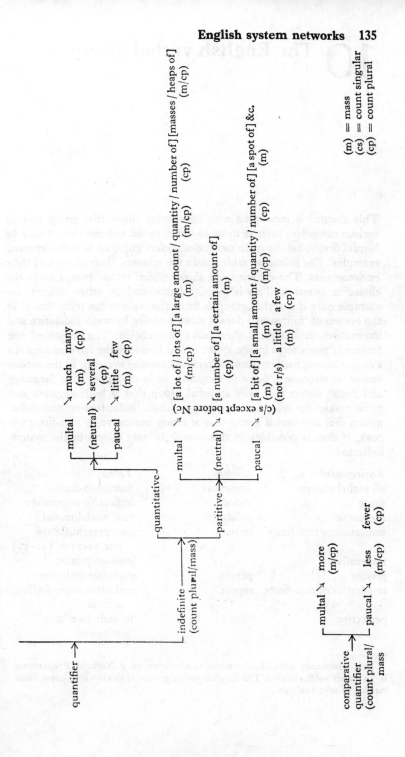

quantifier →

indefinite
(count plural/mass)

quantitative

partitive

multal — (neutral) — paucal

much (m) / many (cp)
several (cp)
little (m) / few (cp)

multal — (neutral) — paucal

[a lot of / lots of] [a large amount / quantity / number of] [masses /heaps of]
(m/cp)   (m)   (cp)   (m/cp)

[a number of] [a certain amount of]
(cp)   (m)

[a bit of] [a small amount / quantity / number of] [a spot of] &c.
(m)   (m/cp)   (cp)   (m)
a little   a few
(m)   (cp)
(not r/s)

(c/s except before Nc)

comparative
quantifier
(count plural/
mass)

multal — paucal

more (m/cp)
less (m/cp)
fewer (cp)

(m) = mass
(cs) = count singular
(cp) = count plural

10 The English verbal group

This chapter is concerned with identifying the verbal group and its various categories such as those of tense, mood and the like. It may be helpful first to list the main categories, before going on to consider some examples. The following table shows the systems, their terms and their environments. The environment shows which verbal groups make the choice in question. This is usually determined by other choices: for example only if a verbal group is finite (i.e. selects the term 'finite' in the system of 'finiteness') does it make a choice between indicative and imperative—and it must then make that choice. The choice of one feature (a given term in one system) thus becomes the environment for a choice among further features (terms in another system). In the entries under 'environment', *and* is conjunct, *or* is disjunct: thus 'negative and finite' means that only a verbal group that is both negative and finite makes the selection in question while 'indicative or non-finite' means that any verbal group that is either indicative or non-finite (or both, if that is possible; in this case it is *not*) selects in the system indicated.

Environment	System	Terms
all verbal groups	finiteness	finite/non-finite
finite	mood	indicative/imperative
indicative	modality	non-modal/modal
indicative or non-finite	tense	past/present/future (etc.; see pp. 141–50)
imperative		jussive/optative
jussive	person	exclusive/inclusive
imperative or non-finite	aspect	perfective/imperfective/ neutral
perfective		'to' infinitive/'zero' infinitive

This previously unpublished paper was written as a Nuffield Programme Work Paper 1966, entitled 'The English verbal group: Notes towards a specimen manual of text analysis'.

Environment	System	Terms
all verbal groups	voice	active/passive
passive		'be' passive/'get' passive
all verbal groups	polarity	positive/negative
positive and finite		unmarked positive/ marked positive
negative and finite		unmarked negative/ marked negative
all verbal groups	contrast ('emphasis')	non-contrastive/ contrastive
all verbal groups	presupposition	non-presupposing/ presupposing
presupposing		elliptical/substitute

Before going on to describe these systems in detail, we shall consider some examples, which will show that there is in fact very little difficulty in recognizing the forms concerned, even though one may not always be aware exactly how one has recognized them. In

they wept like anything to see such quantities of sand

there is one finite verbal group *wept* and one non-finite *to see*. Both of these realize the clause element 'predicator'; a non-finite verbal group has the same function as a finite one in this respect. Other non-finite verbal groups are *hopping* and *scrambling* in

all hopping through the frothy waves, and scrambling to the shore

Compare *pounding* and *purpling* in

Don John pounding on the slaughter-painted poop
Purpling all the ocean like a bloody pirate's sloop

These last are imperfective, while *to see*, above, was perfective; we could write

to see (non-finite: perfective)
hopping (non-finite: imperfective)

where the colon means that the second choice is dependent on the first; only the non-finite verbal group has this choice of perfective versus imperfective.

Both *to see* and *hopping* are present tense; the corresponding past would be *to have seen* and *having hopped*. The choice of tense is thus independent of aspect; in adding the tense feature we can use / to indicate that the choice of tense is independent of the previous choice:

to see   (non-finite: (perfective / present))
to have seen   (non-finite: (perfective / past))
hopping   (non-finite: (imperfective / present))
having hopped   (non-finite: (imperfective / past))

The bracketing works as in mathematics, where $((a+b) \times c)$ has to be distinguished from $(a+(b\times c))$; certain brackets can be eliminated by convention, again as in mathematics where $(a+bc)$ means $(a+(b\times c))$ not $((a+b)\times c)$, but there is no harm in putting them all in.

Now to consider some examples of finite verbal groups. In

they wept like anything

wept is finite, indicative and past. As indicative, it contrasts with imperative *weep* in *weep no more*, or *cut* in

cut us another slice

Since there is no past imperative the choice of tense in *wept* depends on its being indicative:

wept (finite : indicative : past)

This now can be contrasted with *doubt* in '*I doubt it*', *said the Carpenter*:

doubt (finite : indicative : present)

In *the sun was shining on the sea* there is a tense of a different kind:

was shining (finite : indicative : present in past)

while in '*The time has come*', *the Walrus said* we have

has come (finite : indicative : past in present)

These tenses in which there is more than one choice, referred to here by a label of the form 'x in y' (e.g. past in present) are called 'compound tenses'; they are discussed in detail on pages 146–50.

All the examples cited so far have been positive in polarity and active in voice. By contrast *he's being punished* and *he's getting punished* both represent passive voice, the difference between them being somewhat similar to that between *it was cold* and *it got cold*. Negative hardly needs illustration, but the difference may be noted between the reduced or 'unmarked' negative with *n't*, as in

they hadn't any feet

and the non-reduced or 'marked' negative with *not* as in

he did not choose to leave the oyster-bed

A similar contrast appears in the positive, between the 'unmarked' form in *they'd eaten every one* and the 'marked' form *had eaten*. Normally again this corresponds to reduced and non-reduced; but there is a special form in some tenses where no reduction is possible and the 'marked' positive has a form of the verb *do* as in

the Walrus did beseech

which does not make sense in this instance, and so is probably used for purposes of rhyme and rhythm. Written English does not however make all the distinctions necessary for the explanation of either those features or those of contrast in the verbal group, so that they will need to be discussed in phonological terms.

To add just one more illustration, modal forms of the verbal group are those such as *can begin, could not see* in

we can begin to feed
you could not see a cloud

These are formed with items such as *can, may, must* which are followed, not preceded, by the negative element in the verbal group.

We may now turn to a more systematic examination of the forms of the verbal group, beginning with a discussion of the way it is built up.

It will be seen from the preceding section that where complication arises in the verbal group it is in part due to the fact that the way in which a particular verbal group is built up does not directly reflect the choices that have been made in the various systems: its morphology, in other words, does not directly reflect its syntax. For example, *was taken* looks more like *was taking* than it does like *took;* yet *was taken* and *was taking* differ from each other both in tense and in voice, whereas *took* has the same tense (simple past) as *was taken* and the same voice (active) as *was taking*. Sometimes there is, in fact, a simple correspondence, such that a given feature has one and only one clearly recognizable realization: the feature 'negative', for example, is always realized by *not* or *n't*, and likewise the presence of *not* or *n't* is always an indication that the verbal group has the feature 'negative'. But no such simple rule can be given for the features 'passive' or 'past'.

It has already been noted that the verbal group may consist either of one word (e.g. *took*) or of more than one word (e.g. *has taken, will have been taking*). The first step therefore is to identify and label certain forms of the *words* that go to make up the verbal group. These words are verbs; the term 'verb' refers to a class of the word, so that the verbal group *was shining* consists of two words both of which are verbs. Now, with the exception of a small set of verbs which perform an entirely grammatical function in the verbal group (the 'modals', which will be discussed later), English verbs display a 'scatter' of from three to five variants—or, in the case of the verb *be*, eight. From the point of view of their function in the verbal group, these variants need to be grouped into four distinct forms (one of which is then subdivided) which can be specified as follows, where x stands for any verb:

(1) x^o — base form ('zero'-form, 'infinitive', 'dictionary form')
(2) x^f — finite form, subdivided into:
　　　x^s ('present tense')
　　　d^d ('past tense')
(3) x^n — non-finite, present/active form ('present or active participle')
(4) x^n — non-finite, past/passive form ('past or passive participle')

The various labels that have been used for these tend to be cumbersome and somewhat inadequate—inevitably so, since the total range of their functions in the verbal group is rather complex. They can be referred to simply by their symbols, as 'zero'-form, 'f'-form, 's'-form and so on; or by some version of the labels on the right. These forms are as follows:

		be (eight variants)	5-variant verbs (e.g. *take*)	4-variant verbs (e.g. *walk*)	3-variant verbs (e.g. *put*)
(1) x^o		be	take	walk	put
(2) x^f	x^s	am/is/are	take/takes	walk/walks	put/puts
	x^d	was/were	took	walked	put
(3) $x^{\text{ŋ}}$		being	taking	walking	putting
(4) x^n		been	taken	walked	put

All such verbs—that is, all verbs having all four forms—may occur as the lexical element in a verbal group. The lexical verb, whichever form it takes, always occurs in final position in the verbal group (the special case of 'phrasal verbs' is treated separately): so for example the lexical verb *take* appears as *take*^{o} in *I can take*, as x^f in *I take, I took*, as $x^{\text{ŋ}}$ in *I am taking* and as x^n in *I have taken*. The 's'-form and the 'd'-form are grouped together because they have the same potentialities of occurrence in the verbal group: wherever one can occur the other can also. If the lexical verb is in one of these two 'f'-forms, nothing can precede it within the verbal group: it forms a verbal group on its own. If the lexical verb is in one of the other forms, then it may occur alone or it may be preceded by one or more of a small set of verbs known as 'verbal operators'. These operators, in combination with the appropriate forms of the lexical verb, serve to realize the grammatical features of the verbal group.

The operators are of two kinds: non-modal, and modal. The non-modal operators, which mark tense, aspect and other features, have non-finite as well as finite forms. They are:

(1) be: in forms be^f, i.e. is/am/are/was/were
            be^o, i.e. be
            be^{ŋ}, i.e. being
            be^n, i.e. been

(2) have: in forms have^f, i.e. have/has/had
               have^o, i.e. have
               have^{ŋ}, i.e. having (in non-finite verbal groups only)

(3) will/shall: in forms will^f, i.e. will/shall/would/should
                  will^{ŋ}, i.e. going to/about to

(4) get: in forms get^f, i.e. get/gets/got
             get^o, i.e. get
             get^{ŋ}, i.e. getting
             get^n, i.e. got

The modal operators, which have only 'f'-forms, are:
can/could/would/should/may/might
am/are/is/was/were+to   ought+to   used+to
need/dare

For the purpose of the present section *can* is used to represent the whole set. Note that, of the operators, *be have get need* and *dare* also occur as lexical verbs: thus for example *be* and *have* are operators in *he is taking/has taken a holiday* but lexical verbs in *he is a teacher, he has a daughter*.

We can now show how the morphology of the verbal group is built up. For the moment we shall consider only the finite indicative verbal group, since both the imperative and the non-finite, which have fewer possibilities of choice, can be related fairly simply to the finite indicative forms. Leaving aside the forms with *going to*, which will be introduced as a second step, we find the following combinations; the lexical verb *take* is used in the example:

	Formula: forms and items	forms only	Example
1	$take^f$	f	takes
2	$will^f + take^o$	f o	will take
3	$have^f + take^n$	f　n	has taken
4	$have^o + take^n$	f o n	will have taken
5	$be^f + take^{ŋ}$	f　ŋ	is taking
6	$will^f + be^o + take^{ŋ}$	f o　ŋ	will be taking
7	$have^f + be^n + take^{ŋ}$	f　n ŋ	has been taking
8	$will^f + have^o + be^n + take^{ŋ}$	f o n ŋ	will have been taking
9	$be/get^f + take^n$	f　n	is taken
10	$will^f + be/get^o + take^n$	f o　n	will be taken
11	$have^f + be/get^n + take^n$	f　n n	has been taken
12	$will^f + have^o + be/get^n + take^n$	f o n n	will have been taken
13	$be^f + be/get^{ŋ} + take^n$	f　ŋ n	is being taken
14	$will^f + be^o + be/get^{ŋ} + take^n$	f o　ŋ n	will be being taken
15	$have^f + be^n + be/get^{ŋ} + take^n$	f　n ŋ n	has been being taken
16	$will^f + have^o + be^n + be/get^{ŋ} + take^n$	f o n ŋ n	will have been being taken

Each formula represents a small set of possible forms of the verbal group, of which one example is given on the right; $take^f$, for example, stands for *take* (in *I take*), *takes* and *took*; $will^f + take^o$ for *will take, shall take, would take, should take; will* can also be replaced by *can* or any of the other modals. The full set (leaving out only the variants of *will*) are now tabulated in two ways, the first corresponding to the order as given here with columns representing the different *forms* (as in the formulae) the second ordered according to the number of words in the verbal group and with columns representing the different *items*:

TABLE 1

	f	o	(have +) n	ŋ	(be/get +) n
1	take(s); took				
2	will	take			
3	have/has; had		taken		
4	will	have	taken		
5	am/is/are; was/were			taking	
6	will	be		taking	
7	have/has; had		been	taking	
8	will	have	been	taking	
9	am/is/are; was/were; get(s); got				taken
10	will	be/get			taken
11	have/has; had		been/got		taken
12	will	have	been/got		taken
13	am/is/are; was/were			being/getting	taken
14	will	be		being/getting	taken
15	have/has; had		been	being/getting	taken
16	will	have	been	being/getting	taken

TABLE 2

	will	*have*	*be*(+ŋ)	*be/get*(+n)	*take*	
1					take(s); took	1 word
2	will				take	
3		have/has; had			taken	
5			am/is/are; was/were		taking	2 words
9				am/is/are; was/were; get(s); got	taken	
4	will	have			taken	
6	will		be		taking	
7		have/has; had	been		taking	
10	will			be/get	taken	3 words
11		have/has; had		been/got	taken	
13			am/is/are; was/were	being/getting	taken	
8	will	have	been		taking	
12	will	have		been/got	taken	
14	will		be	being/getting	taken	4 words
15		have/has; had	been	being/getting	taken	
16	will	have	been	being/getting	taken	5 words

So far we have recognized sixteen formulae, or what may be called sixteen 'morphological types'. The second step is to include *going to*, which adds a further 32 possibilities, since (i) *going to* can be inserted in all the above types, and (ii) wherever *going to* occurs it is possible to add another 'n'-form. Like *will*, *going to* always demands an immediately following 'o'-form, so that this is represented in the formulae as η–o showing the two always belong together: the same practice can be adopted for f–o where f = will. The additional types are built up as on p. 144.

The original list of 16, plus this further set of 32, gives a total of 48 possible formulae for the verbal group. Each formula represents one morphological type, to which corresponds a small set of actual forms varying according to person, number etc. as explained above. It may be helpful, as a reminder, to list the variants represented by each form of each item:

be^f	stands for	am/is/are/was/were
be/get^f	,,	am/is/are/was/were/get/gets/got
be^o	,,	be
be/get^o	,,	be/get
be^{η}	,,	being
be/get^{η}	,,	being/getting
be^n	,,	been
be/get^n	,,	been/got
$have^f$	,,	have/has/had
$have^o$	,,	have
$will^f$	,,	will/shall/would/should; or any modal
$will^{\eta}$	,,	going to/about to
$take^f$	,,	take/takes/took
$take^o$	,,	take
$take^{\eta}$	,,	taking
$take^n$	,,	taken

To complete this section we will tabulate all the types, following the pattern of Table 1 on page 142; that is, with columns corresponding to the verb *forms* as set out in the formulae. To simplify the table, only third person singular forms are given in the 'f' column; and *going to* is used throughout to represent both *going to* and *about to* (pp. 146–47).

At this point it may well be objected that many of the forms cited will never actually be found to occur; what then is the relevance of such an account? The question is an important one, and there are three parts to the answer.

First, it is true that some of the forms have probably never occurred in a written text. But we cannot be so sure about their non-occurrence in speech; spoken language, especially informal conversation, tolerates

	Formula: forms and items	forms only		Example
17	$be^f + will^ŋ + take^o$	f	ŋ-o	is going to take
18	$will^f + be^o + will^ŋ + take^o$	f-o	ŋ-o	will be going to take
19	$have^f + be^n + will^ŋ + take^o$	f	n ŋ-o	has been going to take
20	$will^f + have^o + be^n + will^ŋ + take^o$	f-o	n ŋ-o	will have been going to take
21	$be^f + will^ŋ + have^o + take^n$	f	ŋ-o n	is going to have taken
22	$will^f + be^o + will^ŋ + have^o + take^n$	f-o	ŋ-o n	will be going to have taken
23	$have^f + be^n + will^ŋ + have^o + take^n$	f	n ŋ-o n	has been going to have taken
24	$will^f + have^o + be^n + will^ŋ + have^o + take^n$	f-o	n ŋ-o n	will have been going to have taken
25	$be^f + will^ŋ + be^o + take^ŋ$	f	ŋ-o ŋ	is going to be taking
26	$will^f + be^o + will^ŋ + be^o + take^ŋ$	f-o	ŋ-o ŋ	will be going to be taking
27	$have^f + be^n + will^ŋ + be^o + take^ŋ$	f	n ŋ-o ŋ	has been going to be taking
—32				etc.
33	$be^f + will^ŋ + be/get^o + take^n$	f	ŋ-o n	is going to be taken
34	$will^f + be^o + will^ŋ + be/get^o + take^n$	f-o	ŋ-o n	will be going to be taken
35	$have^f + be^n + will^ŋ + be/get^o + take^n$	f	n ŋ-o n	has been going to be taken
—40				etc.
41	$be^f + will^ŋ + be^o + be/get^ŋ + take^n$	f	ŋ-o ŋ n	is going to be being taken
42	$will^f + be^o + will^ŋ + be^o + be/get^ŋ + take^n$	f-o	ŋ-o ŋ n	will be going to be being taken
43	$have^f + be^n + will^ŋ + be^o + be/get^ŋ + take^n$	f	n ŋ-o ŋ n	has been going to be being taken
—48				etc.

Each of the last three blocks can be filled out with eight types according to the regular pattern displayed in the formulae for the first block.

considerably greater complexity in certain respects, of which the type of complexity represented in these verb forms is one, than does written language. The following are recorded from conversation:

will have been going to be being tested
must have been going to have finished
is going to have been being discussed

while the slightly simpler ones occur fairly regularly, including those which the native speaker of English feels to be odd if his attention is drawn to them: mainly those involving the sequences *been being* and *will be going to*, as in *he'll be going to do it* and *it's been being discussed*. It is not unknown for a speaker to use without noticing it a form the existence of which he has vigorously denied not long before.

This is not to dispute that some of these forms are extremely rare, and this leads in to the second part of the answer. The forms are rare because the contexts in which they would be appropriate, the particular sets of linguistic and non-linguistic conditions which would call for them, are also extremely rare. A form like *will have been going to be being tested*, which would imply some such context as *at this time every day for a fortnight soon* (whether or not all these items actually figure in the same sentence), presupposes a very unusual set of circumstances and a particular direction in the preceding discussion, perhaps something like this:

'Can I use that machine when I come in at this time tomorrow?'
'No—it's going to be being tested.'
'It'll have been going to be being tested every day for a fortnight soon.'

These forms can occur if called for; the resources are there in the language at the native speaker's command. In coding such items (see pages 156–58), there is no need to treat very simple verbal groups such as *is* or *went* as if each time they occurred the speaker was selecting from this total range; indeed it would be misleading to do so, and this leads in turn to the third part of the answer.

All the highly complex verb forms are built up out of very simple resources; the complexity, which involves only the system of tense, results from the fact that selection for tense may be made more than once in one verbal group. The system, which is a recursive one, and the limitations on it, are given on pp. 153–55. When the speaker chooses a certain tense, he is not making a sudden selection all at once from this huge inventory; he is choosing from a very small set of possibilities, namely 'past', 'present' or 'future', and he will more often than not make this selection only once with each verbal group. But it is open to him to make a second choice from the same set: the verbal group may be both 'past' and 'present' at the same time; and then a third choice, and so on.

f / f-o	n / ŋ	tense	have / be	taken / been	going to	be / have	taken / been	taking
f		takes; took	take	takes				
f-o		will	have	taken				
f	n	has; had	be	been				taking
f-o	n	will	have	been				taking
f	ŋ	is; was	be	been				taking
f-o	ŋ	will	have	been				taking
f	n	has; had			going to	take	taken	
f-o	n	will			going to	have	taken	
f	ŋ	is; was			going to	be	been	taking
f-o	ŋ	will			going to	have	been	taking
f	n	has; had			going to	be	been	taking
f-o	n	will			going to	have	been	taking
f		is; was			going to	be		taking
f-o		will			going to	have		taking
f	n	has; had			going to	be		taking
f-o	n	will			going to	have		taking
f	ŋ	is; was			going to	be		taking
f-o	ŋ	will			going to	have		taking
f	n	has; had			going to	be		taking
f-o	n	will			going to	have		taking
f	ŋ	is; was			going to	be		taking
f-o	ŋ	will			going to	have		taking
f	n	has; had			going to			
f-o	n	will			going to			

f		n	is; was; gets							taken
f-o		n	will	be; get						taken
f	n	n	has; had	have						taken
f-o	n	n	will	have	been; got					taken
f		n	is; was	be						taken
f-o		n	will			going to	be; get			taken
f	n	n	has; had	have	been					taken
f-o	n	n	will	have		going to	be; get			taken
f	n	n	is; was	be		going to		been; got		taken
f-o	n	n	will			going to		been; got		taken
f	ŋ n	n	has; had	have		going to		been; got		taken
f-o	ŋ n	n	will			going to		been; got	being; getting	taken
f	ŋ n	n	is; was	be		going to	have		being; getting	taken
f-o	ŋ n	n	will			going to	have		being; getting	taken
f	ŋ n	n	has; had	have	been	going to	have		being; getting	taken
f-o	ŋ n	n	will		been	going to	have		being; getting	taken
f	ŋ n	n	is; was	be		going to	be	been	being; getting	taken
f-o	ŋ n	n	will			going to	be	been	being; getting	taken
f	ŋ n	n	has; had	have	been	going to	be		being; getting	taken
f-o	ŋ n	n	will		been	going to	be		being; getting	taken
f	ŋ n	n	is; was	be		going to	have	been	being; getting	taken
f-o	ŋ n	n	will			going to	have	been	being; getting	taken
f	ŋ n	n	has; had	have	been	going to	have	been	being; getting	taken
f-o	ŋ n	n	will		been	going to	have	been	being; getting	taken

This leads to a great increase in the morphological complexity of the verbal group; at the same time it accounts for its very great regularity. In analysing these forms therefore, and in suggesting coding for them, we need to reflect this patterning and to avoid suggesting that the choice of a simple 'present' form of a verbal group is like, say, choosing a number between one and fifty. It is more like choosing a number between one and three, and then going on to decide whether or not you are going to do so a second time. This is particularly important in any text analysis where an assessment of relative complexity is involved.

Before the presentation of the total framework suggested for the analysis of the verbal group it will be helpful to make some comments on the components as outlined in the preceding section. The following are some observations which may help to simplify the recognition of the tenses and other categories from the forms as they occur in texts.

The finite verbal group always begins with an 'f'-form; this is absent in the non-finite verbal group (*taking, having taken, (to) take, (to) be taking,* etc.). If no other element is present, this 'f'-form must be the 'f'-form of the lexical verb, e.g. *take, takes, took.* If other elements are present, the lexical verb is pushed over to the right so that it always occurs as final element, in whatever form is appropriate.

We have listed only the 'non-reduced' variants of the 'f'-forms; some of them have also 'reduced' variants represented in orthography as follows:

am = 'm	have = 've	will/shall = 'll
is = 's	has = 's	would/should = 'd
are = 're	had = 'd	

Since both *is* and *has* may be followed by 'n'-forms, ambiguity arises: *it's taken* may be equivalent to *it has taken* (e.g. in *it's taken a long time*) or *it is taken* (e.g. in *it's taken to mean that . . .*); *it's* alone is usually *it is* (*it's cold*), although it can stand for *it has* provided this is the verb *have = have got* (*it's no meaning, he's no sense*)—never with the verb *have = take* (*he has dinner out* cannot be reduced to *he's*). With *'d* the position is simpler. Since *had* can only be followed by the 'n'-form and *would/should* only by the 'zero'-form (*had taken* but *would take*), and moreover *would/should* can only be verbal operators, never lexical verbs, ambiguity only arises where the lexical verb is one of the 3-variant type, such as *put*, where the 'n'-form and the 'zero'-form are identical: *he'd put* may be equivalent either to *he had put* (put^n) or to *he would put* (put^o). There is no way, on the other hand, of deciding whether *'ll* stands for *will* or *shall*, or whether *'d* stands for *would* or *should*; the difference between them, if any, simply disappears in the reduced form.

If the 'f'-form is *will*, or a modal (it has been pointed out earlier that modals have only 'f'-forms), a 'zero'-form must follow immediately.

The resulting sequence f–o can in fact be thought of as a single complex element:

f–o   will/can take   contrasting with   f   take(s); took
,,   will/can have   ,,   f   have/has; had
,,   will/can be   ,,   f   am/is/are; was/were

The fact that *will have* behaves morphologically like a modal rather than like the tense forms *take/took* is suggestive, and is one of the reasons for the existence of two different traditions in the analysis of English tenses. The earlier tradition, based on classical grammars, considers that English has a three-term tense system:

past   took
present   take(s)
future   will take

A more recent tradition, recognizing that the fact that Latin and Greek had a future tense is irrelevant to English, and that morphologically *will take* is more like *can take* than like *take(s)* and *took*, asserts that English has only a two-term tense system:

past   took
present   take(s)

and that *will take* is not a tense form at all but a modal form.

As often in linguistic description there is much to be said on both sides. Semantically *will* has some modal flavour, as in *Will you open the door?*; on the other hand it functions in many respects like a tense form, and the view adopted here is that the earlier tradition was basically sound. The fact that the mechanism for producing a future tense is different from that used in producing present and past is really irrelevant—all languages show such morphological irregularities; while once one recognizes that *going to* is merely the 'ing'-form of *will* the way in which future interacts with past and present in the compound verbal forms is very suggestive. For various reasons the analysis adopted is that into three tenses, so that the first tense selection in the verbal group is made by the initial 'f'-form, in combination with a following 'zero'-form if the tense if future.

All the remaining elements so far introduced in the verbal group except the final 'n'-form make optional further selections in the tense system. Thus in any given instance it may be that, in the selection of tense, only one choice is made:

f   took   past
f   take(s)   present
(f–o)   will take   future

Alternatively, this may be followed by a second choice:

f	n	had taken	past in past
f	n	has taken	past in present
(f–o)	n	will have taken	past in future
f	ŋ	was taking	present in past
f	ŋ	is taking	present in present
(f–o)	ŋ	will be taking	present in future
f	(ŋ–o)	was going to take	future in past
f	(ŋ–o)	is going to take	future in present
(f–o)	(ŋ–o)	will be going to take	future in future

and a third:

f	n (ŋ–o)	had been going to take	future in past in past
f	n (ŋ–o)	has been going to take	future in past in present
(f–o)	n (ŋ–o)	will have been going to take	future in past in future

and so on, up to five:

f	n (ŋ–o) n ŋ	had been going to have been taking	present in past in future in past in past
f	n (ŋ–o) n ŋ	has been going to have been taking	present in past in future in past in present
(f–o)	n (ŋ–o) n ŋ	will have been going to have been taking	present in past in future in past in future

Basically, every time an additional tense selection is made a further reference point is added in time. The full list of tense forms is given on pp. 153–54.

The final element in the verbal group—that is, the one which, if present at all, must be in final position—is an 'n'-form which is distinct from any preceding 'n'-forms in that it is preceded not by *have* but by *be* or, as an alternative, *get: it was taken, it got taken*. This element is concerned not with tense but with voice. Any verbal group having its final element in this 'n'-form (i.e. preceded by *be* or *get*) is passive; any one without it is active.

It will have been noticed that in order to distinguish the various constructions we have had to range the symbols in columns, eight in all, so that e.g. f   ŋ *is taking* had f in column 1 and ŋ in column 7. In fact however the only ambiguity that arises if we eliminate the columns, writing in this case simply f ŋ, is caused by the 'n'-forms: f n might be (columns 1 and 3) *has taken* or (columns 1 and 8) *is taken*. If therefore we write the passive (final) n, that which must be preceded by *be/get*, with some distinguishing symbols e.g. n*, then any formula is unique without being spaced out into columns. Although there can be two preceding 'n'-forms, these need not be distinguished from each other, since in the *going to* forms one always precedes and the other always follows *going to*, while in the other forms there can only be one such n and it does not matter which column it goes in (it was assigned above to column 3 rather than to column 6 simply because column 3 is the earlier).

The last point to be considered in this section is the need to distinguish between complete (i.e. non-elliptical) and elliptical forms of the verbal group. All these forms cited so far have been non-elliptical forms. Elliptical forms are those which presuppose some components from a previous verbal group, as in:

> after we've brought them out so far, and *made* them trot so quick
> do you think it's going to rain? No, I don't think it *is*

where *made* in the second clause is an elliptical form presupposing *have* in (*ha*)*ve brought* in the first; and the *is* in the answer is an elliptical form presupposing *going to rain* in the question. Elliptical forms appear in two types, the preceding examples showing one of each. They may be illustrated as follows

(1) they had been playing on the beach, and
   had been sunbathing $have^t$ be^n $(lexical)^ŋ$
   they had been playing on the beach, and
   been sunbathing be^n $(lexical)^ŋ$
   they had been playing on the beach, and
   sunbathing $(lexical)^ŋ$
(2) I thought they had been sunbathing, and
   they had been sunbathing $have^t$ be^n $(lexical)^ŋ$
   I thought they had been sunbathing, and
   they had been $have^t$ be^n
   I thought they had been sunbathing, and
   they had $have^t$

In the first type, ellipsis begins from the front, so that in the shortest form only the lexical verb is retained; in the second type it begins from the back, so that in the shortest form only the 'f'-form is retained. The first type is more restricted, since it generally requires a relation of co-ordination between the clauses concerned, although it can occur in question-answer sequences: *Have they been swimming? No, sunbathing.* The second is likewise frequent in co-ordination and in question and answer; it also occurs in dependent clauses (with *before, than, when, if* etc.: *they had been sunbathing before we had*), and where there is no specific relation between the clauses concerned other than that implied by the ellipsis itself: *I thought they had been sunbathing. If they had been,* . . .

It is thus not difficult to recognize elliptical forms; the actual difficulty arises only in two instances, both involving type (2) above. The first is that involving *be* or *have*. A verbal group ending in any form of *be* or *have* is ambiguous (in the theoretical sense of 'ambiguous': it is a realization of two (or more) different sets of grammatical features—there may be only one possible interpretation in the context):

has he a home? yes, he *has* (lexical^f) [where lexical verb is *have*; non-elliptical]

has he come yet? yes, he *has* (*have*^{f}) [where *have* is verbal operator; elliptical (presupposing *come*^{n})]

A similar problem arises with *do,* which can also be either lexical verb or verbal operator.

The second difficulty is caused by the fact that where more than one element may be presupposed, it is not always easy to decide which in fact are. In

has he been working? yes he *has*

it can be assumed that *has* represents *has been working*. If there is no tense contrast, it can be assumed that anything that is not explicit is in fact presupposed. If however there is a contrast of tense, as in

has he been working? no, but he *will*

the presupposition is less clear; theoretically at least this might represent he *will work, he will be working* or *he will have been working*. The safest principle is to assume maximum possible identity with the presupposed item, as much of it being presupposed as can be taken over with the minimum of changes, so that this would probably be interpreted as *he will be working*. In fact the context often makes it clear; where it does not the speaker tends to use a fuller form:

has he been working? no but he *will be*

In representing elliptical forms for purposes of text analysis, it is important to show two things about them: one, their relation to the non-elliptical forms they presuppose, and which determines their meaning; the other, the fact that they are elliptical (since it is always possible to select a non-elliptical form instead). This is done by showing that an elliptical form has the FEATURES of the form it presupposes: thus in

I thought they had been sunbathing, and they *had/had been/had been sunbathing*

had, had been and *had been sunbathing* all have the same analysis in terms of features. In terms of structure, however, they differ: *have,* *have*^{t} *be*^{n}, *have*^{t} *be*^{n} (*lexical*)$^\eta$, or simply f, f n, f n ŋ.

Tense (Finite Indicative Verbal Group)

ε	δ	γ	β	α		Tense no.	Block no.
				past	1	
				present	2	I
				future	3	
			past in	past	4	
				present	5	II
				future	6	
			present in	past	7	
				present	8	III
				future	9	
			future in	past	10	
				present	11	IV
				future	12	
		past in	future in	past	13	
				present	14	V
				future	15	
		present in	past in	past	16	
				present	17	VI
				future	18	
		present in	future in	past	19	
				present	20	VII
				future	21	
		future in	past in	past	22	
				present	23	VIII
				future	24	
	past in	future in	past in	past	25	
				present	26	IX
				future	27	
	present in	past in	future in	past	28	
				present	29	X
				future	30	
	present in	future in	past in	past	31	
				present	32	XI
				future	33	
present in	past in	future in	past in	past	34	
				present	35	XII
				future	36	

Tense: Active

1	took / did take	f
2	takes / does take	f
3	will take	(f–o)
4	had taken	f n
5	has taken	f n
6	will have taken	(f–o) n
7	was taking	f ŋ
8	is taking	f ŋ
9	will be taking	(f–o) ŋ
10	was going to take	f(ŋ–o)
11	is going to take	f(ŋ–o)
12	will be going to take	(f–o) (ŋ–o)
13	was going to have taken	f(ŋ–o)n
14	is going to have taken	f(ŋ–o)n
15	will be going to have taken	(f–o)(ŋ–o)n
16	had been taking	f n ŋ
17	has been taking	f n ŋ
18	will have been taking	(f–o) n ŋ
19	was going to be taking	f (ŋ–o) ŋ
20	is going to be taking	f (ŋ–o) ŋ
21	will be going to be taking	(f–o)(ŋ–o) ŋ
22	had been going to take	f n (ŋ–o)
23	has been going to take	f n (ŋ–o)
24	will have been going to take	(f–o) n (ŋ–o)
25	had been going to have taken	f n (ŋ–o) n
26	has been going to have taken	f n (ŋ–o) n
27	will have been going to have taken	(f–o) n (ŋ–o) n
28	was going to have been taking	f (ŋ–o) n ŋ
29	is going to have been taking	f (ŋ–o) n ŋ
30	will be going to have been taking	(f–o)(ŋ–o) n ŋ
31	had been going to be taking	f n (ŋ–o)ŋ
32	has been going to be taking	f n (ŋ–o)ŋ
33	will have been going to be taking	(f–o) n (ŋ–o)ŋ
34	had been going to have been taking	f n (ŋ–o) n ŋ
35	has been going to have been taking	f n (ŋ–o) n ŋ
36	will have been going to have been taking	(f–o) n (ŋ–o) n ŋ

The above table gives the complete list of finite indicative tense forms in active voice, beginning with the 'simple' tenses, those where only one tense selection is made, and continuing through the 'compound' tenses, those with two, three, four or five selections. For the sake of clarity, 3rd person singular forms are used throughout column α: thus *is* stands for *am/is/are*, *was* for *was/were* etc.; and *going to* is used to represent *going to* or *about to*.

It will be seen that, although the system is a recursive one, in that one choice can always be followed by another, and then another, and so on, there are in fact limits to the number of possible tenses. These do not arise because of any arbitrary limit or the *number* of choices but because the system has certain combinatory restrictions, which operate as 'stop rules' and in effect preclude all but the combinations listed above. It may be helpful just to state them here:

1) 'present' can occur only at the outer ends of the series (as first and/or final choice)
2) except at α and β, the same tense cannot be selected twice consecutively
3) 'future' can occur only once other than at α.

Explanation is needed of the names and the column headings: it will be more helpful first, however, to present a small number of simple rules which permit the identification of the tense and voice of any finite indicative verbal group occurring in a text:

$$x^d = \text{past}$$
$$x^s = \text{present}$$
$$\text{will} + x^o = \text{future}$$
$$\text{have} + x^n = \text{past in}$$
$$\text{be} + x^\eta = \text{present in}$$
$$\text{be-going/about-to} + x^o = \text{future in}$$
$$\text{be/get} + x^n = \text{passive}$$

Look at the first word in the verbal group. If x^d, assign feature 'past'; if x^s, assign 'present'; if *will*, do nothing. Then look at each succeeding pair of words, beginning with the first word and overlapping the pairs: first and second word, then second and third word, then third and fourth and so on. Treat *be-going-to* and *be-about-to* as a single word, its form being determined by the form of the *be*. Look at the *item* in the first word of the pair and the *form* of the second, and assign features as above. If final pair is *not* be/get—x^n, assign 'active'. For example:

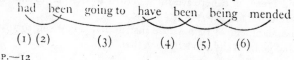

(1) first word: x^d 'past'
(2) first pair: have+x^n 'past in'
(3) second pair: be going to+x^o 'future in'
(4) third pair: have+x^n 'past in'
(5) fourth pair: be+$x^ŋ$ 'present in'
(6) fifth pair: be/get+x^n 'passive'

Then read upwards: 'passive; present in past in future in past in past'.
Similarly:

is doing

(1) first word: x^s 'present'
(2) first pair: be+$x^ŋ$ 'present in'
(3) final pair is *not* be/get+x^n 'active'; so 'active; present in present'

will come

(1) first word: will   (—)
(2) first pair: will+x^o 'future'
(3) first pair is *not* be/get+x^n: 'active'; so 'active; future'.

was going to be asked

(1) first word: x^d 'past'
(2) first pair: be-going-to+x^o 'future in'
(3) second pair: be/get+x^n 'passive'; so 'passive; future in past'.

It is not suggested that anyone analysing a text would look up these rules every time he came to a verbal group; in all but the more complex cases it is easier to remember the items and their labels as wholes. But even here it may serve as a means of checking, and it is a useful procedure for the more complicated tenses. At the same time it illustrates the principle of explicitness in linguistic description; the verbal group is favourable material in the sense that it is more clearly defined and more regularly structured than most areas of English grammar, so that it can be used to exemplify methods of analysis and coding.

The labels assigned in this way represent part of the 'feature description' of the verbal group, and could be written out as in the first section:

    was going to be asked (passive / future in past)

Symbols may be used to represent the tenses; the following have been found convenient and easy to remember: —for past, ϕ for present, +for future. (ϕ is the sign used in linguistics for zero.) The question arises, however, in what order they should be used in representing a compound tense; and here we must return to the names and column headings referred to earlier.

In the assignment of names, the instruction was given to read 'upwards': that is, from right to left, such that

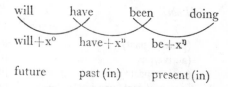

future   past (in)   present (in)

is named 'present in past in future'. The Greek letters used in the column headings, however, go from left to right, so that here 'future' is α, 'past in' β and 'present in' γ. α represents the 'first' choice, both in the sense that it is the one that is realised first in the sequence and in the sense that it is the primary time reference, that which relates directly to the moment of speaking. The tense could be represented as 'α future, β past, γ present', or simply $+-\phi$.

The reason why the names go backwards is just that they make more sense like that and are thus easier to remember: *was going to* is more meaningfully labelled 'future in (the) past' than simply 'past future', and there is a long tradition of naming in this way. In using symbols, however, it is more satisfactory to start from the left, beginning with the α tense. The possible representations would thus be:

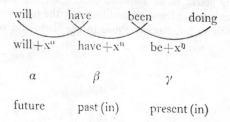

α β γ

future   past (in)   present (in)

coded as (future: past: present), or $(\alpha+:\beta-:\gamma\phi)$, or simply $(+-\phi)$; but read aloud as 'present in past in future'.

Here is a short extract, slightly abridged, from a recorded conversation among a group of children and one adult (the speaker is a nine-year-old girl), with the verbal groups, other than the non-finites which we have not yet dealt with, marked for tense and voice:

And they *got mixed up* . . . because—em—they *thought* that a—a boys' school *was coming* to board with them just while this other school *was being repaired*, but it *was* a girls' school, and they *had* to take these goal—these rugby posts out because—because—er—the people *were coming* in to in—er . . . inspect it: and parents *had come* to inspect the other school that the girls *were* at, and they *had to* try and take the rugby posts up while the boys—em . . . while all the people—men—em—*were touring* the school . . . It *got* so far and they *were just about to leave* and then . . .

Item	Label	Tense symbol	Read as
got mixed up	(passive/past)	—	past
thought	(active/past)	—	past
was coming	(active/ past : present)	—φ	present in past
was being repaired	(passive/ past : present)	—φ	present in past
was	(active/past)	—	past
had	(active/past)	—	past
were coming	(active/ past : present)	—φ	present in past
had come	(active/ past : past)	— —	past in past
were	(active/past)	—	past
had	(active/past)	—	past
were touring	(active/ past : present)	—φ	present in past
got	(active/past)	—	past
were about to leave	(active/ past : future)	—+	future in past

The precise method of coding will necessarily vary according to the purpose in view, the type and extent of the material, and so on. One can conflate the two columns, representing e.g. *were about to leave* as (active / —+); introduce symbols for 'active' and 'passive', or show only passive, leaving active to be assumed otherwise; and other such variations. The aim is to represent unambiguously the features of the verbal group dealt with so far, namely those in the tense and voice systems.

11 Types of process

Transitivity

Transitivity is the representation in language of PROCESSES, the PARTICI-PANTS therein, and the CIRCUMSTANTIAL features associated with them. This is an extension of a narrower meaning whereby the form refers simply to the types of process, as in 'transitive and intransitive verbs'; we shall use it in the wider sense, so that transitivity here refers to the 'content', or factual-notional structure of the clause in its entirety. In other words, all those features of the clause which contribute to the linguistic representation of the speaker's experience come under this heading; the term is thus parallel to 'mood' and 'theme'. Mood, theme and transitivity refer to the organization of the clause in, respectively, its interpersonal, its textual and its experiential function.

The term 'process' is understood in a very broad sense, to cover all phenomena to which a specification of time may be attached—in English, anything that can be expressed by a verb: event, whether physical or not, state, or relation. So *he's throwing stones, it's raining, don't sulk!, the blade's gone rusty, can you see a light?, justice had been done, Jupiter is the largest of the planets* all include the expression of processes. Processes may be of different types and involve different numbers and kinds of participants: for example *you are required by the regulations to pay the full fee to the examining board* involves four participants, while in *it's raining* there is no participant at all.

In English there are two basic distinctions: in the type of process that is being represented, and in the number of participants that are inherently associated with it. It is necessary to say 'inherently associated' because in most types of process it is possible to bring in participants other than those that are essential to the process; and conversely one or other of those that are essential to it may not actually be expressed in the structure: e.g. the process expressed by the verb *pelt* is a three participant one, as in *he pelted the dog with stones*, and this is true even

---

This previously unpublished paper was written as a Nuffield Programme Work Paper, 1969, under the same title.

if one of them is left out (*he pelted the dog;* even two might be left out, e.g. *the dog got pelted*), whereas *throw* is a two-participant process, e.g. *he threw stones,* even if an additional participant is expressed as in *he threw stones at the dog.* One verb may itself belong to more than one type: *the rain pelted down* illustrates another use of *pelt,* expressing a one-participant process.

This brings out two points concerning the notion of a participant. The first is that the term itself is a little misleading as it suggests human beings, whereas in fact a participant is not necessarily human or even animate: the term PARTICIPATING ENTITY would be more accurate, but we shall use 'participant' as being less clumsy. Secondly, although in general a participant is expressed by a noun in direct relation to the verb (that is, by a noun as head of a nominal group functioning as subject or complement), it may be introduced indirectly by a preposition, like *with stones* and *at the dog* above. This distinction, between DIRECT and INDIRECT participants, is a structural one, but it is not irrelevant to the meaning: a direct participant can function as subject, whereas an indirect one cannot. The indirect participants are as it were dressed up to look like circumstantial elements; but note that in *he was throwing stones at the bridge, the bridge* is a participant, whereas in *he was throwing stones on the bridge,* it is part of the circumstance *on the bridge.* A good test for this is provided by the interrogative: participants are questioned by *what* or *who* (or a nominal group with WH-determiner, e.g. *which line, whose hat*), as in *what was he throwing stones at?,* whereas circumstances are questioned by *when, where, how* or *why,* e.g. *where was he throwing stones?*

The notion of participant is itself based on the more fundamental concept of syntactic function or role. The element that enters into the transitivity structure is actually a particular 'role' identified in relation to the process, for example the role of 'actor' or 'beneficiary'. The distinction is important because it is possible to combine two or more roles in a single participant. If we consider the example *they elected John their spokesman, John* is at one and the same time the 'identified' element (person identified by the function of spokesman, cf. *John was the spokesman*) and the 'goal' (person affected by the process of electing, cf. *they elected John*). The combination of syntactic roles in one element of structure is analogous to the combination of social roles in one individual; it is fundamental to the organization of language, since it is this that enables the various components of language function to combine in the formation of integrated structures.[1]

---

1. That is, roles may be combined both between and within components. In the example cited, the roles of *John* as 'identified' and as 'goal' are both functions in transitivity. If we replace this by *John was elected spokesman, John* still has both these roles, but in addition it is now 'subject', which is a function in mood, and 'theme', which is a textual function.

Action clauses

Modern English recognizes three main types of process: ACTION, MENTAL PROCESS, and RELATION, exemplified respectively by *he is throwing stones, can you see a light?* and *Jupiter is the largest of the planets.* Like most linguistic categories, these are distinct enough at the centre but shade into one another at the edges. They do however show certain fairly clear distinguishing features.

Processes of the 'action' type involve, as inherent participant (except in one sub-type: see below), an ACTOR. The actor may be (i) subject, (ii) adjunct with *by*, or (iii) not expressed at all.

If the clause is OPERATIVE or MIDDLE, the verb will be active and there will be an actor as subject. If the clause is RECEPTIVE, then either the verb will be active and there will be no actor or the verb will be passive, in which case either there will be an actor introduced by *by*, or there will be no actor. Examples:

operative	he is tying the string	actor (= subject) *he*	active verb
middle	he is waiting	actor (= subject) *he*	
receptive	this string won't tie	no actor	
	this string has been tied very tight	no actor	
	this string must have been tied by an expert	actor (= adjunct) *an expert*	passive verb

An actor expressed in the form of an adjunct with *by* (or other preposition) in a receptive clause is usually known as an AGENT.

As these examples show, action clauses come in three forms known as VOICES: we are calling these operative, middle and receptive. (Operative and receptive could be known instead by their more familiar names 'active' and 'passive'. However, the division does not correspond to that between active and passive in the verb: receptive clauses may have active verbs, and in addition there is a 'middle' type of clause which has no corresponding special form of the verb. This seems to be a place where it is simpler to introduce new terms.) The difference relates to the participants involved.

A middle clause is one in which the action involves only one participating entity, which is thus always an actor: *John is waiting, the sun is shining, his popularity declined, behave yourself!*

In non-middle clauses, on the other hand, the action involves two participating entities, even though one or other of these may not be present in the structure: it involves an actor and a GOAL, respectively *John* and *the string* in *John is tying the string*. Within the non-middle, the distinction between operative and receptive relates to the function of subject: in the operative the subject is the actor while in the receptive the subject is the goal. The other participant, the one which is not the subject, may be absent in each case: *you wrap and I'll tie* shows a 'goalless' form of the operative, while *this string won't tie* and *this string has been tied very tight* show an 'actor-less' (agentless) form of the receptive.

The choice between operative and receptive—that is, the factors affecting the speaker's decision whether to say *Wren built this gazebo* or *this gazebo was built by Wren*—is not, however, a matter of transitivity but of theme: the difference in meaning between the two is a textual one (and is discussed in chapter 12, pp. 180–2).

The distinction between middle and non-middle does however represent a difference of meaning in transitivity; and it enables us to classify the principal types of action embodied in the semantic structure of the present day English language.

It is clear that this has to do with the distinction into transitive and intransitive verbs: as a first approximation one might suggest that a middle clause is simply one with an intransitive verb, such as *wait* or *shine*, and a non-middle clause is one with a transitive verb. This would be a reasonable account of the state of affairs in an earlier stage of the language, where verbs could be classified as transitive and intransitive and this would correspond to the presence or absence of a goal in the clause. But modern English has changed rather markedly in this respect.

It is no longer very useful to classify verbs simply into transitive and intransitive, because a large number of them, including probably a majority of the more common verbs, can be either.[1] This does not mean, however, that all verbs are alike in their transitivity potential. Verbs do show different tendencies as regards the number of participants with which they are most naturally associated—generally, either actor and goal, or actor only.

It means, rather, that transitivity is to be treated as a feature of the clause, not of the verb; the distinction between middle and non-middle voice in the clause can then be used as the basis for verb classification. With verbs of action, a three-way classification suggests itself. First, there are those verbs, forming a large proportion of the more frequent verbs in the language, which are equally at home with either one or two participants. Examples are *move, turn, open, change, spread, shake, pour, roll, bend, break, smash, mend, cook, boil, stew, burn, melt, dry, loosen, soften, quicken, plug in, fit in, mix, combine, evolve, drive, row, sail, drill, slide.* With such verbs it is not really possible to decide which is the more 'basic' form, that with one participant, like *the water poured out,*

---

1. Of a random sample of 100 verbs taken from *Chambers' Twentieth Century Dictionary* (1959 revised edition), 40 were marked both 'verb intransitive' and 'verb transitive'; of the remaining 60, 27 were obsolete or rare words and about a further 10 could have been marked as transitive or intransitive (e.g. *drill* and *erode* are given only as transitive).

or that with two, like *he poured the water out;* compare *it's moved/he's moved it, they're training/he's training them.* (As illustration of the two-participant use we could also cite the verb in the passive, *the water was poured out, they're being trained* etc., since this implies an actor-goal pattern even when no actor is expressed—these have been called 'agent-less agentive' clauses.) It is immaterial whether or not an external agency is required in the real world: from the point of view of the English language *the water poured out* does not imply the meaning 'someone or something poured it', even though one may reason that it implies this state of affairs.[1]

These verbs, then, fit equally naturally into both middle and non-middle clauses, being associated indifferently either with actor alone or with actor and goal. Let us refer to these as 'neutral' verbs. Two things are noticeable about them. One is that, even when we recognize this new category, it is still not always possible to classify each verb as inherently belonging to one or other transitivity class; we often need to specify the verb together with a noun (or class of nouns). For example, in combination with *door, open* is a neutral verb: we can say either *he opened the door* or *the door opened;* and likewise with *eyes,* and with *meeting* and *school* (and other nouns of the 'institution' class). But we cannot say *a tin of beans opened,* corresponding to *he opened a tin of beans;* or *an account opened at the bank.* It may be only certain types of noun that can occur indifferently as either actor or goal of one of these neutral verbs.

Secondly, looking at these verbs from this standpoint brings out the fact that there are pairs of verbs which are related to each other as *open* in *the door opened* is to *open* in *he opened the door.* Consider first *stand,* which resembles *open: the chair stood by the wall, he stood the chair by the wall.* Let us call the first of these uses, that with one participant, $stand_1$, and the latter, with two participants, $stand_2$. In older English, *set/sit* and *lay/lie* were related to each other in the same way as $stand_2$/$stand_1$. With these particular words the relationship has almost been lost; but there are a number of other pairs which exhibit the same relationship, e.g. *send/go, kill/die, teach/learn, cure/recover.* It is customary to speak of the first member of such pairs as 'causative', and this under-lines the similarity between the notions of 'causative' and 'transitive' (see pages 168–73 below).

Contrasting with verbs of the neutral type (with which we should now perhaps include those grouped into correlative pairs like *send/go*) are those that reflect a more clear-cut treatment of an action as in-

---

1. This point may perhaps be clarified by an analogy from the vocabulary. In the 'real world'—that is, in a biological as distinct from a non-technical classification—spiders are not insects. Nevertheless for most speakers the sentence *I don't like insects* includes spiders in its meaning; and we should be surprised to hear a formulation like *I don't like insects and spiders.*

herently, or preponderantly, of a two-participant type ('transitive', e.g. *throw*) or of a one-participant type ('intransitive', e.g. *swim*). It is still not unusual for such verbs to appear in clauses of the opposite type: *shine* is intransitive but we talk of *shining the silver*, whereas *polish* is transitive but we can say *the silver polishes beautifully*. But these represent more restricted uses, as can be seen in various ways: for example if an intransitive verb is used in an operative clause there must be a goal actually expressed, whereas a transitive verb may occur in a generalized sense without a goal: *what are they doing? they're polishing* (sc. 'things'), but not *what are they doing? they're shining—they're shining* could never mean 'they're shining something'.

There is a small class of action clauses with no participants at all: meteorological clauses such as *it's raining*. In a transitive/intransitive classification, they are intransitive since they have no goal, and when a nominal is associated with them, as in *it's snowing feathers*, it does have participant function (distinguish *they rained down arrows/arrows rained down*, where *rain down* is a neutral verb and *arrows* is goal or actor). These meteorological clauses are a sub-class of the class of 'natural phenomena', most of which are however expressed nominally, e.g. *there was an earthquake, a gale was blowing* (note here that *gale*, not *blowing*, carries the tonic accent).

A broad classification of action-type clauses is given in Table 3 on page 172. In order to give a clearer idea of how the verbs of English are distributed among the various types that can be recognized, cross-reference is made to the relevant sections of *Roget's Thesaurus*.

Mental process clauses

Mental process clauses are characterized by their being associated (i) with different participant functions and (ii) with different circumstantial elements from action clauses. Here we shall be concerned with (i).

If we consider a pair of clauses like *his attitude pleased me* and *I was pleased by his attitude*, these form an operative/receptive pair like a corresponding pair of action clauses *Wren built his gazebo, this gazebo was built by Wren*. But there are other related forms not paralleled in action clauses: *he pleased me by his attitude* and *I liked his attitude;* and corresponding to the second a passive *his attitude was liked* (*by everyone*). This last type is very much the least frequent of those mentioned (with *by me* it would be even less frequent, but that is because personal pronouns are always rare as agents).

All these clause types involve (at least) two participants: a human, or at any rate animate, being whose consciousness—feeling, perception etc.—is involved, and a phenomenon—object quality, event etc.—which impinges on it. Let us call the first of these the PROCESSER and the second the PHENOMENON. Mental process clauses involve, normally, a processer and a phenomenon, the processer being animate (or inanimate object being treated as animate, like a computer).

The processer may be subject, as in *I liked/was pleased by* ..., or complement as in ... *pleased me;* it can also, rarely, figure as complement of the preposition *by*, as in *was liked by me*. The phenomenon may also appear in all these three functions. Notice however that processer and phenomenon do not consistently correspond to any roles in action clauses: with *please* the phenomenon seems to resemble the actor and the processer the goal, while with *like* it is the other way round. And the form *he pleased me by his attitude* is different again. (Note that these last occur only if the phenomenon is a process or quality noun: we can have *he frightened me by his threats*, corresponding to *his threats frightened me*, but not *he frightened me by his dog*.)

It is thus not very helpful to describe mental process clauses in terms of actor and goal: any generalization that we make to cover the transitivity functions in both action and mental process clauses has to be at a more abstract level. For mental process clauses by themselves it is more helpful to recognize as separate functions the processer and the phenomenon. These clauses fall into two classes: those having the phenomenon as subject in active voice, e.g. with the verbs *please, convince, frighten*, and those having the processer as subject in active voice, e.g. with the verbs *like, believe, fear*. With the former type the passive is frequent (much more frequent than the passive in action clauses), with the latter it is rare (much less frequent than in action clauses); this is to be expected in view of the regular function of the passive, that of satisfying the strong thematic preference for personal pronouns as subject in English—passive with *please* will give the processer as subject, which is often a personal pronoun, while passive with *like* gives phenomenon as subject.

Mental process clauses are of four main types: perception (e.g. verbs *see, look*), reaction (e.g. *please, like, smile*), cognition (e.g. *convince, believe, wonder*), and verbalization (e.g. *say, speak*). The last is in fact rather different from the other three (see below).

It is mainly in reaction and cognition that both types of verb appear, those such as *please* as well as those such as *like*, although in perception there are some locutions that have the phenomenon as subject, e.g. *a strange sight assailed him/his eyes* (cf. *a thought struck him*). It is reasonable to think of these as the 'transitive' type of mental process clause, the others being 'intransitive' even though they have a complement: thus in *I like his attitude*, *his attitude* is not in any real sense a goal. There are also clauses without phenomena, often having verbs which are similar in meaning to those of the *like* type. The pattern could be exemplified as follows (there is no suggestion that the verbs are exactly matched: e.g. *enjoy* would correspond to *please* just as well as *like* does):

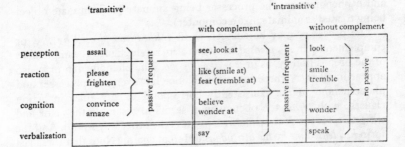

	'transitive'		with complement		'intransitive' without complement	
perception	assail	passive frequent	see, look at	passive infrequent	look	no passive
reaction	please frighten		like (smile at) fear (tremble at)		smile tremble	
cognition	convince amaze		believe wonder at		wonder	
verbalization			say		speak	

The most distinctive and important feature of mental process clauses is that the phenomenon, that which is 'processed' (perceived, reacted to etc.), is not limited to the kinds of 'things' which function as actor or goal in action clauses—persons, objects and the other phenomena on the plane of experience. That which is perceived or felt or thought may also be what we might call a 'metaphenomenon'. To put it another way, in mental process clauses words as well as things may play a part in the process.

In action clauses, the participants are all things in this broad sense: persons, objects, abstractions, events, qualities, states or relations—elements of what is sometimes called the 'ideational content of language'. In mental process clauses, on the other hand, the participants may be things but may also be words: that is, facts and reports—elements that have been as it were 'processed' by language. This distinction is a fundamental one, probably in every language; here we will merely illustrate it briefly.

With the verb *see*, we may have clauses such as *I saw John* (person), *I saw the tower* (object), *I saw the point* (abstraction), *I saw the game* (event); also *I saw Leeds play(ing) Chelsea* (event), *I saw what* (= the thing that) *you gave John* (object). All these are things, phenomena of experience. But in clauses such as *I see that he's honest, but I don't see that he's right*, *that he's honest* and *that he's right* are not things but facts—we could actually insert *the fact* before *that* without changing the meaning. In *I see that Leeds are playing Chelsea*, *that Leeds are playing Chelsea* is likewise not a thing but a report. And in its other meaning, the clause *I saw what you gave John* has the sense of 'I know the answer to the question "what did you give John?" ' where, again, what 'I saw' is a fact, not a thing.

The fact that *see* has different meanings in some of these examples does not affect the point: indeed it rather underlines it, since 'seeing' a fact or a report is different from 'seeing' a thing. In what is known as 'indirect speech', pieces of discourse—words as words, instead of as names—are entering as participants in the process. What is perceived or reacted to or 'cognited' may in fact be language; and it may be perceived, etc., at the semantic level (fact) or at the formal level (report). This distinguishes mental process clauses from clauses of action in which only things, not words, can play a part.

What is called 'reported speech' is, in fact, 'report' in the clauses of verbalization. Verbalization clauses differ from the others in that they accept only reports, not facts, as 'processed' phenomena: naturally, since they are 'reporting' clauses. They accept 'things' only in the restricted sense of the names of (classes of) metaphenomena, e.g. *he spoke only two words, don't talk nonsense!*—compare similar items in other clauses of mental process, e.g. *he didn't believe the rumour, I appreciate the fact.*

Relational clauses

Relational clauses are clauses in which the 'process' takes the form of a relation between two participating entities, or between one participating entity and an attribute. Both these two types may have the verb *be*, which tends to obscure the difference between them; they are perhaps less closely alike than they look.

In the latter type, those with an ATTRIBUTE, e.g. *Mary is a teacher, Mary looks happy*, the only role of *Mary* is as the carrier of the attribute *a teacher* or *happy:* we might call this the role of ATTRIBUEND. Attribution is a relation of class inclusion: the meaning is 'Mary belongs to the class of teachers'. It is thus a relation between entities of the same order of abstraction but differing in generality; either both are realized as nouns, or the attribute is an adjective—which is still however a type of nominal, meaning 'a happy one', thus 'Mary belongs to the class of happy ones'. This shows that the attribute is not as sharply distinct from the notion of a 'participant' as it might seem at first sight.

The other type is exemplified by *John is the leader* or *the leader is John*, where there are two clearly nominal elements and the order of the two is reversible. Here the clause is equative, not attributive: the relation between the elements is one of identity, not inclusion. It is the relation of IDENTIFIED (strictly this should be 'element to be identified') and IDENTIFIER (or 'identity'), where the two are alike in generality but of a different order of abstraction: the former is a participant requiring identification, the focus of an implied question 'which is . . .?', while the latter is an entity by reference to which the identification is made. The identifier may be of a higher order of abstraction than the element to be identified, e.g. (*which is John?*) *John is the treasurer*, where *the treasurer* expressed John's function; or of a lower order of abstraction, e.g. (*which is John?*) *John is the tall one*, where *the tall one* expresses John's form, stating how he is to be recognized.

Identification and attribution are logical relations of a similar but distinct kind. Although both may be expressed by the verb *to be*, the other verbs occurring in the two types are different. In the equative, the other verbs are those such as *equal, represent, resemble, stand for*. In the attributive, they are of two sub-classes (i) *get, turn, keep, remain, turn out*, etc., (ii) *seem, look, sound, appear*, etc.; these are unique among verbs in English in that they regularly occur unstressed. If the clause is a WH-question, the attributive usually has *what* or *how* whereas the equative has *who* or *which;* and in general, though not automatically, an attributive may be expected to be indefinite (*a teacher*) while an identifier will be definite (*the leader*).

We have already noted that the identified—identifier relation is reversible in sequence; in fact it produces pairs of clauses related in voice, like the operative/receptive ('active' type/'passive' type) pairs of action clauses and clauses of mental process. Thus in a sense *John is the leader* is the passive of *the leader is John* ('the leader is been by John'). Note that in the normal intonation pattern (that is, the unmarked information structure, with tonic at the end; see chapter 12, pp. 175–9) the two types answer different questions, exactly in the same way as do pairs of action clauses related in voice:

Wren built *this gazebo* (what did Wren build?)
this gazebo was built by *Wren* (who built this gazebo?)
John is *the leader* (which is John?)
the leader is *John* (who is the leader?)

With attributive clauses, on the other hand, there are no such pairs: *happy is Mary* is impossible (or rather, it occurs only as a stylistic variant; it does not answer the question *who is happy?*). Instead of this there is a different contrast in voice, relating *Mary is happy* to *John made Mary happy*. Here another participant is introduced, which we might call the ATTRIBUTOR: the one who brings about the attribution in question. In this example it is necessary to introduce the verb *make*, but a number of verbs used in attributive clauses can occur in the 'causative' form without change, e.g. *get, turn, keep: the children kept quiet, the teacher kept the children quiet.*

Transitive and causative

The last example brings out very clearly one of the basic factors in transitivity: the relationship between the transitive and the causative. Languages vary as to how alike these notions are; in modern English they are rather closely connected, especially in the spoken language.

We can regard as the basic concept a process with one associated participant, or participant function. Let us call this function the AF-FECTED, since it is just that—in the most general terms, the entity that is affected by the process: *John* in *John fell down, the door* in *the door opened*. There will always be an 'affected' participant; there may also be a second participant involved, as CAUSER of the process: *a car* in *John was knocked down by a car*, *Mary* in *Mary opened the door*.

A process where the 'affected' participant is human, e.g. *depart+John*, is likely to be brought about by that participant himself: in *John departed*, *John* is the 'causer' of the process as well as being the one 'affected' by it. Thus we often find the middle voice—the one-participant form—as the norm in clauses expressing processes centering around a human participant. On the other hand, a process where the 'affected' participant is non-human, and especially where it is inanimate, is likely to be brought about by an external agency, e.g. *throw+stones;* so in such cases we tend to find the 'non-middle', two-participant form as the unmarked one: *the boy was throwing stones*.

However, there is as we have seen a tendency in English for the two types of process to become less clearly separated, so that an increasingly large class of processes is coming to be expressed equally readily either with one or with two participants: *the door opened*, *Mary opened the door*. Thus we will hear exchanges like *look, it's shivering—well you're shivering it;* and with the possibility of switching between indirect (prepositional) and direct (nominal) representation of the same function—a possibility which is similarly increasing: cf. above—forms such as *it caught (on a nail)* in preference to *a nail caught it*.

But to the extent that a two-participant process is interpreted as relating an entity that is affected by the process to an entity that causes it, to that extent the distinction between transitive and causative is obscured or eliminated: 'doing something to someone' is the same thing as 'making someone do something'. The distinction often seems greater than it is because of the particular verb used: we do not accept *he made the ball throw* as a paraphrase or *he threw the ball*, but we do accept both *he made the ball bounce* and *he bounced the ball*. With verbs of the neutral type (see p. 163), both forms occur—*he opened the door, he made the door open*—but it is not quite clear whether they are paraphrases or not.

These developments are not unrelated to other trends in the language. The clause is the domain of transitivity, of mood and of theme, all of whose options have to be accommodated in its structure; and there seems to be a more complex interaction among them than at earlier stages in the language. We cannot say that the structure of the clause is determined by its transitivity pattern, with other components providing only optional extras. The choice of subject, for example, depends largely on thematic options, since it is the participant functioning as theme rather than that functioning as actor that is normally chosen as the subject; and this is in turn linked to the fact that 'actor' is relevant only to one type of clause—action clauses, which are less frequent than mental process clauses in most types of discourse—and even here is becoming

TABLE I : Voice

		Non-middle: operative	Middle	Non-middle: receptive
ACTION	transitive type	I can tie the string | I can tie	the string tied itself	the string doesn't tie | the string wasn't tied (by me)
	neutral type	Mary opened the door | [Mary will open]	the door opened	this door opens | the door was opened (by Mary)
	intransitive type	John bounced the ball |	the ball bounced	the ball won't bounce | the ball was bounced (by John)
MENTAL PROCESS	'transitive-like'	the book pleased John | the book pleases		John pleases | John was pleased (by the book)
		it doesn't convince you | it doesn't convince		you don't convince | you aren't convinced (by it)
	'intransitive-like'	John enjoyed the book you believe it/that . . . Mary watched the game he said nothing/he said that . . .	John enjoyed himself Mary watched he spoke	[the book was enjoyed (by John)] it is believed that . . . [the game was watched (by Mary)] nothing was said; it was said that . . .
RELATION	Attributive	John made Mary happy the girls kept the room clean	Mary was happy the room kept clean	Mary was made happy (by John) the room was kept clean (by the girls)
	Equative	the chairman was John a tick represents an acceptance		John was the chairman an acceptance is represented by a tick

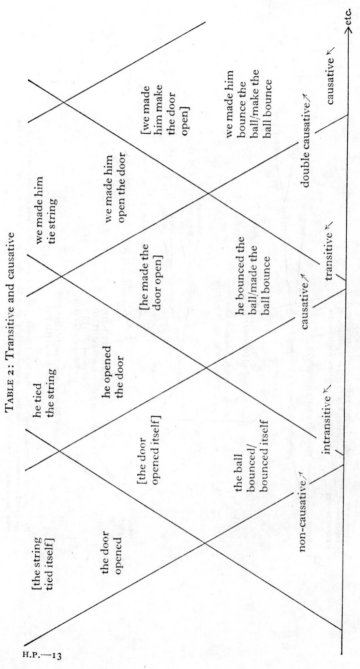

Table 2 : Transitive and causative

TABLE 3: Clause types

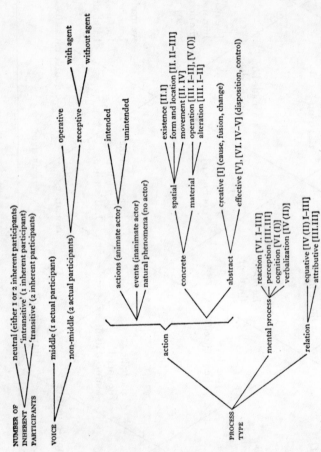

References are sections in *Roget's Thesaurus* in which many verbs occurring in the clause type in question are listed; these are broad correspondences, and there is considerable overlap. Note that the table, although exhaustive, does not show restrictions on combination of types (it is not a 'system network').

less clear cut (with the development of the neutral clause type, and the merging of 'transitive' into 'causative'). The location of the subject in the clause—before or after the finite element of the verb—is an expression of mood; and the reasons why the location of the subject expresses mood are thematic reasons. (See chapter 12, page 180.) Whether a particular element can be subject or not depends in principle on whether it is to be expressed as a direct or as an indirect participant (as a nominal or following a preposition), and this is primarily a question of transitivity; but even here there is considerable variation of a thematic kind, as in *he was sat next to by a complete stranger*.

Within transitivity itself, the action clause type is not really more fundamental than those of relation and mental process, nor can the actor-goal structure be thought of as a model for the whole system. If there is any general pattern of transitivity functions, common to all clause types, it is probably to be sought in the concept of 'affected' and 'causer' rather than in those of actor and goal, although this should not be pressed too far; action, mental process and relational clauses embody fairly distinct functions, even if all of them exhibit some form of causative relation. The notions of actor and goal are helpful in accounting for the potentialities of action clauses, but even here there are signs that the language is moving away from them.

12 Theme and information in the English clause

Introduction

This chapter is concerned with the English clause considered from the point of view of its organization as a message. Work in this aspect of English syntax, which is referred to here under the general heading of 'thematic organization', has been being pursued by linguists in the United States and in Europe for some considerable time; the labels that have been used are terms such as topic and comment, theme and rheme, functional sentence perspective, and the like. Yet this aspect of the clause remains a relatively neglected area, one that is still generally regarded as in some sense subordinate to its actor and process, or 'subject-predicate', organization. The purpose of this chapter is to suggest a reexamination of thematic structures, the contention being that there are rather more distinct patterns involved than have usually been taken into account. In particular there have been, it seems, two main problems, one caused by the partial congruence among what are in fact independent variables, the other by the assumption that all thematic patterns must be explained by reference to the structure of discourse (that is, organization above the sentence), although this is precisely one of the factors that distinguishes some of these patterns from others.

In general, thematic systems form part of the clause system network, although as will be shown, there is one subset that must be derived from a different point of origin. With this reservation, thematic systems can be said to be of two kinds: those which assign structure to the whole clause, and those which assign substructures at certain points in the clause. This chapter will be concerned only with those of the first kind.

These thematic systems fall into three sets, each forming a small sub-network within the total network of systems. They will be labelled information, thematization and identification; the structures they assign are, respectively, given–new, theme–rheme and known–unknown.

Extract from 'Some aspects of the thematic organization of the English clause' Santa Monica: The Rand Corporation (memorandum R. M. 5224 P-R) 1967.

Information, thematization and identification represent, but do not exhaust, the resources that the speaker of English has at his disposal in organizing the clause as a message; they may be regarded as mapping distinct structures on to one another and on to structures generated by other systems, such as those of transitivity. Information choices, those concerned with given–new, are realized phonologically, by intonation features. Thematization, yielding a theme–rheme structure, is realized by the sequence of elements in the clause. Identification, the known–unknown pattern of organization, is realized by certain structural devices. Information systems will be considered first.

Information

Information is a form of discourse organization. Any discourse is organized as a linear succession of information units, each such unit being realized as one tone group. (For the phonological representation see pages 215–223.) Thus for example the following utterance by one speaker in a recorded conversation consists of eight information units:

//4 and / what one / really ought to / do is //4 not be / mean as //4 I am and //4 hire a / catalogue for a / shilling but //1 buy one for about // 1 ten / shillings and / then sort of //1 — study it be //1 — fore one /goes the/ second / time //

The information unit is not coextensive with any constituent type derived from other sources; it must rather be accounted for as a constituent in its own right. This is the instance referred to above as requiring derivation from a different point of origin. It seems necessary to postulate, for spoken English, a form of discourse organization that generates a structure whose elements may require to be mapped on to others of any rank from (at least) the clause complex (see Huddleston, 1965) downwards. No attempt is made here to suggest how this might be done; and since the frame of reference for the present discussion is the clause, these systems may be considered here solely from the point of view of their interaction with other clause systems. In fact, the number of information units in a discourse tends to be roughly equal to the number of clauses, if one includes dependent clauses; the passage cited above is typical in having eight information units and eight clauses, and in the text from which it is taken the first hundred clauses were organized in 111 information units. But it is important to recognize that the boundaries do not coincide, and any given information unit may be more than or less than a clause.

Distribution into information units thus represents the speaker's organization of the discourse into message blocks. There seems little doubt that there is more than one layer of organization here, since intuitively one can recognize patterns in the sequences of tone groups, characterized by the selection of particular tones: one or more tone groups of tone 4 followed by one of tone 1, and so on. These are being further investigated at the moment (see Afaf Elmenoufy, 1969). At the same time each information unit has its own internal structure, and it is this that imposes on the discourse a recurrent pattern in terms of given and new information. This works as follows.

Within each information unit is/are located either one or two points of prominence, representing the speaker's choice of information focus. Information focus is realized as phonological prominence, specifically the assignment of tonic value to a given syllable (more accurately, to a given foot); this corresponds fairly closely to what is often called 'primary stress'. This is shown in the transcription by underlining; thus in

//4ʌ and / what one / really ought to / do is //

there is one point of information focus, whereas in

//13ʌ I'd / love to have / seen that exhi / bition //

there are two—as shown also by the tone symbol, which specifies either a compound tone (here tone 13) or a simple tone (here tone 4). Since each information unit contains not less than one and not more than two points of focus, it might seem that the distribution into information units would be fully predictable from the information focus, but it is not: in the following pair, the focus is identical, but the information is differently distributed:

//1 buy one for about //1 ten / shillings and / then sort of //1 — study it //

//1 buy one for about //1 ten / shillings and //1 — then sort of / study it //

In the second case the last information unit begins at *then*. The delimitation of information units and the assignment of structure within each such unit are thus independent of each other within the limits specified.

Information focus relates each information unit to the preceding discourse by assigning to it a structure whose elements may be labelled 'given' and 'new'. The terms 'given' and 'new' are to be interpreted, not as 'previously mentioned' and 'not previously mentioned', but as 'assigned, or not assigned, by the speaker, the status of being derivable from the preceding discourse'. Thus what is treated by the speaker as given may not in fact have been said, and what is treated as new may be contrastive or contradictory. It is in this sense that the element to which information focus is assigned can be said to have the value 'new' in the structure. Whether the remaining elements have the value 'given', however, depends on whether the focus is marked or unmarked.

The rule whereby information focus falls on the final lexical item in the information unit in fact merely specifies unmarked focus, and in this case the remaining elements are unspecified as to given and new. But the focus may appear at any point in the information unit; and if it is elsewhere than on the final lexical item the remaining elements are thereby specified as given. This can be seen from the fact that an information unit with unmarked focus does not imply a specific WH- question, whereas one with marked focus does. Thus

|| John washed the car yesterday ||

implies 'who washed the car yesterday?'. Similarly,

||John washed the car yesterday ||

implies 'what did John do with the car yesterday?', and

|| John washed the car yesterday ||

implies 'when did John wash the car?'. But

|| John washed the car yesterday ||

does not necessarily imply 'what did John wash yesterday?'—it may imply no more than 'what happened?'. For this reason the initial information unit in a discourse normally has unmarked information focus.

Thus if the system of information focus structures the information unit into two elements that may be labelled 'given' and 'new', we must make clear (1) that 'given' and 'new' represent the speaker's interpretation of the relation of what is being said to the preceding discourse—the 'given' may, but will not necessarily, be overtly anaphoric; and (2) that in the case of unmarked focus 'given' is to be interpreted as 'unspecified as regards any relation to the preceding discourse'. Furthermore, while the element 'new' is obligatory, the element 'given' is optional: the information unit may contain only the element having information focus.

The rule assigning unmarked focus to the final lexical item can be explained in these terms. The specification 'lexical' reflects the fact that non-lexical, closed system items are intrinsically 'given': that is to say, they are either anaphoric, like third-person pronouns, or situation-dependent, like first- and second-person pronouns—therefore if a closed system item carries information focus it must be contrastive or contradictory. This is the reason why *yesterday*, which is likewise situation-dependent (it is interpretable only by reference to 'today'), does not carry the unmarked information focus: contrast the examples above with

|| John washes his car every day ||

where the unmarked focus is on *day*. The specification 'final (lexical)' reflects the simplest form of organization of the message, that in which what is marked as new is culminative in the information unit; any other focus has the effect of delimiting a distinct 'post-focal' position in the information unit, any material coming within which is thereby shown to be explicitly 'given' in the sense referred to in (1) above.

But the essential factor in information focus is that, like all thematic systems, it affords the speaker a choice; it is a choice within which one term, the 'unmarked' term, represents the minimum of organization and will thus be expected to have the highest text frequency—nevertheless this term is merely unmarked, not obligatory. The 'unmarked' term is that which is selected in the absence of positive specification to the contrary. Thus in the recorded example

//1∧you / had to / walk from / one to the / other . . . // 1∧ but you / didn't

know / where to start / looking for the / other //

the marked focus on *looking* in the second information unit reflects the fact that *the other* is a repetition, and shows that it is to be interpreted anaphorically.

A number of specific contrasts within English grammar, which at first sight might seem to be unrelated, can be seen to be special instances of choices in information structure associated with certain statable environments: the fact that they are realized by the same set of intonation features is not merely coincidental. Thus for example

// my brother the dentist //

where the *dentist* is a postmodifier defining *my brother*, is one information unit; whereas

// my brother // the dentist //

where the two nominal groups are in apposition, is two information units. Apposition in English is in fact realized by tone concord: two consecutive tone groups having the same tone—so both tone groups will have tone 2 in

//2 was it your / brother the //2 dentist //

As a second example, the domain of initial adjuncts is specified by the information structure: it is always one information unit, which may or may not include the adjunct itself. Thus compare

// nevertheless he said so and I believe him //

with

// nevertheless he said so // and I believe him //

With certain other items, such as *too*, the domain is specified by the preceding information unit; contrast

// I saw John // and Mary // too //

where *too* links *and Mary* to *I saw John*, with

// I saw John and Mary // too //

where *too* links *I saw John and Mary* to the preceding discourse.

To summarize, then, the information unit, realized as the tone group, represents the speaker's organization of the discourse into message units; the information focus, realized as the location of the tonic, represents his organization of the components of each such unit such that at least one component, that which is focal, is presented as not being derivable from the preceding discourse. If the information focus is unmarked (focus on the final lexical item), the non-focal components are unspecified with regard to presupposition, so that the focal is merely culminative in the message (hence the native speaker's characterization of it as 'emphatic'). If the information focus is marked (focus elsewhere than on the final lexical item), the speaker is treating the non-focal components as presupposed. Thus for example

//4ʌbut on a / weekday one / wouldn't ex / pect to have / quite such /

crowds //

was anaphoric to

//1+ʌI was a / mazed because there was //1+ such a crowd of //1—

people there //

The point of reference in the preceding discourse may be at quite some distance; the information unit

//4ʌI was a / student / then //

was related to the earlier (answer to 'I thought it was half price for students')

//1ʌit / is but I'm //1 not a / student un / fortunately //

from which it was separated in the text by 83 information units.

Thematization

The second choice to be considered here is that of thematization: the organization of the message into theme and non-theme, or theme and rheme. Here the constituent is the clause, and the element selected by the speaker as theme is assigned first position in the sequence. Thus, in those cases where the clause is coextensive with the information unit, there is an association of theme–rheme with given–new. It follows from what was said about information focus that the clause-initial element will be focal only under certain specific conditions, so that in the majority of text instances the theme is included in the given (or rather in the 'non-new', since as has been pointed out, 'given' is to be interpreted as 'unspecified' if the information focus is unmarked). But the two are independently variable, and derive from different sources; given–new is a discourse feature, while theme–rheme is not. The difference may be summed up in the observation that, in dialogue, 'given' means 'what you were talking about' while 'theme' means 'what I am talking about'; and, as is well known, the two do not necessarily coincide. Information structures the item in such a way as to relate it to the preceding discourse, while thematization structures it in a way that is independent of what has gone before.

The meaning of the choice of theme is perhaps best understood by reference to the English mood system. If we consider the declarative/interrogative opposition, we find that the realization of the terms in this system involves the assignment of different elements to initial position in the clause: thus *John did it, did John do it, who did it*. In other words, a different element is selected as theme in each case. In a wh- interrogative the reason why the wh- element occurs in thematic position in the clause is that the wh- element is, by definition as it were, the theme of the clause in which it appears; it is what is being talked about, the point of departure for the message. This explanation can be generalized to interrogatives as a whole. In yes/no interrogatives, what is in question is the polarity: is the answer positive or negative? Since it is the finite element of the verbal group that carries the realization of polarity, this element, and this element alone, is marked out as the theme of the clause and therefore precedes the subject.

It is thus possible to specify an unmarked theme by reference to the system of mood. The unmarked theme is the subject in a declarative clause, the wh- element in a wh- interrogative and the finite verbal element in a polar interrogative. Any clause in which the element so designated does not occur initially is said to have marked theme. (Note that 'subject' in the present grammar is derived from the mood system, and thus corresponds to the 'surface subject' of a transformational grammar; a discussion of the concept of 'deep subject' lies outside the scope of this paper, but this corresponds rather to a mapping of functions derived from a number of different systemic sources.) Thus the theme is closely related to sentence function; and the meaning of theme as point of departure for the clause as message is further reflected by the fact that it is very much rarer to introduce a marked theme (complement or adjunct) in an interrogative clause, where the question point is itself the point of departure, than in a declarative, where the subject is merely a way of getting off the ground. It may not be unreasonable to suggest that the preference for the 'inverted' interrogative structure in English, by contrast with a number of other languages that have basically the same resources, is due to the relative importance assigned to thematic organization in the syntax of the English clause.

In other words, precisely the same factor favours 'inversion' for mood as also favours 'inversion' for transitivity, as seen in the relatively high frequency of the passive construction. The passive may be regarded as the structural device for dissociating the roles of actor and theme while leaving the theme unmarked. (It is suggested in Halliday (20) that 'causer' is a more appropriate label than 'actor' in modern English.) If theme and actor do not coincide, the clause may still be active (actor as subject), as in

// these houses my grandfather <u>sold</u> //

The difference between this and the passive (theme as subject)

// these houses were sold by my <u>grandfather</u> //

is twofold. In the first place, in the active *these houses* is a marked theme, and its selection as point of departure for the message thus constitutes a special 'foregrounding'; this point is returned to in the next paragraph. In the second place, if the focus is unmarked it falls on the actor in the passive form but on the verbal element, the process, in the active form. The passive is therefore the preferred form unless the actor is required to be overtly specified but non-focal in the clause. That is to say, modern English favours the passive structure (by contrast, again, with certain other languages having like resources) because of the predominance accorded by the speaker to the thematic organization of the clause: the passive allows the actor to remain unspecified or, if specified, to occur at the end of the clause and thus carry unmarked information focus.

The significance of the distinction between marked and unmarked theme can be seen from the fact that marked theme is regularly associated with a particular information structure, in which the theme is isolated as an information unit on its own. Thus in the examples above, the active is likely to take the form

// these <u>houses</u> // my grandfather <u>sold</u> //

To put this another way: in a clause consisting of two information units the tendency is for the first information unit to contain only the theme, which is thereby set apart in a function that the speaker feels may appropriately be glossed (and sometimes does gloss) by some such locution as 'as for'. This is not uncommon even with unmarked theme; but with marked theme it is the predominant pattern, thus showing that marked theme represents a 'foregrounding' of the speaker's point of departure. Further confirmation of this is provided by the third of the three systems to be discussed in this paper, that of identification; it may be helpful first to cite text examples illustrating the points made in the last two paragraphs.

passive with actor unspecified
//1$_\wedge$it's been / very very well / <u>publicized</u> //

passive with focus on actor
//1$_\wedge$ it was / led by the / local / <u>clergyman</u> //

marked theme as separate information unit

//4ₐ in Ma / drid it was // 1 terribly / cold //

unmarked theme as separate information unit

//4ₐ the / catalogue had //4 obviously been pre / pared be // 1 fore
they'd / hung the pictures //

Identification

Identification refers to the set of choices whereby a clause in English is
matched by a group of agnate clauses of the 'equative' type: thus to
John broke the window are related *what John broke was the window*, *the
one who broke the window was John*, etc. These need to be distinguished
from the somewhat different type, which will not be discussed here,
involving the sub-predication of one element (usually the theme) as in
it was John who broke the window.

Clauses such as *what John broke was the window*, *the one who broke
the window was John*, etc., for which the general term 'identifying
clauses' will be used here, are characterized by their being structured
into two parts, one of which is nominalized, the two being linked by the
equative verb *be*. For the purpose of the discussion it will be useful first
to give a brief account of equative clauses, which are resembled by
identifying clauses [see the author's discussion of this construction on
page 167] in most though not all respects (Halliday 20). An equative
clause has three elements, a 'known', an 'unknown' and a relator. The
relator is the verb *be*, or rather is that one of the three verbs *be* that
belongs to the class of transitive verbs, forming a sub-class together with
equal and some others.

Which term in an equative clause is the known and which the unknown can be stated by specifying an implied question to which the
equative clause stands in the relation of an answer: thus if *John is the
leader* implies 'which is John?', *John* is the known and *the leader* the
unknown, while if *John is the leader* implies 'which is the leader?', *the
leader* is the known, and *John* is the unknown. It is thus not the sequence
that carries the information regarding the known–unknown structure.
Rather it is the information focus, which in the unmarked case falls on
the unknown; thus normally

// John is the leader //

will be interpreted as implying 'which is John?',

// John is the leader //

as implying 'which is the leader?'. (As always, this may be overridden
by contrastive (marked) focus, as in 'John's the organizer, but which is
the leader?'

// John's the leader (// too) // .)

Thus the generalization that unmarked information focus falls on the final lexical item in the information unit must be replaced, in the environment 'equative', by the rule that the unmarked information focus falls on the unknown; this is clearly explicable since 'unknown' is obviously related to 'new', but we cannot simply define 'unknown' as ' "new", in the environment "equative" ' since the two are in fact separable, as the preceding example showed.

As pointed out above, the sequence of elements in an equative clause does not serve to specify the implied question; thus to *which is the leader?* we may get either the answer *John is the leader* or the answer *the leader is John*. It is this that differentiates the equative *be* from the copulative (attributive) *be* as in *John is happy*. Thus to the question 'what is Mary's husband?' we cannot answer, except in Middle English, *a teacher is Mary's husband*, whereas to 'who (which) is Mary's husband?' we can answer either *John is Mary's husband* or *Mary's husband is John*.

It is not enough, however, to characterize an equative clause as a simple structure of the form known–unknown. The equative relation may take either of two forms: finding a value for a given variable, or finding a variable with a given value. For example, the question *which am I?* has *I* as variable, for which a value has to be found; this may be called an 'encoding' equative. Here the answer *you're the leader* means as it were 'that's the semantics of you, your function' (as in the assignment of a role). The question *which is me?* has *me* as value, for which a variable has to be found; this may be called a 'decoding' equative. Here the answer *the leader is you* means as it were 'that's the phonetics of you, your manifestation' (as in pointing out on a photograph).

In the question, which is likewise either an encoding or a decoding equative, the sequence of elements is determined by the normal interrogative rule that assigns the wh- element to initial position; in general, only if the known is a case-marked pronoun will a distinction be made between an encoding and a decoding question (although, as will be mentioned below, there is some tendency to mark the distinction by number (/person) concord even when this is not determined pronominally: cf. *which are/is you?*). But in the answer, as shown in the above examples, the variable comes first. In fact, however, the rule that the variable precedes the value merely specifies the active form of an equative clause; and to each active corresponds a passive that is simply the other one of the pair. In the passive, therefore, the value comes first. Thus given the encoding question *which is the leader?*, where *the leader* is variable (i.e., 'how do I interpret the leader?', 'what person does the leader realize?'), the answer is

(active) // the leader is John //

(passive) // John is the leader //

—that is, active *the leader* (variable) *is* (encodes) *John* (value), passive *John* (value) *is* (is encoded by, decodes) *the leader* (variable). Given the decoding question *which is the leader?*, where *the leader* is value (i.e., 'how do I recognize the leader?', 'what person realizes the leader?'), the answer is

(active) // John is the leader //

(passive) // the leader is John //

—that is, active *John* (variable) *is* (encodes) *the leader* (value), passive *the leader* (value) *is* (is encoded by, decodes) *John* (variable). The respective equivalents of these four, using instead the verb *equal*, are

// x equals 2 //

// 2 is equalled by x //

// 2 equals x //

// x is equalled by 2 //

the only difference being that the verb *be* has no morphological passive whereas *equal* has. (It appears that in American English the verb *resemble* is to be classified with *be* in this respect, whereas in British English it forms the passive in the normal way.)

Thus equative clauses combine two simultaneous but independent structures: a known–unknown structure, and a value–variable structure. Using the symbols K 'known', U 'unknown', X 'variable', N 'value', we can represent the structure of the four examples above as follows:

	'the leader realizes John' (encoding question)	'John realizes the leader' (decoding question)
active	// the leader is John //	// John is the leader //
	K/X U/N	U/X K/N
passive	// John is the leader //	// the leader is John //
	U/N K/X	K/N U/X

where K/X, U/N, etc., are composite symbols representing the conflation of two structural functions, like S/WH meaning 'wh- element as subject' in a clause such as *who saw John?*

In identifying clauses, with which we are concerned here, the same two structures come together, but with the restriction that the nominalization is always the known: it is the nominalization that realizes the known, in fact. That is to say, in *the one who broke the window was John* the known can only be *the one who broke the window*. This does not mean that a nominalization can never function as an unknown, but that if it does, it is not agnate in the same clause paradigm; thus if

//John is the one who broke the window //

is an answer to the question *which is John?*, then it is not an identifying clause systemically related to *John broke the window*—as shown by the fact that *John broke the window* could not occur here as an answer, while

|| <u>John</u> broke the window ||

could occur in answer to *which is the one who broke the window?* Either part of an identifying clause may, however, be value or variable. Thus, assuming active voice,

|| the one who broke the window was <u>John</u> ||

answers the encoding question 'someone broke the window; who was it?' (*the one who broke the window* encodes *John*), while

|| <u>John</u> is the one who broke the window ||

answers the decoding question 'which of these people broke the window?' (*the one who broke the window* decodes *John*). Decoding usually has *be* in the present tense, while in encoding *be* has the tense of the nominalization, and therefore of the agnate non-identifying clause. The coding also determines the choice of number, referred to above, in such instances as *what frightened him was the crowds* (encoding: 'something frightened him'), *what frightened him were the crowds* (decoding: 'there were frightening things around').

In general, any subset of the elements of the clause can be nominalized to form the known in an identifying clause. The most frequent type is that in which only one element falls outside the nominalization, as the unknown; but this is not obligatory, as shown by examples such as *what happened to the window was (that) John broke it*. Certain alignments are however very rare, the general rule being that if the unknown does consist of more than one element, it must normally include the verb.

The relation of the composite known–unknown and variable–value structure of equative and identifying clauses to the structures derived from information and thematization may be summarized briefly as follows. With regard to thematization, 'variable' can be regarded as being ' "actor" in the environment "equative" '. That is to say, as can be seen from examples such as *which am I?*, *which is me?*, just as in non-equative clauses the unmarked theme is actor in the active and goal in the passive, so in equative clauses the unmarked theme is variable in the active and value in the passive. With regard to information, it was noted earlier that in equative clauses the unmarked information focus falls on the unknown whatever the sequence of elements in the clause. Both these generalizations are valid also for identifying clauses, with however one proviso to be made concerning information focus.

The identifying clause is a favourite clause type not only in scientific discourse but also in informal conversation; and a particularly frequent sub-type is that having a demonstrative as the unknown: *that's what I want*. Here however the unknown is frequently non-focal, as in

// that's what I want //

There is in fact an important contrast between

// that's what I want //

and

// that's what I want // ,

a contrast derivable from a general property of English demonstratives. Unlike other closed-system items, demonstratives are regularly focal, as in

// I want that one //

The reason is that, while other such items are anaphoric (that is, intrinsically 'given'), and therefore non-focal, demonstratives may or may not be anaphoric; their meaning differs according to the intermediary through which they are to be interpreted. When anaphoric, they are normally (that is, unless contrastive) non-focal; but when referential to the situation, they are focal. Contrast for example

// that's the trouble // ('what you've just said')

with

// that's the trouble // ('that bit of wire there')

Similarly they are focal when cataphoric, as in

// this is the trouble // ('what I'm just going to tell you')

When therefore a demonstrative is the unknown in an identifying clause, it will carry the information focus as predicted provided it is referential or cataphoric:

// this is what puzzles me // (either 'this object' or 'the following fact')

but if the demonstrative is anaphoric, the result being an incongruent association of known–unknown with given–new (with unknown mapped on to given), the given–new structure, being more general, takes precedence, and the focus falls on the known:

// this is what puzzles me // ('what's just been said').

The very high frequency of demonstrative identifying clauses is not perhaps unexpected, since they combine two features both of which contribute significantly to the role played by the message as part of a discourse. The speaker encodes one part of the message as the known, and then identifies it with an unknown that is at the same time shown deictically to be retrievable from the preceding discourse, either that of his interlocutor or—sometimes to forestall interruption—his own. In the latter case, that is, where the referent of the anaphoric demonstrative is in the speaker's own previous utterance, the demonstrative often constitutes a separate information unit and thus does carry information focus (which, since the item is anaphoric, is contrastive), as in

//1 where did he / hear about / that //1 that's what //4 puzzles me //

But this in turn relates to a general feature of identifying clauses, namely their greater tendency, by comparison with non-identifying clauses, to be organized into two information units, the known and the unknown each constituting one. Here identifying clauses follow the usual pattern by which, as noted earlier, the first information unit is coextensive with the theme; and if the identifying clause has the sequence known–unknown, the whole of the nominalization functioning as the known is thematic—so that in *the one who broke the window was John* the theme is *the one who broke the window*, and the expected pattern, given a structure of two information units, is

// the one who broke the window // was John //

The association of information focus with an anaphoric demonstrative, which is unusual in other environments, is thus predictable in identifying clauses from the fact that here the demonstrative is at the same time both the unknown and the theme.

One final point may be referred to briefly in connection with identifying clauses, namely the distinction between the two types represented by *what I need (is . . .)* and *the thing I need (is . . .)*. In *the thing I need* the *the* is cataphoric, as always in the nominalization part of an identifying clause; and it may be noted in passing that cataphora is textually more frequent than anaphora as a specification function of the definite article, in spite of the persistent belief that *the* always specifies by anaphora—it is in fact quite normal, therefore, to begin a discourse with *the*. In demonstrative identifying clauses the type *what I need* tends to be associated with an anaphorically specified unknown, as in

// that's what I need // ('what you've just mentioned')]

The second type, *the thing I need*, tends to be associated with a situationally specified unknown, as in

// that's the thing I need // ('that thing over there')

This distinction is matched in the non-demonstrative type by a preference for the use of the *what I need* type when the unknown is a non-specific and unmodified noun phrase: thus *what I need is a knife* but *the thing I need is a curved knife*.

For this reason personal proper names do not accept the *what* type: *that's who I'm looking for* but not *John's who I'm looking for;* proper names, being intrinsically specific, do not take defining modifiers. It may be noted further that it is the specificity of the noun phrase rather than the class of noun that determines which of the 'general' (or 'substitute') nouns appears as head in a *the thing that* type of identifying clause, *thing* being non-specific and *one* specific whether human or non-human: compare *the thing she uses is a knife, the one she uses is the curved knife; the thing she wants most is a daughter, the one she wants most is her daughter.* Here *one* has, in fact, its usual function of being merely a carrier for defining modifiers. Much further investigation, however, remains to be done in this area.[1]

---

1. In subsequent writings, Halliday used 'identified' for 'known' and 'identifier' for 'unknown' (cf. chapter 11, p. 167).

13 Modality and modulation in English

Modality in English poses one very special problem, which may be stated by means of an example: what is the relation between the two meanings of *must* in (1.1) and (1.2)?

(1.1)   you must be very careful

(1.2)   you must be very careless

The first means 'you are required to be', the second 'it is obvious that you are'; an example such as *you must be very sympathetic* may readily be interpreted in either sense and this brings out the ambiguity. But what kind of an ambiguity is it? Is it the same as that which is the source of the humour in *Mary can't think that! Mary can't think (period!)*? And why is *you couldn't have done that yesterday* ambiguous whereas *you can't have done that yesterday* is not? (The first may mean either (i) 'you were not able to do it' or (ii) 'it is impossible that you did it'; the second has only the latter meaning.) To put the last question in another form, why can we say *I could have been in Mexico* but not, or only very restrictedly, *I can have been in Mexico*?

As a startingpoint let us consider a small set of related clauses indicating possibility. In Greenwich, in south-east London, there is a small brick gazebo which is attributed to Sir Christopher Wren, architect of St. Paul's cathedral. It is a rather undistinguished structure which, if it was by Wren, might have been a task set for homework while he was at school. At any rate, we can say

(2.1)   possibly this gazebo was built by Sir Christopher Wren

We can express more or less the same content by saying

(2.2)   this gazebo may have been built by Sir Christopher Wren

with *may have been* instead of *possibly . . . was*; and we can also combine the two:

(2.3)   possibly this gazebo may have been built by Sir Christopher Wren

---

Extract from 'Functional diversity in language, as seen from a consideration of modality and mood in English' *Foundations of Language* 6.3, 1970, pp. 327–51.

TABLE I

rank \ function	IDEATIONAL Experiential	Logical	INTERPERSONAL	TEXTUAL
CLAUSE	TRANSITIVITY types of process participants & circumstances (identity clauses) (things, facts & reports)	condition addition report	MOOD types of speech function modality (the *WH*-function)	THEME types of message (identity as text relation) (identification, predication, reference, substitution)
Verbal GROUP	TENSE (verb classes)	catenation secondary tense	PERSON ('marked' options)	VOICE ('contrastive' options)
Nominal GROUP	MODIFICATION epithet function enumeration (noun classes) (adjective classes)	classification sub-modification	ATTITUDE attitudinal modifiers intensifiers	DEIXIS determiners 'phoric' elements (qualifiers) (definite article)
Adverbial (incl. prepositional) GROUP	'MINOR PROCESSES' prepositional relations (classes of circumstantial adjunct)	narrowing sub-modification	COMMENT (classes of comment adjunct)	CONJUNCTION (classes of discourse adjunct)
WORD (incl. lexical item)	LEXICAL 'CONTENT' (taxonomic organization of vocabulary)	compounding derivation	LEXICAL 'REGISTER' (expressive words) (stylistic organization of vocabulary)	COLLOCATION (collocational organization of vocabulary)
INFORMATION UNIT			TONE intonation systems	INFORMATION distribution & focus

Logical column also includes: POLARITY

HYPOTACTIC COMPLEXES OF CLAUSE, GROUP & WORD

PARATACTIC COMPLEXES (all ranks)
co-ordination
apposition

COHESION ('above the sentence': non-structural relations) reference; substitution & ellipsis; conjunction; lexical cohesion

TABLE II

MODALITY (interpersonal function)

| | | PROBABLE | POSSIBLE-CERTAIN | | |
			POSSIBLE	VIRTUALLY CERTAIN	CERTAIN
NEUTRAL	POS NEG (i) NEG (ii)	probably will won't	possibly may, can* (could) may not [can't (couldn't)]		certainly must (will) can't (couldn't) [may not]
UNDERTONE: tentative, deduced	POS NEG (i) NEG (ii)	presumably would (will) wouldn't (won't)	perhaps might, could might not [couldn't (can't)]	assuredly should, ought to shouldn't, oughtn't to [might not]	obviously must couldn't (can't) [might not]
OVERTONE: assertive, with reservation (tonic)	POS NEG (i) NEG (ii)	predictably (tone 1) *would* *wouldn't*	conceivably (tone 4) *may, might, could* *might not* [*can't, couldn't*]	surely (tone 4) *should, ought to* *shouldn't, oughtn't to* [*might not*]	surely (tone 1) *must* *can't, couldn't* [*may not, might not*]

* normally *may* in declarative, *can* in interrogative

( ) alternative forms

[ ] 'modality negative' forms

To show that this is a general pattern, here is a similar triad; note that the italicized elements are tonic (carry the intonation pattern associated with primary stress) and have the same tone in each case:

(3.1)   *surely* he'll stop talking soon

(3.2)   he *must* be going to stop talking soon

(3.3)   *surely* he *must* be going to stop talking soon

And there are a number of others. The principal system, as it is for a widespread variety of British English, is set out in Table II.

These forms represent the speaker's assessment of the probability of what he is saying, or the extent to which he regards it as self-evident. They are thus restricted to finite, declarative, independent clauses, and finite dependent clauses such as conditionals; there is also a minor system in interrogative, whereby the speaker invites the hearer to express his assessment, as in

(4)   could they perhaps have left a note somewhere?

i.e. 'do you consider that there is a chance that . . .?'

These meanings are what we understand by 'modalities'. A modality is expressed by either or both of two elements, one verbal and the other non-verbal (where 'verbal' means 'functioning syntactically as a verb'). The verbal forms are the modal auxiliaries *will would can could may might should must ought to* and *need*. Their properties are well known, but it may be helpful to list them here:

1. They have only finite forms: there is no *to can*, *canning* (forms such as *to be able* are not modalities; see below).

2. They form negative and interrogative without expansion, the negative also being reducible: *he cannot (can't)*, *can he?*, not *he doesn't can*, *does he?*

3. They are used as 'code verbs' in ellipsis: '*can you swim?*' *yes I can*; *so can I*.

4. They have three prosodic values, remiss (unstressed), ictus (secondary stress) and tonic (primary stress): // ∧ he can / *go* //, // ∧ he / can / *go* //, // ∧ he / *can* / go //, the unstressed form being normally reduced; these are systemic variants, differing in meaning in a regular way.

They are further distinguished from the other verbal auxiliaries *be, get, have* and *do* by the fact that:

5. They do not take *-s* on the third person singular: *he can*, not *he cans*. The absence of *-s* relates to the fact that these forms are not present but tenseless, like the corresponding forms of the non-finite verb: *can go* is like *to go*, *going* (and not like *goes*) in this

respect. This is not true of the 'quasi-modals' (see below); *can go* in sense 'is able to go' *is* present tense, so that the absence of *-s* is here unmotivated. (It is noticeable that *is to*, which occurs as quasi-modal but not as 'true' modal, does have the form of a present tense verb.) The absence of *-s* is one of the signs that modality rather than modulation is the underlying meaning of the modal auxiliaries (see p. 199 below).

Finally

6. They do not occur in imperative.
7. They do not combine with each other. Where there is double modality one must be expressed non-verbally, e.g. *certainly . . . might* (see below). Sometimes a speaker does produce a combination of verbal modals, such as in *he might ought to be here* meaning 'perhaps he ought to be here'; but in such cases the second of the pair appears always to be 'modulation'. Professor William Labov has drawn my attention to the occurrence of 'double modals' in certain Confederate dialects, and I believe the same restriction applies there—at least the second member of the pair must be a modulation. Note also that verbal modality cannot be incorporated into a non-finite clause; we have *the proof that he can't have been here is . . .* but not *his not canning have been here is proved by . . .* (the form *his not having been able to be here* is of course not equivalent, being again modulation not modal).

The non-verbal forms are lexical items such as *possible, certain*, which may occur in any of five different patterns, although most of them do not occur in all five, e.g. *certainly, it is certain that, I am certain that, he is certain to, there is a certainty that*. Specifically:

1. As adverb ('modal adjunct'): *perhaps, possibly, presumably, obviously* &c.
2. As adjective (predicative in impersonal matrix clause *it is . . . that . . .*): *possible, likely, obvious, conceivable* &c. (The form *it is possible (for . . .) to . . .* is not a modality; see below.)
3. As adjective (predicative in interpersonal, speaker-hearer matrix clause *I am . . . that . . ., are you . . . that . . .?*): *sure, certain* &c.; also *doubtful (whether . . .)*. (Compare *I think that . . .*, &c.)
4. As adjective (predicative in clauses such as *he is sure to have known*): *sure, certain, likely*.
5. As noun (complement in impersonal matrix clause *there is a . . . that . . .*): *possibility, chance, likelihood, presumption* &c.

The verbal and the non-verbal forms do not correspond one to one. In my own speech *possible* tends to go with *may* and *perhaps* with *might*, but the two are interchangeable and other speakers probably have different patterns. Nor do the different non-verbal forms of the same lexical item necessarily correspond with each other: *obviously* is not the same as *it is obvious that*, *surely* as *I am sure that*. But there are discernible groupings, and a clear distinction can be drawn between pairs which are felt to be equivalent, and thus reinforce each other (as 'concord') when both are present, as in *perhaps he might have built it*, and those which are not equivalent and are thus cumulative in meaning, as in *certainly he might have built it* ('I insist that it is possible' or 'I grant that it is possible').

There is thus no one single place in the clause where modality is located. It is a strand running prosodically through the clause (see Mitchell 1958); and this effect is further enhanced by the fact that in addition to the forms above it may be realized also by the intonation contour, or tone. For example the meaning 'possibility, but with an overtone of reservation' (i.e. 'maybe, BUT . . .') is typically realized by tone 4 (fall-rise contour with rising onset and main intensity on fall) in association with other modal forms, the modal elements themselves carrying the tonic:

(5) //4 ∧ he / *might* have / built it //4 ∧ con/*ceiv*ably //

from which we know that the speaker is thoroughly sceptical about the possibility which he is in process of conceding. This clause as a whole has the features

(modality: ((committed: possibility) / (overtone of reservation)))

and these are realized, as a whole, by the tone, the modal auxiliary in the verb, and the modal adjunct.

The system of modality may be set out in the form of a simple network:

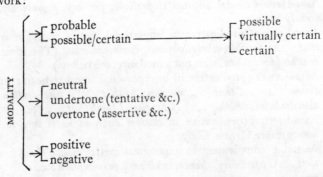

The basic distinction is that between 'probable' and the rest. This is a distinction between the intermediate value in the speaker's assessment of probability and the outer, or polar, values which are 'possible' and 'certain'. That this is the basic opposition in the system can be seen from the negative. In modal clauses, there are two possible domains for the negative: either the modality may be negative (*it is not possible that . . .*), or the thesis may be (*it is possible that . . . not . . .*). In the case of the intermediate value 'probable' these two are not in contrast: for the negative of

(6.1)   this gazebo will probably have been built by Wren

it makes no difference whether we associate the negative with the thesis, as in

(6.2)   it is probable that this gazebo was not built by Wren

or with the modality, as in

(6.3)   it is not probable that this gazebo was built by Wren

—either of these can be expressed as

(6.4)   this gazebo won't have been built by Wren

But this is not true of the outer values; there is a difference between

(7.1)   it is possible that this gazebo was not built by Wren

and

(7.2)   it is not possible that this gazebo was built by Wren

such that if the two are expressed verbally a different auxiliary is required:

(7.3)   this gazebo may not have been built by Wren

(7.4)   this gazebo can't have been built by Wren

At first sight, it would seem that we should express this by adding to the intersection of 'possible/certain' and 'negative' a further system distinguishing 'modality negative' from 'thesis negative':

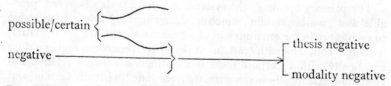

possible/certain {

negative ———————————————————————→ { thesis negative

modality negative

But this is surely wrong, since the total number of negative modalities is no greater than the total number of positive modalities. We are simply dealing with the complementarity of 'possible' and 'certain': 'it is possible that . . . not' equals 'it is not certain that' and 'it is certain that . . . not' equals 'it is not possible that'. Hence for each pair there is only one verbal equivalent; (7.3) above can be analysed either (i) as 'possible' plus 'thesis negative', *it is possible that this gazebo was not built by Wren* (= (7.1)), or (ii) as 'certain' plus 'modality negative', *it is not certain that this gazebo was built by Wren.* Of the two, the former analysis is the preferred one, since the realization of modality is then the same whether negative or positive: *possible* and/or *may* in each case. This is always true for the non-verbal forms. For the verbal forms, there is an alternation of *must* and *can't*: *certainly this gazebo must/can't have been built by Wren.* Note also the 'smeared' form *this gazebo can't possibly have been built by Wren* where *can't possibly* = *certainly . . . can't*; cf. *couldn't conceivably.* There are also marginal instances of *may, might, must* in 'modality negative' form, e.g. *John must be very worried—well, no he mustn't, but he may be*; these are text negatives, or verbal crossings out, and the use of the reduced form of the negative shows that it is the modality that is being negated. Compare *John might be pleased—No he mightn't* where the negation of 'unlikely but possible' has to be interpreted as 'not ((merely) unlikely (but possible) but not (even)) possible'. Note that *can* is occasionally used in positive declarative by syntactic 'back-formation' from interrogative: *Can John be busy, I wonder?—Possibly he can be.*

There is no such thing, therefore, as a negative modality; all modalities are positive. This is natural, since a modality is an assessment of probability, and there is no such thing as a negative probability. A modality may combine, of course, with a thesis which is negative; but the modality itself is not subject to negation—it does not enter the system of polarity, which thus has no place in the modality network. Negative polarity in the clause may be realized through the structural association of negative and modal elements (cf. *I don't think he built it*), but systemically they are unrelated. Thus, if the clause is (independently) both negative and modal, certain further, syntactically more delicate options arise, illustrated by forms such as *he probably didn't build it, I think he didn't build it, I don't think he built it, I'm not sure he built it*, &c.

The primary option in the system, therefore, is that between 'probable' and 'possible/certain', which are differentiated by their relationship to each other in the environment of a negative clause. Within the latter, 'possible' contrasts with 'certain' as the lower versus the higher value; and finally within 'certain' there is a distinction between relative and absolute certainty—between what we have called 'virtually certain' and 'certain' (see Table II). Simultaneous with this variable is another one, whereby the modality may be as it were either straight or modified, by undertone or overtone. If 'toned down', it has the sense of tentative, or else presumed by deduction. If 'toned up', it takes the form of an emphatic assertion, or an assertion contrasting with some kind of reservation; in the case of *would* the sense is 'that's just what I expected', with an implication of perversity as in

(8)   they *would* telephone just as I was going to sleep

Note that this form with *would*, often treated as aberrant, is in fact entirely regular in the system.

The following paradigm illustrates the range of different assessments of probability that typically make up an English speaker's system of modality. Each one corresponds to one main cell in Table II, reading down the columns from left to right. The negative form (i.e. the form taken by the modality when the thesis is negative) is shown on the right, under (i), with alternative non-reduced negatives *should not be | ought not to be* in (9.7) and (9.8), and *must not be* in (9.9)–(9.11).

(i)

(9.1)	probably this gazebo will be by Wren	won't
(9.2)	presumably this gazebo would be by Wren	wouldn't
(9.3)	*predictably* this gazebo *would* be by Wren (tone 1)	*wouldn't*
(9.4)	possibly this gazebo may be by Wren	may not
(9.5)	perhaps this gazebo might be by Wren	might not
(9.6)	*conceivably* this gazebo *might* be by Wren (tone 4)	*might* not
(9.7)	assuredly this gazebo should / ought to be by Wren	shouldn't
(9.8)	*surely* this gazebo *should	ought to* be by Wren	
	(tone 4) *shouldn't*	
(9.9)	certainly this gazebo must be by Wren	can't
(9.10)	obviously this gazebo must be by Wren	couldn't
(9.11)	*surely* this gazebo *must* be by Wren (tone 1)	*can't*

One or two of these would be more natural in another form, e.g. (9.7) where the likely form of expression would be *I'm sure this gazebo . . .* rather than *assuredly . . .*; the aim has been to bring out the full regularity of the paradigm. Some pairs are quite similar in meaning, but in no case, I think, identical; for example, (9.8) and (9.11) both have *surely* in an intensified form, but they differ in tone and in the modality in the verb. The former, which has the 'virtually certain' form *should* together with the 'yes but' falling-rising intonation, more readily admits the possibility of being wrong. In fact, there is also a difference in meaning between what are treated here as alternative (verbal and non-verbal) realizations of the same features, such as *possibly* and *may*, but it is a difference in thematic structure and not in modality: *possibly it was Wren* differs from *it may have been Wren* in that in the former the speaker has selected the modality as his theme. In *possibly it was Wren* the meaning is 'as far as the probabilities of the situation are concerned' or 'if you want to know what I think, . . .'.

Modality is a form of participation by the speaker in the speech event.

Through modality, the speaker associates with the thesis an indication of its status and validity in his own judgment; he intrudes, and takes up a position. Modality thus derives from what we call (Table I) the 'inter-personal' function of language, language as expression of role. There are many other ways in which the speaker may take up a position, and modality is related to the general category that is often known as 'speaker's comment', within which a number of other types have been syntactically distinguished; like modality, these are typically, though not uniquely, expressed by adverbs of different classes, e.g. those represented by (taking just one example from each class) *frankly*; *generally*; *wisely*; *fortunately*; *officially*; *reasonably*; *personally*; *incidentally*; *doubtfully* (see Davies 1967). Speaker's comment is then, in turn, one among the syntactic complexes which together make up the interpersonal or 'social role' component in language.

This, we are suggesting, is not a minor or marginal element in language, but one of its three primary functions, that concerned with the establishment of social relations and with the participation of the individual in all kinds of personal interaction. Language, in this function, mediates in all the various role relationships contracted by the individual, and thus plays an essential part in the development of his personality. If we consider the language of a child, there is good evidence to suggest that control of language in its interpersonal function is as crucial to educational success as is control over the expression of content, for it is through this function that the child learns to participate, as an individual, and to express and develop his own personality and his own uniqueness (see Turner and Pickvance 1969). Modality represents a very small but important part of these resources—of the semantics of personal participation; and the means whereby we express modalities are strung throughout the clause, woven into a structure, with other elements expressing different functions. This is why there is grammar in language; grammar is the weaving together of strands from the various components of meaning into a single fabric that we call linguistic structure. Into this go elements of the representation of experience, and of the expression of role and personality, together with those of discourse to provide the texture. If we take apart a piece of text in order to see how it works, in this way we reveal its origins in a diversity of functions.

We should not have advanced very far in the understanding of modality if we had assumed that the modal auxiliaries in the verb were to be treated on their own, and that the list of these could be taken as representing the system. We have had to identify the CATEGORIES of modality and show how these are realized; and the realization involves some fairly complex syntagmatic and paradigmatic patterns of relationship. Some general meanings have been able to be recognized; it is clear that *may* has something to do with possibility, for example. But we have not up to now accounted for all the uses of *may* and the other auxiliaries. We have not, for example, accounted for any of the following instances:

(10.1)   You must build a gazebo.
(10.2)   I can't build gazebos. If I could I would.
(10.3)   Well you ought to be able to.

These have nothing to do with the speaker's assessment of probabilities. In these examples the auxiliaries *must, can* &c. express various types of modulation of the process expressed in the clause; modulation in terms of permission, obligation and the like. They are part of the thesis—part of the ideational meaning of the clause.

Although by and large the same verbal auxiliaries are used for 'modulation' as for modality, there are some rather fundamental differences between the two. One of these which appears most clearly relates to tense. The modalities, being outside the ideational meaning of the clause, are also outside the domain of tense; like other forms of speaker's comment, they relate only to speaker-now. It is true that there exist different tense forms of the non-verbal expressions of modality, such as

(11.1)   it was certain that this gazebo had been built by Wren until the discovery of the title-deeds

But this has become objectified, and is thus removed from the realm of modality. Hence there are no corresponding verbal forms; we cannot say

(11.2)   this gazebo must have been built by Wren until the discovery of the title-deeds

Nor can *it was certain that* be replaced by *certainly*, which would give

(11.3)   certainly this gazebo had been built by Wren until the discovery of the title-deeds

At the same time, although modality itself is not subject to variation in tense, it combines freely with any tense. If it is expressed non-verbally, by *surely* &c., then all tenses of the finite tense system can occur: *surely he built | builds | will build | had built | has built | will have built | was building | is building | will be going to build | was going to have built | . . .*

If it is expressed verbally, by *must* &c., then the modality replaces the primary tense and the tense system with which it combines is the non-finite one, in which the absence of primary tense leads to some neutralization. One non-finite tense corresponds to up to three finite ones, e.g. *must have built* corresponds to (i) *surely . . . built*, (ii) *surely . . . has built*, and (iii) *surely . . . had built*, as the following makes clear:

(12.1)   surely he left yesterday   he must have left yesterday
(12.2)   surely he has left already   he must have left already
(12.3)   surely he had left before   he must have left before you came
          you came

Compare the non-finite form *having left* which is also the equivalent of all three:

(13.1)   having left yesterday, he . . .
(13.2)   having already left, he . . .
(13.3)   having left before you came, he . . .

It may be helpful to give some further examples:

(14.1)   Smith *can't be* so busy (surely . . . isn't)
(14.2)   Smith *can't have been* so busy (surely . . . wasn't / hasn't been / hadn't been)
(14.3)   Smith *can't be working* at this hour (surely . . . isn't working)
(14.4)   Smith *can't be going to work* all night (surely . . . won't work / isn't going to work)
(14.5)   Smith *can't be going to have finished* all that work by tomorrow (surely . . . won't have finished / isn't going to have finished)
(14.6)   Smith *can't have been working* all night (surely . . . wasn't working / hasn't been working / hadn't been working)
(14.7)   Smith *can't be going to be working* at it all weekend (surely . . . won't be working / isn't going to be working)
(14.8)   Smith *can't have been going to finish* all that work today (surely wasn't going to finish / hasn't been going to finish / hadn't been going to finish)

and so on. There are four more, to be exact (twelve non-finite tenses as against thirty-six finite); see chapter 9 pages 127–30. The analysis of tense is based on a three-term system (past, present, future) but with tense selection recursive. Note that *going to* and *about to* are regarded as (alternative) realizations of secondary future. There may be a slight preference for *going to* in finite and *about to* in non-finite forms.

Thus modality itself has no tense; but it may combine with any of the tenses of the verb. The categories of the second type (10.1–3), on the other hand, which are not true modalities—they are a kind of quasi-modality, which we are calling 'modulation'—have their own complete set of tenses. Modulations are not speaker's comments, but form part of the content of the clause, expressing conditions on the process referred to; they are thus subject to modification by temporal categories. However, all their tenses except simple present (and, very restrictedly, simple past) are realized not by modal auxiliaries, which have no tense variants, but by periphrastic forms such as *be able to* and *be allowed to*. Thus:

(15.1)   Jones *can* / *is allowed to* go out today
(15.2)   Jones (*could* /) *was allowed to* go out yesterday
(15.3)   Jones *will be allowed to* go out tomorrow

(15.4) Jones *had been allowed to* go out before the relapse
(15.5) Jones *has been allowed to* go out since this morning
(15.6) Jones *will have been allowed to* go out by the time you see him
(15.7) Jones *was being allowed to* go out at that time
(15.8) Jones *is being allowed to* go out just at the moment
(15.9) Jones *will be being allowed to* go out soon at this rate
(15.10) Jones *was going to be allowed to* go out until this happened

and so on. These 'modulations' catenate with a non-finite verb, here *go out*, which for its part is restricted to the unmarked 'tenseless' form, the simple infinitive. (This is a slight oversimplification as it ignores the possibility of interpreting forms like *you should be going to finish it soon, you should have finished it by tomorrow*, as modulations. On the other hand the exception seen in such forms as *you should have finished it earlier* is only apparent. Both these types are briefly discussed later.) So whereas in modality the process may have any tense but the modality is outside it, in these 'quasi-modalities' the modulation is subject to the full tense system, but the process that is modulated is tenseless.

Modulation, when it is not expressed through the modal auxiliaries, is realized not by non-verbal forms like *possible, possibly, possibility* &c. but by verbal structures consisting of *be*+adjective+*to*, e.g. *be able to*, or *be*+passive participle+*to*; e.g. *be obliged to*. These realizations are alternatives and cannot be combined: 'ability' is expressed either as *can* or as *be able to* but not both—there is no possibility of the two occurring in concord, as do the two forms of modality. A combination of modulations is always cumulative, e.g. *Jones must be allowed to go out*, even where the same one appears twice, e.g. *Jones may be allowed to go out now, nurse* 'you are allowed to allow him to go out'. There would be no reason for modulation to extend prosodically through the clause, since it is a part of the thesis rather than a commentary on it.

The principal categories of modulation are given in Table III. There is a fairly clearcut distinction between an 'active' and a 'passive' type, corresponding to the distinction in realization between adjective and passive verb referred to above. In the active modulations, those of ability and inclination, the modulation relates to and is intrinsic to the actor: *Jones will / is willing to drive, Jones can / is able to drive*. Where the clause is active, the subject is actor with respect to the modality as well as with respect to the process.[1] In the passive modulations, on the other hand, the modulation likewise relates to the actor, but is extrinsic: *Jones may /*

1. If the clause is passive, however, there is a distinction between the 'able' and the 'willing': *they were able to be helped* means 'someone had the ability to help them' (cf. *this problem has been able to be solved*); but *they were willing to be helped* does not mean 'someone had the willingness to help them' (hence we cannot say *this problem has been willing to be solved*). The 'able' term is the odd one out in the modulation system as a whole (cf. Huddleston, 1969, 165–76).

TABLE III
MODULATION (ideational function)

	INCLINATION AND ABILITY	PERMISSION	OBLIGATION	COMPULSION
	ACTIVE	PASSIVE	PASSIVE (NECESSITY)	PASSIVE (NECESSITY)
	willing; insistent*	allowed	obliged, supposed	required
NEUTRAL POS	will	can, may	should, ought to	must
NEUTRAL NEG (i)	won't	needn't	shouldn't, oughtn't to	can't, mustn't
NEUTRAL NEG (ii)		mustn't, can't	needn't	needn't
OBLIQUE: hypothetical, tentative POS	would	could, might	should	
OBLIQUE NEG (i)	wouldn't	needn't	shouldn't, mightn't	
OBLIQUE NEG (ii)		mustn't, couldn't	needn't	
	able	entitled	desired, expected**	designated, intended
NEUTRAL POS	can	can	shall	is to
NEUTRAL NEG (i)	can't	needn't	shan't, mayn't	isn't to
NEUTRAL NEG (ii)		mustn't, can't	needn't	needn't
OBLIQUE: hypothetical, tentative POS	could	could	should	was to
OBLIQUE NEG (i)	couldn't	needn't	shouldn't, mightn't	wasn't to
OBLIQUE NEG (ii)		mustn't, couldn't	needn't	needn't

* verbal forms phonologically weak in sense 'willing', salient in sense 'insistent'

** normally in first person interrogative only, e.g. *shall we come with you?*

is allowed to go out. Where the clause is active, therefore, the subject is actor with respect to the process but goal with respect to the modality. Here is a paradigm giving examples of the principal types:

Active type: (i)   (ii)

(16.1)   Jones will / is willing to tell you   won't
(16.2)   Jones can / is able to tell you   can't

Passive type:

(16.3)   you may / can / are allowed to tell   needn't   can't
(16.4)   you can / are entitled to tell   needn't   can't
(16.5)   you should / ought to / are   shouldn't,   needn't
              supposed to tell   oughtn't to
(16.6)   shall I / am I expected to tell   mayn't, shan't   needn't
(16.7)   you must / are required to tell   mustn't   needn't
(16.8)   you are to / are intended to tell   aren't to   needn't

In modulation too there is complementarity in the negative forms, although with a difference. Corresponding to *you can smoke* are

(17.1)   (process negative) you needn't smoke ('are allowed not to')
(17.2)   (modulation negative) you can't smoke ('are not allowed to').

In the above list of examples, 'process negative' forms are given in column (i) and 'modulation negative' forms in column (ii). The distinction looks parallel to that between 'thesis negative' and 'modality negative' in the discussion of modality above. But whereas in modality there are reasons for recognizing only one system of positive/negative, that associated with the thesis, in modulation there are two distinct systems, one associated with the modulation and one with the process. We can have, for example, *he is not allowed not to tell.* We also find double negatives in modality, as in *he can't not have done it;* but there, both negatives are negations on the process, so that the non-verbal equivalent is *certainly he didn't not do it* (cf. *he must not be here = apparently he isn't here*). Furthermore, of the two it is the negative associated with the modulation that is less restricted, being the only one that can be expressed by modulation: there is no verbal modal form equivalent to *Jones is willing not to tell.* Thus modulations are clearly subject to the sys em of polarity, as they are to that of tense.

Some of the modulations are 'oblique' forms, used in environments demanding sequence of tenses: past reported, tentative, and hypothetical. In some instances these pair off with the simple forms: thus oblique *could* corresponds to unmarked *can, would* to *will, should* to *shall, was to* to *is to;* and, up to a point, *should, ought to* and *need to* to *must.* The correspondences are not complete; but the set of oblique forms is, in fact, clearly specifiable, since they alone occur in the particular pattern referred to earlier—that exemplified by *you should have known, they ought to have warned you.* In this pattern we may have

Active:	could have	but not	can have
	would have	but not	will have
Passive:	could have	but not	can have
	might have	but not	may have
	should have	but not	shall have
	ought to have, need have	but not	must have
	was to have	but not	is to have

This is not to say that the forms on the right never occur, but that they never occur as modulations, only as true modalities, e.g. *Smith must have known* 'it is certain that Smith knew'; the only one that never occurs at all is *is to have,* but that is to be expected, since *is to* / *was to* never functions as a true modality.

Forms like *you should have known* look like instances of the non-finite tense *(to) have known,* which as we have already noted is in fact the one that occurs in modality—in *Smith must have known,* for example. But they are not. In *you should have known* it is still the modulation that is in the past; the meaning is 'you were supposed to know, but didn't'. Thus there is an explicit contradiction between the modulation of the process and the process itself. Other examples:

(18.1) Jones would have driven you   'was willing to (but didn't)'
(18.2) Jones could have shown you   'was able to (but didn't)'
(18.3) they might have arrested you   'were entitled to (but didn't)'
(18.4) should I have apologized?   'was I expected to (I didn't)?'
(18.5) we needn't have given one   'weren't required to (but did)'

This form is thus the realization of the features 'modulation, past, unfulfilled'.

We are now getting near to the point of this lengthy discussion of modality. It is clear that in modality and modulation we have to do with two different systems which are at the same time in some sense semantically alike. Let us recapitulate some of the differences between them. Modality is a system derived from the 'interpersonal' function of language, expressing the speaker's assessment of probabilities. It is therefore not subject to variations or constraints of tense or polarity (or, we might add here, of voice): it has no tense, voice or polarity of its own but combines freely with all values of these variables in the clause. There is one exception to the latter: where modality is expressed in the verb, it excludes the possibility of the selection of primary tense. The verb may select either primary tense or modality but not both. This is explained by the system of finiteness. The function of finiteness in the verb is to relate what is being said to the 'speaker-now', both by allowing options of mood and by giving a reference point either in time or in the speaker's judgment. Hence the finite element always combines with one or other of the two categories that serve to provide the reference point, namely primary tense and modality; but they cannot both function in this way at the same time. The fact that primary tense and modality are both realized by 'anomalous finites' reflects the similarity between them; they are both 'deictic' in the extended sense, and differ merely in the type of deixis involved—'at the time at which I am speaking' or 'in my opinion'. The two can co-occur if modality is expressed otherwise than in the verb; but it remains true that, because of the deictic function of finiteness, neither can be present except in the environment of a finite clause.

The system which we have called 'modulation' is very different: it is ideational in function, and expresses factual conditions on the process expressed in the clause. These are 'quasi-modalities', in the sense that they may be realized through the medium of what is essentially a modal structure—by finite verbal auxiliaries; but they are not themselves necessarily finite, and they carry the full range of options in tense and polarity, while the main verb with which they catenate must be non-finite and tenseless. On the other hand, they do not display a voice option; each one is either inherently active or inherently passive. Consequently, while they may combine with either active or passive in the main verb, the nature of the active/passive opposition in these cases varies according to the particular type of modulation involved.

The complex nature of the relationship between modality and modulation is brought out by a consideration of the ambiguities that arise— which appear sometimes as ambiguities and sometimes as blends. In the first place, naturally no ambiguity arises at all where the realization is other than by a modal auxiliary, since in such cases there is no overlap except that the form *it is possible for . . . to . . .* can occur in both systems (and perhaps other locutions with *possible*). Where a modal auxiliary is used, ambiguity arises under the following conditions:

(i)   non-oblique modal+simple infinitive (e.g. *must do*)
(ii)   oblique modal+simple infinitive (e.g. *should do*)
(iii) oblique modal+past infinitive (e.g. *should have done*)

These may be either modalities or modulations. (But not non-oblique modal plus past infinitive, e.g. *must have done*, which as we have seen can only be a modality.) We shall look briefly at each of them in turn.

Under condition (i), if the form in question is a modality then the tense must be simple present: *John may go = possibly John goes* (and not *possibly John is going*). Any given instance will therefore be ambiguous only where this tense makes sense, for example *John must go round the world about once a month these days*, i.e. 'he certainly goes . . .'. The difference is realized through the stress pattern. In modality, the *must* is salient: // ∧ he / must go . . .; in modulation, it is weak: // ∧ he must / go . . . . It is difficult, for example, to interpret *you must tie a knot here* as a modality: 'I'm sure you tie a knot here regularly'. If the form is a modulation this restriction does not apply, since the tense is in the modulation and here (modulations being stative) simple present is the norm: *John must go = John is required to go*. Thus the number of ambiguous instances is not as great as might at first seem likely. In action clauses, which typically have the *be . . .ing* form to express the sense of 'present', the simple present tense is fairly restricted; and while this tense is normal in clauses of other types—mental process clauses and relational clauses—the former are less subject to modulation anyway (an example was given above, *Mary can't think!*). So the most usual source of ambiguous instances is the relational clause with *be* and similar verbs, where the interpretation, as modality or as modulation, often depends on the nature of the complement; *he must be crazy* is unlikely to mean 'he is required to be crazy'—thought it might, in referring to an actor—whereas in *he must be firm* the interpretation 'is required to behave . . .ly' is the more likely one (cf. the examples with *careful* and *careless* at the beginning of the paper). One thing however is common to all instances of the non-oblique type—condition (i)— namely that it is necessary to distinguish the two interpretations. They are truly ambiguous, and the hearer has to select one or the other.

This is much less true of the oblique forms, conditions (ii) and (iii), especially those with past infinitive: *could have, should have* &c. Here we find instances which are more like blends, where there appears to be no requirement of selecting just one or the other interpretation; for example *he could have escaped if he'd tried*, 'that he would have escaped if he'd tried is possible' or 'if he'd tried he would have been able to escape'. Compare *the home team ought to have won, if they'd had reasonable luck* 'that they would have won is predictable' or 'they would have been under obligation to win'. The distinction between modality and modulation tends to be neutralized in a hypothetical environment. This is true even with a simple infinitive, if there is a hypothetical element somewhere around (for example futurity, with *could* or *might = possibly would*, e.g. *he could finish it tomorrow*; or another modulation, e.g. *they ought to be able to get it right*); otherwise, such forms are ambiguous, or even seem to permit both discrete and overlapping interpretations (e.g. *they couldn't trust Smith* 'surely they don't', 'they wouldn't be able to', 'surely they wouldn't be able to').

Some interesting further light is shed on this by a consideration of equatives. There is a general constraint whereby encoding equatives (those like *the leader is John*) are not subject to active modulation at all: we cannot have *the leader is willing | able to be John*. To any clause is related a paradigm of thematic variants which are in fact encoding equatives: e.g. to *Smith told them* corresponds (among many others) *the one who told them was Smith*, where the matrix clause is of the type of *the leader is John*. Since these clauses cannot be modulated by ability or inclination the clause *the one who told them could have been Smith* is not ambiguous in spite of the *could have been*: it can only be a modality 'possibly the one who told them was Smith'. If, on the other hand, the *could have* had been in the constituent clause, which is not an equative, the clause would have remained ambiguous: *the one who could have told them is Smith*. Passive modulation, which in this and other respects is intermediate between active modulation and modality, can be combined with encoding equative, but the result is incongruent: *the leader must be John* (in sense 'we demand that . . .'; cf. *the one who told them should have been Smith* 'it was supposed to be Smith who told them, but it wasn't— i.e. someone else did').[1]

Summarizing: not all forms with a modal auxiliary can belong to both systems. Non-oblique past tense forms, such as *can have . . .*, can only be modalities; likewise some equatives; and some negative forms are specialized to one or the other (these have not been discussed, but are shown in the Tables). Among those that are ambivalent, we find a range of semantic differentiation: clearly ambiguous pairs at one end, e.g. *may do* = either *possibly does* or *is allowed to do*, the two being quite distinct, and blends at the other, e.g. *might have done* = either *possibly would have done* or *were / would have been allowed to* ('but didn't'), without any very clear distinction between them. Blending is associated with the remote or hypothetical end of the scale; the more immediate the environment, the more discrete the meanings of the two systems.

How do we account for this? Let us represent the systems of modulation in a simple network as we did with those of modality earlier:

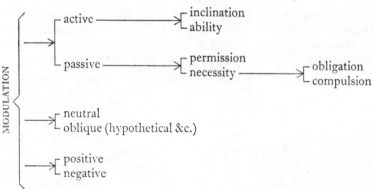

1. For a discussion of 'encoding' and 'decoding' equatives see Halliday 20 esp. pp. 235–7; cf. above, chapter 12, pp. 183–5.

A noticeable feature is that, although as set out independently, the two systems look very different, in fact they match very closely term for term, and this is obviously not to be dismissed as coincidence. There is also movement from one to the other, and dialectal variation. For example in American but not in British English *has to* is used as a modality: *that has to be the best dinner ever!* There is also some transfer of non-verbal expressions, e.g. *possible*: *it is possible (for John) to* . . . cannot be used in sense 'John has learnt to' (e.g. swim), but can in sense 'John has the capability, strength &c. to' (e.g. climb that mountain). Compare *is supposed to*, *is expected to* where the interpretation is related to person: these forms are more likely to be modalities with subject *he* ('probably is/will'), modulations with subject *you* ('ought to'). The notions of 'probable; or if not, then either possible or (virtually or absolutely) certain' and of 'willing; or if not, then either permitted or (virtually or absolutely) compelled' are in some sense to be equated. It is not very easy to express their identity through labels, but this is not an unfamiliar problem: labelling linguistic systems is a use of language rather than an essential component in a description of language, and the categories do not correspond exactly to any everyday concepts, or to any logical structures either. We can, provisionally, use the modal auxiliaries themselves as labels; the system does not in fact reduce taxonomically to classes of modals, but if we select only the non-oblique forms, and ignore neutralizations and diversifications, we can represent it thus:

We also ignore here sub-categories that are not readily identifiable across the two systems. If we now attempt to label the conflated categories in some metaphorical way, based on 'content-substance' as grammatical labels always are, we might arrive at something like the following:

where 'uncommitted' means 'probable (modality) or willing (modulation)', 'committed' means 'possible/certain (modality) or permitted/compelled (modulation)', and so on. The network is corrected to show that 'relative' (i.e. virtually certain/compelled) is found only in the oblique form: it is only in hypothetical, tentative &c. environments that there is a distinct category of 'nearly certain/compelled but not quite'. It looks as though the relative/absolute distinction is of fairly recent origin and is still only in process of emergence: the simple opposition 'strong: neutral (= absolute)' *must* / 'strong: oblique (= relative)' *should* is being replaced by one in which oblique/neutral and relative/absolute are independently variable, but the combination 'neutral: relative' is not (yet) found. The forms themselves are set out in Table IV; again, only categories common to both systems are shown, but with their specific as well as their general labels and with negative forms included to indicate where these differ, as between the two systems—for example, the negative of *must* is *can't* in modality but *mustn't* in modulation.

The partial reduction of modality and modulation to a single network expresses the closeness of fit of the two systems; but although they are systematically related they are not identical. This 'same but different' phenomenon is nothing new; much of linguistic description consists in accounting for the fact that things are different and yet identical at the same time—the notion of realization expresses just that. But in this instance the 'same but different' phenomenon rests on the functional diversity of language. Modality and modulation are the same system in different functions, where 'function' refers to components of the linguistic system (Table I): the one is interpersonal, the other ideational. In both cases we have to do with some kind of qualification of the process expressed in the clause, or rather of the complex of 'process+participant'; either this qualification resides in the speaker's own mind, or it resides in the circumstances. If the former, then it is interpersonal in function: it relates to the speaker's own communication role. The declarative mood is tempered with a modality showing the value attached to the declaration. If the latter, then it is ideational in function: it relates to a particular part of the content of the clause. The transitivity structure is accompanied by a modulation showing the conditions that circumscribe the process.

But the likeness is not merely one of parallelism; there is also some actual overlap between the two systems, and this accounts for the blending that can occur. In the passive type of modulation—permission or necessity—the qualification comes from outside the participant; he is committed by someone or something other than himself, e.g. *Jones must resign.* The agent in the process (*Jones*) is the goal of the modulation. Then what is the agent of the modulation? Very often it is the speaker.

TABLE IV
MODALITY/MODULATION (unified system)

		Committed			Uncommitted
		POSSIBLE-CERTAIN/PASSIVE			PROBABLE/ACTIVE
		Strong		Weak	
		CERTAIN/NECESSITATED		POSSIBLE/PERMITTED	PROBABLE/WILLING
		Absolute	Relative		
		CERTAIN/COMPELLED	VIRTUALLY CERTAIN/OBLIGED		
NEUTRAL	POS	must		can, may	will
	NEG	can't (modality)/ mustn't (modulation)		may not (modality)/ needn't (modulation)	won't
OBLIQUE tentative, hypothetical etc.	POS	must	should, ought to	could, might	would
	NEG	couldn't (modality)/ mustn't (modulation)	shouldn't, oughtn't to	might not (modality)/ needn't (modulation)	wouldn't

It is the speaker's opinion that there is some qualification on the process; his own judgment is involved—in which case it is very close to a modality. The difference between *I think it possible* and *I permit it* is small, especially in a hypothetical or tentative environment; the *I* is prominent in both cases. Note that this lies behind the difference between the two forms of modulation: between *Jones must resign* and *Jones is required to resign*. The first is speaker-based, meaning 'I insist on it'; hence it is realized by a modal auxiliary. The second is external to the speaker, and means 'someone else insists on it'. Compare *you can go now* 'I permit it', *you are allowed to go now* 'someone else permits it'. The position is more complex if the main verb is passive: cf. the difference between *John must be warned* and *John must be sacked*. Modulation, especially of the passive type, is a condition imposed by someone; and if that someone is the speaker himself then it becomes a kind of modality—the speaker in his normal, modal function interfering as it were in the event, in the ideational content of the clause. Hence the term 'quasi-modality' which I used above.

Modality, then, is the speaker's assessment of probability and predictability. It is external to the content, being a part of the attitude taken up by the speaker: his attitude, in this case, towards his own speech role as 'declarer'. It is thus clearly within the interpersonal component; but at the same time it is oriented towards the ideational, because it is an attitude towards the content that is being expressed. Modulation, on the other hand, is part of the ideational content of the clause; it is a characterization of the relation of the participant to the process—his ability, &c., to carry it out. But while reference to ability does in fact characterize the participant in question—*Smith can swim* is a fact about Smith—reference to permission or compulsion does not. *Jones must swing* is not a characterization of Jones' participation in the process but of someone else's judgment about Jones' participation; and that 'someone else' is, typically, the speaker. Thus the same forms can be used to express both. When we say that the opinions a person expresses often tell us more about the speaker than about the subject he is pronouncing on it is likely to be his use of these 'quasi-modalities' that we have in mind: his *musts* and *mays* and *shouldn'ts*. So while modulations are incorporated into the thesis as ideational material, they represent that part of it that is oriented towards the interpersonal—it is the content as interpreted by or filtered through the speaker that is being expressed.

It appears, therefore, that the similarity between the two systems has two aspects to it. On the one hand, there is a semantic region where the two functions, the ideational and the interpersonal, overlap, that of speaker's commentary on the content. The interpersonal function includes all kinds of commentary by the speaker; where his comment specifically relates to the probability of the content it is expressed through

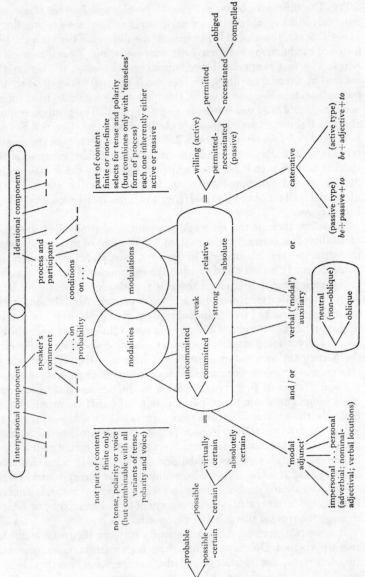

TABLE V

the syntactic system of modality. The ideational function includes all aspects of the content; those that specifically involve the speaker are expressed through the syntactic system of modulation. Hence the two overlap in meaning, and there is the possibility of semantic blends. On the other hand, the two systems are, up to a certain point (in delicacy), formally identical, so that we could in fact set up a single syntactic system, on the lines suggested above, which then operates in different functional environments. The system may be entered either from the interpersonal function, in which case it expresses modality, or it may be entered from the ideational function, in which case it expresses modulation. Hence the two are parallel but distinct, and there is the possibility of ambiguities. But the explanation is a functional one in each case, and both the ambiguity and the blending are accounted for in functional terms.

I have suggested at various places that the internal organization of the grammar of languages provides strong reasons for adopting a functional approach, since grammatical systems group themselves into sets of related systems and these groupings turn out to reflect a basic functional diversity in language. But the present illustration has gone further than merely demonstrating the assignment of systems to functional components. Modality and modulation do derive from different functional origins, and hence they are related to different neighbour systems in the grammar of English: modality to mood and other interpersonal systems of the clause, modulation to transitivity and the grammar of processes and participants. But they are also remarkably similar, so that having once taken them apart we have to put them back together again; and this reveals another aspect of the functional diversity, namely that it provides the conditions for bringing together in the grammar what are essentially distinct sets of semantic options. The interrelation between them, in realization and in meaning, is summarized schematically in Table V; the actual picture is, as we have tried to show, somewhat more indeterminate than this implies.

14 Intonation and meaning

1.1. **Rhythm.** The rhythm of spoken English is based on a unit known as the *foot*. The foot, therefore, is like the 'bar' in music; and a spoken sentence consists of a succession of feet, in the same way as a piece of music consists of a succession of bars. Each foot, in turn, consists of a number of *syllables*, one or more; and the first syllable in the foot is always *salient*. The salient syllable carries the beat. 'Salient' can be thought of as meaning 'stressed'; but we shall use the term 'salient', suggested by Professor David Abercrombie, in preference to 'stressed' because 'stressed' has been made to mean so many different things that its use here could be confusing.

Each foot normally consists either of one salient syllable alone or of one salient syllable followed by one or more non-salient, or *weak*, syllables. Thus, again like the bar in music, the foot always begins with a beat. But a musical bar may also begin with a rest, a *silent beat*; and this explains the use of the word 'normally' just above, because the same is true of the foot in English speech. A foot may begin with a silent beat, without the rhythm becoming disrupted or lost.

'Salient' and 'weak' are properties of syllables in connected speech. They are related to *word accent*, in the following way. 'Word accent' is the potentiality that certain syllables, in certain words, have for being salient when put into sentences. In general, the syllables which become salient in connected speech are:

(1) one-syllable words of the 'content' class (lexical words)
(2) the *accented* syllables of words with more than one syllable

while those which become weak syllables in connected speech are

(1) one-syllable words of the 'form' class (structural words)
(2) the non-accented syllables of words with more than one syllable.

Extract from *A Course in Spoken English: Intonation*, London: Oxford University Press, 1970, Chapter 1.

For example, in the word *April* the accent is on the first syllable; this means that when it is put into a sentence the first syllable will usually be salient and the second weak. In *July*, on the other hand, the accent is on the *-ly*, so that the first syllable will be weak and the second salient. (Note, however, that in words of two or more syllables where the accent is not on the first syllable it may nevertheless be the first syllable that becomes salient in connected speech, unless it is (part of) a prefix and immediately precedes the accent; thus, depending on structural and rhythmic factors, we may have examples like *the idea of a July finance crisis* with *idea*, *July*, and *finance* all having the first syllable salient, though the accent is on the second.)

In all examples consisting of more than one foot, the foot boundaries are marked by / (slash). A silent beat is marked by ∧ (caret) at the beginning of the foot; / ∧ / thus shows a foot consisting solely of a silent beat. Thus, for example, the third sentence of the first paragraph of this section (above) might, if read aloud, have the following rhythm:

each / foot in / turn con/sists of a / number of / syllables / ∧ / one or / more / ∧ and the / first / syllable in the / foot is / always / salient

with the silent beat after *more*, and a foot consisting just of a silent beat coming before the word *one*. This is not the only way in which it could be read; we might have silent beats before and after *in turn*:

each / foot /∧ in / turn /∧ con/sists of . . .

or there might be no silent foot before *one or more*:

. . . con/sists of a / number of / syllables / one or / more . . .

and other variations are possible.

It will be seen from this that there is not always just one way of dividing a sentence up into feet; often there is more than one possibility. One reason for this is that with some sentences two distinct rhythms are possible, the one having twice as many beats as the other. For example the sentence *Peter spends his weekends at the sports club* might be spoken with three feet:

Peter spends his / weekends at the / sports club

or with six:

Peter / spends his / weekends / at the / sports / club

But in general with any sentence there is one rhythm that is the most likely; and it is this that will be adopted in the examples in this book.

To say that the foot is a rhythmic unit implies that the time taken by each foot is more or less the same, again like the musical bar. Of course the whole *tempo* may change: one may decide to speak more quickly, or more slowly. Supposing however that the tempo is not changed, but is kept constant; then each foot does take up a roughly equal amount of time. Therefore, if there are more syllables in the foot they will need to be spoken more quickly in order to maintain the same tempo; and this is in fact what happens. In the example above, the foot *syllable in the* has five syllables, but it takes up hardly more time than the one-syllable foot *first* which comes just before it; so the words *syllable in the* have to be squashed together and the word *first* has to be stretched out.

This point should not be exaggerated; the time taken by each foot is, as was said above, 'roughly equal', not exactly equal. A foot with five syllables will usually take longer than a foot with one syllable; but not five times as long, or even twice as long, in normal speech. However, since rhythm is important, not only in its own right, for the purpose of understanding and being understood, but also because of the part it plays in intonation, it is useful to practice speaking in *strict tempo* even though in most styles of speech one would not in fact maintain a perfect regular beat. (One would do so, on the other hand, in certain styles, for example children's verses.)

1.2. **Tonic prominence** The unit of intonation in English is the *tone group*. The tone group consists of a number of feet, in the same way that the foot consists of a number of syllables: there may be just one, or any number up to about seven or eight, or even ten and more in rapid informal conversation. In general, the more formal the speech, the fewer the feet in each tone group.

The tone group does not coincide with any grammatical unit. In many cases, in conversational English, it corresponds to a clause, and this can be taken as the basic pattern: one clause is one tone group unless there is good reason for it to be otherwise. The 'good reason' principle is an important one in intonation, and we shall meet it again; there are many instances where a particular pattern occurs in all cases except where there is some definite motive for things to be otherwise.

The term 'clause' has to be interpreted here in the sense of a 'non-rankshifted' clause. But it is not the case that every clause is one tone group, because the tone group is a meaningful unit in its own right. The tone group is one unit of information, one 'block' in the message that the speaker is communicating; and so it can be of any length [see pages 175–6]. The particular meaning that the speaker wishes to convey may make it necessary to split a single clause into two or more tone groups, or to combine two or more clauses into one tone group. And in reading aloud, or in more formal speech, clauses tend to be divided into quite a number of tone groups, because they are rather long and full of information.

Within the tone group there is always some part that is especially prominent; broadly speaking, this is the part that the speaker wants to show to be the most important in the message. The part that is prominent is called the *tonic*, and prominence of this kind in the tone group is called *tonic prominence*. The tonic always starts on a salient syllable (that is, at the beginning of a foot), and this syllable is known as the *tonic syllable*. The tonic syllable is often longer, and may be louder, than the other salient syllables in the tone group; what makes it prominent, however, is mainly neither length nor loudness but the fact that it plays the principal part in the intonation of the tone group.

The tonic syllable carries the main burden of the pitch movement in the tone group, and it does this in one of two ways. Usually this means that it covers the widest pitch range: so if, for example, the tone group is on a falling tone the tonic syllable will have a greater falling movement than any of the other syllables—it will fall more steeply, and over a wider range. The alternative possibility is for it to occur immediately following a pitch jump, where instead of a continuous rising or falling movement there is a jump up or down (a musical interval) between syllables.

The tonic syllable is marked by underlining; for example in

Peter spends his / weekends at the / <u>sports</u> club

the tonic syllable is *sports*. If this was changed to *tennis club* the tonic syllable would be the first syllable of *tennis*:

Peter spends his / weekends at the / <u>ten</u>nis club

This notation is used in all examples except those consisting of one foot which itself consists of one syllable only; in such cases this is always to be taken as a tonic syllable and is not underlined.

The tone group boundary is shown by // (double slash):

// Peter spends his / weekends at the / <u>ten</u>nis club //

There are two kinds of tone group: those with single tonic and those with double tonic. The first are called *simple tone groups*, the second *compound tone groups*. Simple and compound tone groups are described in the next section.

1.3. **Structure of the tone group.** Each simple tone group consists of a *tonic*, or *tonic segment*, which extends from the tonic syllable right up to the end of the tone group; and this may or may not be preceded by a *pretonic* (or *pretonic segment*). For example, in

// <u>eve</u>rybody / seems to have / gone away on / holiday //

the tonic begins on the first syllable and extends over the whole tone group; there is no pretonic. On the other hand in

// Jane may be / going on / holiday at the / end of the / month //

the first two feet form a pretonic segment and the remainder form the tonic.

The difference between the simple and the compound tone group is that the compound tone group has a double tonic: that is, two tonic segments one following immediately after the other. For example,

// Robert can / have it if / you don't / want it //

where the first tonic begins at *Robert* and the second at *you*. Compound tone groups may also have a pretonic segment, but only one, and it precedes both tonics, as in the following example:

// Arthur and / Jane may be / late with / all this / rain we're / having //

which has pretonic *Arthur and Jane may be*, first tonic *late with all this* and second tonic *rain we're having*.

Note that no pretonic segment can come in between the two tonic segments of a compound tone group. This is what is meant, in fact, by calling these 'compound tone groups'; if they were merely sequences of two (simple) tone groups, each would be able to have its own pretonic segment.

It will be seen that each segment, tonic or pretonic, consists of at least one complete foot. There may be only one foot in any segment; but there must be at least one foot with a salient syllable in it (that is, one foot not having a silent beat). For this reason an example such as

it's / Arthur

has no pretonic segment, even though the tonic begins at *Arthur*; there is no salient syllable before the tonic. The syllable *it's* in this example could be regarded as a foot with a silent beat; and we shall in fact show that the tone group begins on a weak syllable by marking it as for a silent beat, with a caret:

//ᴧ it's / Arthur //

But it is important to point out that such a tone group has no pretonic segment, because the pretonic has a particular function in the intonation system and that function is not fulfilled unless there is at least one 'complete' foot (one with a salient syllable in it) before the tonic syllable.

1.4. **Melody.** It is the tone group that carries the melody of English speech. When we say that the tone group is the unit of intonation, we imply that it is a melodic unit; that the spoken language is couched in a succession of melodies, and each melody takes up one tone group.

The melody of speech is made up of continuous variations in pitch, or *pitch contours*. These are continuous stretches of falling, rising and level pitch movement. There is no limit to the number of different pitch contours that it is theoretically possible to produce, and the human ear can discriminate very finely between them. But not all the variations in pitch that the speaker uses when speaking his language are significant. The very large set of possible pitch contours can be thought of as being grouped into a small number of distinct pitch contours called *tones*, rather in the same way that we group the large number of colours that we can tell apart into a small set which we recognize as different colours, and which we label 'yellow', 'red', 'green', and so on.

Some tones may have fairly simple contours: just a falling movement, for example, or just rising. Others have rather complex pitch movements; but these can all be analysed into sequences of falling, rising, and level pitch, together with jumps and stepping movements. A *jump* is a sudden shift from a higher pitch to a lower one, or from a lower to a higher, across an interval (contrasting with a *glide*). A *stepping movement* is a series of small jumps in the same direction (contrasting with a *continuous movement*).

English makes extensive use of a simple falling movement and a simple rising movement, and also complex movements involving one *change of direction*; falling-rising, and rising-falling. These can be thought of as the elementary melodic resources out of which the tones of the language are built up. In the complex pitch movements, falling-rising and rising-falling, there are two ways of 'turning the corner' in the change of direction from fall to rise, or from rise to fall. One is more sudden and may involve a jump; the other is more smooth and gradual. These are referred to as 'pointed' and 'rounded'.

In living speech, if an utterance is complete there will always be some point of tonic prominence; and, as we have said, the location of this prominence—the placing of the tonic—makes a difference to the sound: the tonic syllable falls or rises the most, or makes a jump.

There are no level tonics in normal English speech. In some cases, it happens that the tonic can only come in one place: for instance a steadily rising pitch occurs only when the tonic prominence is right at the beginning. In other cases there is more than one possibility: a steadily falling pitch, for example, may occur with tonic prominence at any point:

// <u>dinner</u>'s / ready / everybody //

// jolly good / <u>luck</u> to him / then //

// just what the / doctor / <u>ordered</u> //

It is not always easy to hear where the tonic prominence is located in a sentence spoken with a steadily falling pitch; the tonic syllable does stand out, but often less clearly than in other types, and it may be found difficult to recognize at first.

There is no significant difference, in English, between a continuous movement, falling or rising, on the one hand, and a stepping movement, a series of very small steps up or down, on the other. The pitch movement, in other words, may be either glissando (gliding) or a succession of small intervals like the notes of a scale. This makes no difference to the meaning, and generally depends on the number of syllables in the foot. In a sentence like

// where've / you / <u>been</u> //

spoken on a falling pitch, the fall would be fairly continuous throughout; whereas in

// never seen / anything / like it be/fore in my / <u>life</u> //

the continuity would be likely to be broken up into a series of small steps, with each syllable very short and level. But the tonic syllable will never be level; even in the second example there will still be a clear falling movement, though starting already quite low in pitch, on the word *life*.

2.1. Tone. To repeat the point made in the last section: the very large number of different pitch contours used in speech can be reduced to a very small number of distinct tones. We can recognize, in English, five simple tones, plus two compound tones which are made up of combinations from these five.

These are referred to by numbers. The *simple tones* are tone 1, tone 2, tone 3, tone 4, and tone 5. The *compound tones* are tone 13 ('one three' not 'thirteen', because it is a combination of tone 1 and tone 3) and tone 53 ('five three' not 'fifty-three', for a similar reason).

We say 'we can recognize' five tones because the question 'how many tones are there?' is rather like asking 'how many colours are there?' The answer might be 'red, yellow, and blue' or 'red, orange, yellow, green, blue, and purple'; or we might want to add black and white, or brown, grey, pink, metallic colours like silver and gold, etc.; and all these would result in a different number.

The answer that we give is the one that is most relevant in the light of the particular context: why the question is being asked, what we are trying to do, and so on. There is nothing surprising in the fact that different books about English intonation give different numbers of tones. This does not mean that one or the other is wrong; it simply means that the authors are using different methods for explaining and teaching the language.

Here we shall make a distinction between primary tones and secondary tones. The five (plus two) tones just referred to are the *primary tones*. These represent the first stage in the classification. Any utterance in English is spoken on one or other of these five, or five plus two, tones.

But each of these primary tones can be subdivided, giving a rather larger number of *secondary tones*. The secondary tones represent more subtle distinctions within the primary tones. Again, we can compare this with colours. We can describe any colour as red, orange, yellow, green, blue, or purple, together with white and black. But these can be further divided; within red, for example, we can recognize scarlet, vermilion, crimson, magenta, and so on. These narrower, finer colours such as scarlet would correspond to the secondary tones.

Primary tones are indicated simply by the use of a number written at the beginning of the tone group, after the double slash; for example

//1 where've / you / been //

means that the sentence is spoken on tone 1. The compound tones are shown in the same way:

//13 Robert can / have it if / you don't / want it //

2.2. Pitch contour and primary tone. The primary tones are differentiated from one another by the pitch movement in the tonic segment. It is the pitch of the tonic, and particularly the tonic syllable, that determines whether the tone group is tone 1, tone 2, tone 3, tone 4, or tone 5.

So when we say that tone 1 is 'falling', we mean that in any utterance having tone 1 the pitch in the tonic segment will be falling; and in particular the tonic syllable will have a recognizable fall in pitch. Similarly, when tone 2 is said to be characterized by a 'rising' pitch it is implied that it is the tonic segment of the tonic group that carries the rise—most prominently, again, on the tonic syllable.

This does not mean that the pitch movement in the pretonic segment, if there is one, has no significance. Pitch movement in the pretonic is significant; but it distinguishes secondary tones, not primary tones. As far as the primary tones are concerned, the pretonics are fully determined, and there is no separate choice involved; once a choice of tone has been made this not only specifies how the tonic is to be spoken but sets limits to the form of the pretonic as well.

The secondary tones are in fact of two types: those in the tonic segment and those in the pretonic segment. The *tonic secondary tones* are the finer grades of pitch movement in the tonic segment: for example, within the primary tone 1 (falling tonic) we can distinguish, as secondary tones, a wide fall (high to low), medium fall (mid to low) and a narrow fall (mid-low to low). The *pretonic secondary tones* are the different pitch contours in the pretonic segment: for example, within tone 1 we can distinguish an 'even' pretonic (the contour having few or no changes of direction) and an 'uneven' pretonic (the contour having many changes of direction).

The primary tones, therefore, can be described in terms of the set of fairly generalized pitch contours that are used in their tonic segments. The five simple tones are as follows:

    tone 1   falling
    tone 2   high rising, or falling-rising (pointed)
    tone 3   low rising
    tone 4   falling-rising (rounded)
    tone 5   rising-falling (rounded)

The compound tones, as already noted, are simply combinations of these:

    tone 13   falling plus low rising
    tone 53   rising-falling (rounded) plus low rising

A more detailed account of the primary tones is given in the next section (2.3). In the descriptions, *pitch movement* is characterized as *falling*, *rising*, or *level*, and combinations of these; *pitch height* as *high*, *mid-high*, *mid*, *mid-low* and *low*; *pitch range* as *wide*, *medium*, or *narrow*. The terms for pitch height, 'high', 'mid-high' and so on, do not imply any fixed musical intervals; and they are, of course, relative to the natural pitch of the speaker's voice.

In the pictorial representation, // (double bar) is used to mark the beginning of the tonic segment. The solid line to the right of the double bar thus indicates the pitch movement in the tonic. The broken line, to the left, shows the movement in the pretonic. This is shown as a broken line because in many cases the pitch movement in the pretonic depends on the foot, with each foot displaying the contour in question; here, therefore, each section of the line can be taken to represent one foot. Thus for example ‒ ‒ ‒ ‒ ||/ would mean 'tonic rises from low to high; pretonic, if present, has each foot high level'. A form such as ◡◡◡◡|| would indicate that, no matter how many feet there are in the pretonic, each one falls and then rises.

As has already been mentioned, there is considerable variation of pitch movement within each of the primary tones. A tone 1 may have a wide, a medium, or a narrow tonic; combined with an even or an uneven pretonic, and so on; yet in all these varieties it is still a tone 1. These are simply the various secondary tones of tone 1.

From any such set of secondary tones it is possible to pick out one which is *neutral*, in the sense that it is the one used in the absence of any 'good reason' (cf. 1.2. above) for preferring one of the others. In tone 1, the neutral form of the tonic is the 'medium'; the neutral form of the pretonic is the 'even'. If, then, we select the pitch contour of the medium tonic and the even pretonic, in its most usual form, we shall get the simplest and most useful kind of tone 1. This we call the *basic form* of the tone. (The sections dealing with secondary tones are omitted here.)

We can identify a 'basic form' for each primary tone. This is the form which will be described and illustrated in the next section.

2.3 **Primary tones.** The details of the primary tones are as follows:

Tone 1

Tonic: falling ‖\\

The tonic of tone 1 falls, and ends on a low pitch. It may start at any point from mid-low upwards; the neutral type (see secondary tone) starts mid or mid-high. There is also great variation in the pretonic; the neutral type has an even contour, which often remains fairly level at about mid or mid-high pitch. This gives a basic form in which the tonic starts at about the same pitch as that where the pretonic ends.

Basic form: - - - - ‖\\

Example: ———— ——— ——— ‖_____

‖ 1 Arthur and / Jane / left for / Italy this / morning ‖

Tone 2

Tonic: high rising ‖/   or falling-rising (pointed) ‖\/

In both cases the tonic rises to a high pitch and the rise is fairly steep. The high rising form is the neutral type; it often starts about mid-low. There are also two types of pretonic; the neutral one, called 'high' (see secondary tone), may take various forms, but the basic form can be taken to be high level.

Basic form: - - - - ‖/

Example: ——— ——— ‖/_____

‖2 do they / take the / car when they / go a/broad ‖

Tone 3

Tonic: low rising ‖

The tonic is a gentle rise from low to about mid-low. There are two types of pretonic (see secondary tone); the neutral one is the 'mid' which starts and usually remains level. In the basic form, as in tone 2, the tonic rises until it reaches the height of the pretonic.

Basic form: ‑ ‑ ‑ ‑ ‖

Example: ‑‑‑‑‑ ‑‑‑‑‑ ‖

//3 Arthur / likes to / <u>have</u> it / while he's / there //

Tone 4

Tonic: falling-rising (rounded) ‖

As can be seen from the picture, there is actually a slight rise in the *approach*, as the speaker moves into the falling tonic; it may not be audible, but it can be felt (as a kind of 'silent rise', like the 'silent beat' of the rhythm). The maximum *force*, or intensity, comes on the fall. When there is more than one syllable in the tonic the lowest point is reached by the second syllable (the one immediately following the tonic syllable). The height varies (see secondary tone); the neutral type tends to start about mid-high and have a fairly narrow range, falling only to about mid or mid-low. The accompanying pretonic steps down from high to mid.

Basic form: ‑ ‑ ‑ ‖

Example: ‑‑‑‑‑ ‑‑‑‑‑ ‖

//4ʌ they / didn't / take the / car / <u>last</u> time they / went //

Tone 5

Tonic: rising-falling (rounded) ‖

The tonic is the converse of tone 4 and, like that of tone 4, has an approach from the contrary direction (which, likewise, may not actually be heard). The main force comes on the rise; and provided the tonic has more than one syllable the highest point is often reached by the syllable immediately after the tonic syllable. Again there is a distinction between a 'high' and a 'low' variety (see secondary tone); the neutral type is the high, which starts about mid and may rise as far as high. The pretonic steps up slightly, about mid to mid-high.

Basic form:

Example: .

//5ʌ I / didn't / know they'd / ever / been to / Italy //

Tone 13

Tonic: first tonic falling, second tonic low rising

As tone 1 followed by tone 3; pretonic as for tone 1.

Basic form:

Example:

//13 Arthur's / been there / twice in the / last / year or / so //

Tone 53

Tonic: first tonic rising-falling (rounded), second tonic low rising

As tone 5 followed by tone 3; pretonic as for tone 5.

Basic form:

Example:

//53ʌ he's / never / taken / Jane on / any of his / visits / though //

It will have been noticed that a sequence of falling followed by rising pitch movement occurs in no less than three places in the system:

tone 2, tonic secondary tone: falling-rising (pointed)
tone 4, tonic: falling-rising (rounded)
tone 13: first tonic falling, second tonic low rising

4.1. Intonation and meaning. The importance of intonation is not so much that a good pronunciation always includes correct intonation as well as correct articulation and rhythm. The importance of intonation is that it is a means of saying different things. If you change the intonation of a sentence you change its meaning. In English, there are very few instances of a sentence which has only one possible intonation pattern. There are some idioms and fixed phrases which have their own inherent tone; and a few of these are complete sentences, like *far from it* which is nearly always spoken on tone 5. But in the vast majority of cases, even though for any sentence we may make a guess at a likely intonation, to be used except for 'good reason' (there will probably be one tone we would give it if we were just reading it aloud out of context), there are always various possible intonation patterns; and all these will carry different meanings.

These different meanings are part of English grammar. When we talk of grammatical distinctions we are accustomed to thinking of such things as tense, or mood, or different types of subordinate clause, where the difference in meaning is obvious: there is clearly a difference in meaning between present tense and past tense, or between indicative and imperative, or between *because* and *although*. But the distinctions expressed by the choice of different tones are also distinctions in meaning, and they are of the same general kind; so they too belong in the realm of grammar (and, within grammar, the realm of syntax). Intonation is one of the many kinds of resources that are available in the language for making meaningful distinctions.

It may be that, in calling these distinctions 'syntactic', we are extending the meaning of the word 'syntax' slightly beyond its usual limits. For example, the difference between

//1 where are you / going //   and

//2 where are you / going //

is a difference of the speaker's *attitude*: the first is a normal question, neither abrupt nor deferential, while the second is deferential: it is a question accompanied by a request for permission to ask, 'where are you going, may I ask?'. Differences of this kind are not usually thought of as syntactic. But in fact, and this is what we are emphasizing, there is no clear line between these differences of 'attitude' and differences in meaning such as found in a pair like

//2 would you like / tea //1$_\wedge$ or / coffee //   and

//2 would you like / tea //2$_\wedge$ or / coffee //

where the intonation expresses a clearcut logical distinction between two kinds of 'or': the first means 'which would you like?', the second means 'would you like either?'.

Many of the distinctions made by intonation are intermediate between these two examples. For instance,

//1$_\wedge$ I / know / John //   and

//4$_\wedge$ I / know / John //

where the first is a simple statement while the second means 'but I don't know ... (someone else mentioned, e.g. his wife)'; the second conveys contrast, reservation, an implied 'but'. Or

//1 where are you / <u>go</u>ing //   and

//2 <u>where</u> are you / going //

(note the position of the tonic in the second case) where the second means 'please remind or confirm': it is an 'echo question' (cf. 1.4. above). Examples like these show that one cannot draw a sharp line between the expression of meanings on the one hand and the expression of attitudes and emotions on the other.

It is more helpful to think of attitudes and emotions as part of meaning; to consider that all intonation patterns convey meaning, and then ask what kinds of meaning they convey. In this way it is possible to make some useful generalizations. In general, tone expresses *speech function*, while tonic prominence expresses the structure of *information*. That is to say, the choice of tone—tone 1, tone 2, etc.—relates to mood (kinds of statement, question, etc.), modality (assessment of the possibility, probability, validity, relevance, etc. of what is being said) and key (speaker's attitude, of politeness, assertiveness, indifference, etc.); in other words all the factors which go to make up the relation between the speaker and the hearer, in a speech situation. The choice of tonic prominence—where to put the tonic; also, in fact, where to divide up into tone groups—relates to how the message is divided into units of information, where the main 'new information' lies, and how it ties up with what has been said before: anything that contributes to the structure of the discourse.

4.2. Meaning of the tones: general Basically, a falling contour means certainty and a rising contour means uncertainty. This is true in many languages, though by no means all. In English, it takes this particular form: a falling contour means certainty with regard to yes or no. We go down when we know whether something is positive or negative, and we go up when we do not know. In other words we go down when we know the *polarity* of what we are saying.

This means that we use a falling tone in statements; and in one type of question, the 'WH-' (or 'special') question, the type which has an interrogative word like *who/what/why* in it. The uncertainty in a WH-question is not an uncertainty about yes or no. We use a rising tone, however, in the other type of question, the 'yes/no' (or 'general') question, when the uncertainty is precisely that between negative and positive. (Commands, calls, and exclamations lie outside this particular distinction.)

Tone 1, therefore, is the normal, or *neutral*, tone for declarative clauses, which express statements, and for interrogative clauses of the WH-type. Tone 2 is the neutral tone for interrogative clauses of the 'yes/no' type, those where the question is one of polarity.

This principle, whereby falling pitch means 'polarity known' and rising pitch means 'polarity unknown', gives a clue to the meaning of the tones which change direction. Both tone 4 and tone 5 contain two components of meaning, with a 'change of mind' in the middle. Tone 4 falls and then rises, meaning something like 'it may seem as though all is clear, but in fact there is more involved'; characteristically it is used to make statements carrying some reservation, implying a 'but', and also to express conditions. Tone 5, which phonetically is the contrary of tone 4, is also its converse in meaning: it conveys 'there may seem to be a doubt, but in fact all is certain'—in other words //5 that's / all there / is / to it //: this sentence is almost always spoken on tone 5. Tone 5 also makes statements that are rather assertive, implying 'how could you doubt that, or not know it?' And just as the sense of reservation of tone 4 may imply a tentative opinion, 'that's what I think; how about you?', so the assertiveness of tone 5 may express surprise: 'that's what you say, but are you sure?'.

Tone 3, the low rise, is a sort of compromise between a fall and a rise; it expresses not so much uncertainty as some form of dependence or incompleteness. Characteristically it either confirms a previous statement, or an expectation, meaning something like 'yes it is so, but you knew it already'; accedes to a request; or indicates that the information conveyed is unfinished or of secondary importance.

So for example

//1∧ he / could do // (simple statement)

//2∧ he / could do // ('is that what you think? could he?')

//3∧ he / could do // ('I think he could, but it's of no importance')

//4∧ he / could do // ('but he won't', 'but it won't help you', etc.)

//5∧ he / could do // ('so don't you imagine he couldn't!')

4.3. Meaning of the primary tones.

The specific meanings of the primary tones are dependent on speech function. To explain them we need to recognize seven distinct speech functions, four 'major' and three 'minor':

Major speech functions:
statements; WH- questions; yes/no questions; commands
Minor speech functions:
responses; exclamations; calls

The major speech functions are always expressed in complete sentences. The minor speech functions may be expressed by reduced, or *elliptical*, sentences, not necessarily containing a predication.

The normal, or neutral, tone is tone 1 for all major speech functions except yes/no questions, for which it is tone 2. Whether or not the minor speech functions can really be said to have a neutral tone is a little doubtful. However, if they have, it would also be tone 1.

This does not necessarily mean that tone 1 is the most frequent tone in every case. It is the most frequent tone overall; but in certain particular categories, such as prohibitions (negative commands), it probably is not. The significance of the 'neutral' tone is that it is the one that always can be used, in the given speech function. It implies no previous context—and can always be selected, therefore, if there is doubt about the appropriateness of the other tones. (Note, however, that tone 1 is rather abrupt in commands, especially negative commands!)

Examples are given below of each of the various speech functions, showing which tones are possible, other than the neutral tone, and how the others differ in meaning from the neutral tone. The meanings are given in general terms such as 'reservation' or 'contrast'; in addition in most cases a gloss has been provided showing how this general meaning might be interpreted in the particular example. Thus in

//4ʌ it's / very ef/ficient //

the tone 4 implies some form of reservation or contrast; this might be, in the particular context, 'but I don't like it', 'but it's too expensive', 'although you don't think so', etc., so that the specific interpretation given is just one of the meanings that the sentence might have in an actual speech situation.

1 *Major speech functions*

(a) statement: tone 1, neutral; tone 4, expressing reservation, or contrast, or a personal opinion offered for consideration

//1ʌ it's / very ef/ficient //

//4ʌ it's / very ef/ficient // ('it may not be beautiful', etc.)

//1 I̲ / like it // (tone 1 with tonic on *I* suggests 'too')

//4 I̲ / like it // ('even if you don't', 'I don't know about anyone else')

//1ʌ she's / rather / clever //

//4ʌ she's / rather / clever I / think // ('don't you?')

//1ʌ it's a / bit of a / risk //

//4ʌ it's a / bit of a / risk // ('but as long as you know that you can try it if you want')

Tone 4 is the second most common of the English tones, being considerably more frequent than any except tone 1; and this is probably the most important single opposition in English intonation.

(b) statement: tone 1, neutral; tone 3, acceding to request or to unexpressed expectation—hence also reassurance, for example about the future

//1ᴧ I'll / see what / I can / do //

//3ᴧ I'll / see what / I can / do // ('since you ask me')

//1ᴧ they'll / soon be / here //

//3ᴧ they'll / soon be / here // ('don't worry!')

(c) statement: tone 1, neutral; tone 5, asserting, or expressing some other form of commitment

//1ᴧ he wasn't / telling the / truth //

//5ᴧ he wasn't / telling the / truth // ('I'm quite certain', 'that's the whole explanation')

(d) wh- question: tone 1, neutral; tone 2, mild (tentative or deferential)

//1 what's the / time //

//2 what's the / time // ('may I ask, please?')

(e) yes/no question: tone 2, neutral; tone 1, strong (forceful or impatient)

//2 are you / satisfied //

//1 are you / satisfied // ('you ought to be')

For tone 1 in the sense of 'second attempt' question, see (h) below.

(f) statement-question: tone 1, expressing observation or deduction; tone 2, seeking confirmation

//1 Peter isn't / here yet // ('I notice; is that correct?')

//2 Peter isn't / here yet // ('is that what you're saying?')

Note that tone 1 is ambiguous here and is often misinterpreted as a simple statement: —'oh, isn't he?'—'no, I'm asking you: isn't he?'.

(g) statement-question with tag: this has many variants. The statement may take any of the forms (a)–(c) above, followed by a tag on a separate tone group with tone 1, 2, or 5; or the statement and tag may both be on a single tone group, tone 1, 2, 4, or 5. Moreover the tag may change the polarity of the statement (negative tag on positive statement, or vice versa) or may keep the polarity unchanged (positive on positive or, less commonly, negative on negative). The following are among the most usual: tones 1 & 2, polarity changed, neutral; tones 1 & 1, polarity changed, expressing certainty or demanding an admission; tones 1 & 2, polarity unchanged, expressing new understanding together with forcefulness, accusation or criticism.

//1 Peter's here //2 isn't he //

//1 Peter's here //1 isn't he // ('I'm sure he is'; 'admit it!')

//1 Peter's here //2 is he // ('I've just heard'; 'that explains it')

//1 Peter's here / is he // ('I see', 'well he shouldn't be')

(h) multiple question: tones 2 & 1, alternative question; tones 2 & 2, list question

//2 did you play / tennis //1ʌ or / golf // ('which?')

//2 did you play / tennis //2ʌ or / golf // ('yes or no?')

Note that it is this sense of tone 1 which explains its use in 'second attempt' questions, e.g.: //2 can you / eat it //—'no!'—//1 can you / drink it // (often introduced by *well then*: //1ʌ well then / can you / drink it //).

(i) command, positive: tone 1, neutral; tone 3, mild, expressing request; tone 13, pleading or persuading

//1 tell me / all a/bout it // (instruction)

//3 tell me / all a/bout it // (invitation)

//13 do tell me / all a/bout it // ('won't you, please?')

Tone 13 is more common in negative; see next.

(j) command, negative (prohibition): tone 1, forceful; tone 3, polite, expressing request; tone 13, pleading or dissuading

//1 don't stay / out too / long // ('I mean it')

//3 don't stay / out too / <u>long</u> // ('I know you won't, 'I don't really
mind', 'I'm not serious')

//13 <u>don't</u> stay / out too / <u>long</u> // ('like you did last time', 'please—I
know you probably will')

The explanation of tone 13 here (and cf. (i) above) is to be found
in the meaning of tone 3 as something already known or 'given'.
The action being prohibited has already been referred to, or is
clearly in progress. For this reason the tone 1 tonic falls on the
imperative element *don't*, and not on the verb *stay* (*out*).

(k)   command: tone 1, neutral; tone 4, expressing compromise or con-
cession

//1 give him a / <u>chance</u> //
//4 give him a / <u>chance</u> // ('at least', 'even though he may fail')

2 *Minor speech functions*

(l)   response, favourable: tone 1, neutral; tone 3, confirmation or reassurance. Question: 'have you got the tickets?'; response:

//1 <u>yes</u> // [or] //1 <u>yes</u> //1ᴧ I / <u>have</u> // [or] //1 <u>yes</u> //1ᴧ I / <u>have</u> / got the /
tickets // (not, however, //1ᴧ I've / got the / <u>tickets</u> //)

//3ᴧ yes I've / got the / <u>tickets</u> // ('that's all right', 'it's as you thought')

(m)   response, unfavourable: tone 1, neutral; tone 2, contradiction,
denial or disappointing of expectation. Statement (or statement-
question): 'you've got the tickets'; response:

//1 <u>no</u> // [or] //1 <u>no</u> //1ᴧ I / <u>haven't</u> // [or] //1 <u>no</u> //1ᴧ I / <u>haven't</u> / got the /
tickets //

//2ᴧ no I / <u>haven't</u> // [or] //2ᴧ no I / <u>haven't</u> / got the / tickets // ('out of
the question!')

Note that 'unfavourable' merely means 'not confirming (what is
asked or expected)'; it does not necessarily imply pejorative. We
may have, for example, //2ᴧ it's / not too / <u>bad</u> // in response to
'terrible weather, isn't it?'.

(n)   exclamatory response or exclamation: tone 1, neutral, indicating
simply 'information received, and noted'; tone 2, neutral, seeking

confirmation; tone 5, expressing surprise. Statement: 'they're coming home on Saturday'; response:

//1 oh //1 are they //1ᴧ on / Saturday // ('I see', 'noted!')

//2 oh //2 are they //2ᴧ on / Saturday // ('is that so?')

//5 oh //5 are they //5ᴧ on / Saturday // ('that's unexpected', 'are you sure?')

Any one, or any two, of the three parts of the utterance as given here (e.g. *oh? are they?*) would constitute a normal response. Either tone 1 or tone 2 could be considered neutral. If the utterance is purely an exclamation, not a response, tone 2 is not used; tone 1 is neutral, and fairly cool and dispassionate, while tone 5 expresses surprise, or some form of personal reaction, favourable or unfavourable:

//1 wonderful i/dea //

//5 wonderful i/dea // ('I'm amazed, and delighted')

//1ᴧ I / think that's a / dreadful / hat //

//5ᴧ I / think that's a / dreadful / hat // ('you're not going to wear *that*!')

Tone 5 also conveys sudden realization: //5ᴧ so / that's why you / said you were / too busy//, //5ᴧ no / wonder they're / always / bankrupt //

(o) call: tone 1, summons or command; tone 2, enquiry; tone .3 (pretonic and tonic), call signal, request for attention; tone 3, warning; tone 4, intimate call signal, request for personal attention; tone 5, insistent call; tone 5̠, reproach

//1 Eileen // ('come here!', 'stop that!')

//2 Eileen // ('is that you?', 'where are you?')

//.3 Ei/leen // ('listen!', 'I've got something to say to you')

//3 Eileen // ('I'm warning you!')

//4 Eileen // ('listen carefully!', 'don't tell anyone', 'be honest')

//5 Eileen // ('now I've told you before!', 'take a look at that!')

//5̠ Eileen // ('you shouldn't have done that')

Note that some distinctions of secondary tone have been included here; primary and secondary tone distinctions cannot be separated in the case of calls. Tone .3 here is mid level followed by low rising, with the word *Eileen* split into two feet, a pretonic and a tonic. This would happen even with a one-syllable name,

e.g. // .3 Jo . . . / . . . <u>ohn</u> //.

In all these types of call, however, the name is frequently split into two feet.

Tone <u>5</u> is the low rise-fall, often with breathy voice quality.

Appendix I

References

Berger, P. and Luckmann, T. 1971. *The Social Construction of Reality*. Harmondsworth: Penguin.

Bühler, K. 1933. *Sprachtheorie*. Jena.

Chomsky, N. 1957. *Syntactic Structures*. The Hague: Mouton.

Chomsky, N. 1964. 'Topics in the theory of generative grammar'. In T. A. Sebeok (ed.), *Current Trends in Linguistics* 3. The Hague: Mouton.

Daneš, F. 1960. 'Sentence intonation from a functional point of view'. *Word*, **16**, 34–54.

Daneš, F. 1964. 'A three-level approach to syntax'. In *Travaux Linguistiques de Prague* **1**. Prague: Editions de l'Académie Tchecoslovaque des Sciences.

Davies, E. 1967. 'Some notes on English clause types'. *Transactions of the Philological Society 1967*, 1–31.

Elmenoufy, A. 1969. *A Study of the Role of Intonation in the Grammar of English*. University of London Ph.D. thesis.

Firth, J. R. 1951. 'General linguistics and descriptive grammar'. *Transactions of the Philological Society 1951*, 69–87.

Firth, J. R. 1957a. *Papers in Linguistics 1934–1951*. London: Oxford University Press.

Firth, J. R. 1957b. 'A synopsis of linguistic theory'. *Studies in Linguistic Analysis*. Oxford: Blackwell.

Haas, W. 1966. 'Linguistic relevance'. In C. E. Bazell, J. C. Catford, M. A. K. Halliday and R. H. Robins (eds.) *In Memory of J. R. Firth*. London: Longman.

Hjelmslev, L. 1947. *Prolegomena to a theory of language* (translated by F. J. Whitfield). Madison: Wisconsin University Press. (Originally published 1943, Copenhagen: Munksgaard.)

Hockett, C. F. 1954. 'Two models of grammatical description'. *Word*, **10**, 210–33.

Huddleston, R. D. 1965. 'Rank and depth'. *Language*, **41**, 574–86.

Huddleston, R. D. 1969. 'Some observations on tense and deixis'. *Language*, **45**, 777–806.

Hymes, D. 1970. 'On communicative competence'. In Gumperz and

Hymes (eds.) *Directions in Sociolinguistics*. New York: Holt, Rinehart & Winston.

Lamb, S. M. 1964a. 'The sememic approach to structural semantics'. *American Anthropologist*, **66**, 57–78.

Lamb, S. M. 1964b. 'On alternation, transformation, realization and stratification'. In C. I. M. Stuart (ed.) *Report of the 15th Annual (First International) Round Table Meeting on Linguistics and Language Studies.* (Monograph Series on Languages and Linguistics, 17.) Washington: Georgetown University Press.

Longacre, R. E. 1964. *Grammar Discovery Procedures*. Janua Linguarum, Series Minor, 33. The Hague: Mouton.

Lyons, J. 1963. *Structural Semantics*. Publications of the Philological Society, 20. Oxford: Blackwell.

Malinowski, B. 1923. 'The problem of meaning in primitive languages'. In C. K. Ogden and I. A. Richards *The Meaning of Meaning*. London: Routledge & Kegan Paul.

Malinowski, B. 1953. *Coral Gardens and their magic*, Vol. II. London: Allen & Unwin.

Mitchell, T. F. 1957. 'The language of buying and selling in Cyrenaica'. *Hesperis*, **44**. 1 and 2. pp. 31–71.

Mitchell, T. F. 1958. 'Syntagmatic relations in linguistic analysis'. *Transactions of the Philological Society 1958*, 101–18.

Nida, E. 1966. *A Synopsis of English Syntax*, 2nd revised edition. The Hague: Mouton.

Novák, P. and Sgall, P. 1968. 'On the Prague functional approach'. *Travaux Linguistiques de Prague* 3. (Prague: Editions de l'Académie Tchecoslovaque des Sciences). 291–97.

Palmer, F. R. 1964a. 'Sequence and Order'. In C. I. M. Stuart (ed.) *Report of the 15th Annual (First International) Round Table Meeting on Linguistics and Language Studies*. (Monograph Series on Languages and Linguistics, 17). Washington D.C.: Georgetown University Press. 123–30.

Palmer, F. R. 1964b. 'Grammatical categories and their phonetic exponents'. *Proceedings of the Ninth International Congress of Linguists*. The Hague: Mouton. 338–44

Pike, K. 1967. *Language in Relation to a Unified Theory of the Structure of Human Behaviour*. Janua Linguarum, Series Major. The Hague: Mouton.

Robins, R. H. 1953. 'Formal divisions in Sundanese'. *Transactions of the Philological Society 1953*, 109–42.

Robins, R. H. 1961. 'Syntactic Analysis' (review article). *Archivum Linguisticum* **13**, 78–89.

Sinclair, J. McH. 1966. 'Beginning the study of lexis'. In C. E. Bazell, J. C. Catford, M. A. K. Halliday and R. H. Robins (eds.) *In Memory of J. R. Firth*. London: Longman.

Sinclair, J. McH., Jones, S., and Daley, R. 1970. *English Lexical Studies*. (OSTI Report on Project C/LP/08.) Department of English, The University, Birmingham.

Svoboda, A. 1968. 'The hierarchy of communicative units and fields as illustrated by English attributive constructions'. *Brno Studies in English*, **7**, 49–102.

Tesnière, L. 1959. *Eléments de Syntaxe Structurale*. Paris: Klincksieck.

Turner, G. J. and Pickvance, R. E. 1971. 'Social class differences in the expression of uncertainty in five-year-old children'. *Language and Speech*, **14**

Vachek, J. 1966. *The Linguistic School of Prague*. Bloomington: Indiana University Press.

Appendix II

Books and articles by M. A. K. Halliday

1. 'Grammatical categories in Modern Chinese' *Transactions of the Philological Society* 1956. 177–224.
2. 'The linguistic basis of a mechanical thesaurus' *Mechanical Translation* 3.3, 1956. 81–8.
3. 'Some aspects of systematic description and comparison in grammatical analysis' *Studies in Linguistic Analysis* Oxford: Blackwell (Special Volume of the Philological Society), 1957. 54–67.
4. *The Language of the Chinese 'Secret History of the Mongols'* Oxford: Blackwell (Publications of the Philological Society 17), 1959.
5. 'Categories of the theory of grammar' *Word* 17.3, 1961. 241–92 [Reprinted as Bobbs-Merrill Reprint Series No. Language—36.]
6. 'Linguistique générale et linguistique appliquée à l'enseignement des langues' *Études de Linguistique Appliquée* 1, 1961. 5–42.
7. 'Linguistics and machine translation' *Zeitschrift für Phonetik, Sprachwissenschaft und Kommunikationsforschung* 15.1/2, 1962. 145–58.
8. 'Class in relation to the axes of chain and choice in language' *Linguistics* 2, 1963. 5–15.
9. 'The tones of English' *Archivum Linguisticum* 15.1, 1963. 1–28.
10. 'Intonation in English grammar' *Transactions of the Philological Society* 1963. 143–69.
11. 'Descriptive linguistics in literary studies' Alan Duthie (ed.), *English Studies Today: third series* Edinburgh University Press, 1964. 25–39 [Reprinted in Donald C. Freeman (ed.), *Linguistics and Literary Style* New York: Holt, Rinehart & Winston, 1970. 57–72.]
12. 'The linguistic study of literary texts' Horace Lunt (ed.), *Proceedings of the Ninth International Congress of Linguists* The Hague: Mouton, 1964. 302–7 [Revised and reprinted in Seymour Chatman and Samuel R. Levin (eds.), *Essays on the Language of Literature* Boston: Houghton Mifflin, 1967. 217–23.]
13. (with Angus McIntosh and Peter Strevens) *The Linguistic Sciences and Language Teaching* London: Longman (Longmans Linguistics Library), 1964. [Bloomington, Indiana: Indiana University Press, 1966; English Language Book Society (The Teacher's Bookshelf), 1970.] [Chapter 4 reprinted in Joshua A. Fishman (ed.), *Readings in the Sociology of Language* The Hague: Mouton, 1968. 139–69.]

14. 'Syntax and the consumer' C. I. J. M. Stuart (ed.), *Report of the Fifteenth Annual (First International) Round Table Meeting on Linguistics and Language Study* Washington, D.C.: Georgetown University Press (Monograph Series in Languages and Linguistics 17), 1964. 11–24.

15. 'Some notes on "deep" grammar' *Journal of Linguistics* 2.1, 1966. 57–67.

16. 'The concept of rank: a reply' *Journal of Linguistics* 2.1, 1966. 110–18.

17. 'Lexis as a linguistic level' C. E. Bazell, J. C. Catford, M. A. K. Halliday and R. H. Robins (eds.), *In Memory of J. R. Firth* London: Longman (Longmans Linguistics Library), 1966. 148–62.

18. (with Angus McIntosh) *Patterns of Language: Papers in General, Descriptive and Applied Linguistics* London: Longman (Longmans Linguistics Library), 1966. [Bloomington, Indiana: Indiana University Press, 1966.]

19. 'Linguistics and the teaching of English' James Britton (ed.), *Talking and Writing: A Handbook for English Teachers* London: Methuen, 1967. 80–90.

20. 'Notes on transitivity and theme in English (Parts 1–3)' *Journal of Linguistics* 3.1, 1967. 37–81; 3.2, 1967. 199–244; 4.2, 1968. 179–215.

21. *Some Aspects of the Thematic Organization of the English Clause* Santa Monica: The RAND Corporation (memorandum RM—5224—PR), 1967.

22. *Intonation and Grammar in British English* The Hague: Mouton (Janua Linguarum Series Practica 48), 1967. [Revision of 9 and 10 above.]

23. *Grammar, Society and the Noun* London: H. K. Lewis (for University College London), 1967.

24. 'Language and experience' *The Place of Language (Educational Review,* University of Birmingham, 20.2), 1968. 95–106.

25. 'Options and functions in the English clause' *Brno Studies in English* 8, 1969. 81–8.

26. 'Systemic grammar' *La Grammatica; La Lessicologia* Rome: Bulzoni (Atti del I e del II Convegno di Studi, Società di Linguistica Italiana), 1969.

27. 'Linguistics and the language learner' (in Chinese) *Bulletin of the Teachers' Training College, Singapore,* November 1969.

28. 'Relevant models of language' *The State of Language (Educational Review,* University of Birmingham, 22.1), 1969. 26–37.

29. *A Course in Spoken English: Intonation* (Part 2 of Ronald Mackin, M. A. K. Halliday and J. McH. Sinclair, *A Course in Spoken English)* London: Oxford University Press, 1970.

30. 'Language structure and language function' John Lyons (ed.), *New Horizons in Linguistics* Harmondsworth: Penguin Books, 1970. 140–65.

31. 'Functional diversity in language, as seen from a consideration of modality and mood in English' *Foundations of Language* 6.3, 1970. 322–61.

32. 'Linguistic function and literary style: an enquiry into the language

of William Golding's *The Inheritors*' Seymour Chatman (ed.), *Literary Style: A Symposium* New York: Oxford University Press, 1971. 362–400.

33. 'Language in a social perspective' *The Context of Language* (*Educational Review*, University of Birmingham, 23.3), 1971. 165–88.

34. 'A "linguistic approach" to the teaching of the mother tongue?' *The English Quarterly* (Canadian Council of Teachers of English) 4.2, 1971. 13–24.

35. 'Language acquisition and initial literacy' Malcolm P. Douglass (ed.), *Claremont Reading Conference 35th Yearbook*, 1971. 63–8.

36. *Towards a Sociological Semantics* Urbino: Centro Internazionale di Semiotica e di Linguistica, Università di Urbino (Working Papers and Prepublications 14), 1972.

37. 'The functional basis of language' Basil Bernstein (ed.), *Class, Codes and Control II: Applied studies towards a sociology of language*. London: Routledge & Kegan Paul (Primary Socialization, Language and Education), 1973. 343–66.

38. 'Foreword' Basil Bernstein (ed.), *Class, Codes and Control II: Applied studies towards a sociology of language*. London: Routledge & Kegan Paul (Primary Socialization, Language and Education), 1973. ix–xvi.

39. 'National language and language planning in a multilingual society' *East African Journal*, November 1972.

40. *Explorations in the Functions of Language* London: Edward Arnold (Explorations in Language Study), 1973. [Revision of 28, 32, 33, 36 and 37 above.]

41. 'Foreword' David Mackay, Brian Thompson and Pamela Schaub, *Breakthrough to Literacy: Teachers Resource Book*. Glendale, California: Bowmar, 1973. iii–x.

42. 'A sociosemiotic perspective on language development' *Bulletin of the School of Oriental and African Studies* 37.1 (W. H. Whiteley Memorial Volume), 1974. 98–118.

43. *Language and Social Man* London: Longman (Schools Council Programme in Linguistics and English Teaching: Papers, Series II, Vol. 3), 1974.

44. 'Discussion with M. A. K. Halliday' Herman Parret, *Discussing Language*. The Hague: Mouton, 1974. 81–120.

45. *Learning How to Mean: Explorations in the development of language* London: Edward Arnold (Explorations in Language Study), 1974.

46. 'The place of "functional sentence perspective" in the system of linguistic description' František Daneš (ed.), *Papers on Functional Sentence Perspective*. Prague: Academia (Czechoslovak Academy of Sciences), 1974. 43–53.

47. 'Language as social semiotic: towards a general sociolinguistic theory' Adam Makkai and Valerie Becker Makkai (eds.) *The First LACUS Forum*. Columbia, South Carolina: Hornbeam Press, 1975. 17–46.

48. 'Sociological aspects of semantic change' Luigi Heilmann (ed.), *Proceedings of the Eleventh International Congress of Linguists*. Bologna: Il Mulino, 1975. 853–79.

49. ' "The teacher taught the student English": an essay in applied

linguistics' Peter A. Reich (ed.), *The Second LACUS Forum*. Columbia, South Carolina: Hornbeam Press, 1976. 344–49.

50. (with Ruqaiya Hasan) *Cohesion in English* London: Longman (English Language Series) 1976.

51. 'Text as semantic choice in social contexts' Teun A. van Dijk and Janos Petöfi (eds.), *Grammars and Descriptions*. Berlin and New York: De Gruyter (in press).

Index